The Ultimate Plant-Based Cookbook 2023

1600+ Days of Easy, Mouthwatering, and Nutrient-Rich Recipes for Beginners to Embrace a Sustainable and Vibrant Plant-Based Lifestyle, Incl. 30-Day Meal Plan

Gerard Tipton

Copyright© 2023 By Gerard Tipton

All rights reserved worldwide.
No part of this book may be reproduced or transmitted in any form or by any means, electronic or mechanical, including photo- copying, recording or by any information storage and retrieval system, without written permission from the publisher, except for the inclusion of brief quotations in a review.

Warning-Disclaimer
The purpose of this book is to educate and entertain. The author or publisher does not guarantee that anyone following the techniques, suggestions, tips, ideas, or strategies will become successful. The author and publisher shall have neither liability or responsibility to anyone with respect to any loss or damage caused, or alleged to be caused, directly or indirectly by the information contained in this book.

Table of Contents

Introduction   1

Chapter 1   Plant-Based Diet: a Healthy Way to Eat   3

Chapter 2   Basics   18

Chapter 3   Breakfasts   24

Chapter 4   Beans and Grains   33

Chapter 5   Vegetables and Sides   41

Chapter 6   Stews and Soups   49

Chapter 7   Snacks and Appetizers   60

Chapter 8   Desserts   71

Chapter 9   Salads   79

Chapter 10   Staples, Sauces, Dips, and Dressings   87

Appendix 1:   Measurement Conversion Chart   97

Appendix 2:   The Dirty Dozen and Clean Fifteen   98

Appendix 3   Recipes Index   99

INTRODUCTION

In a world where dietary choices are as diverse as the cultures that inhabit it, the concept of a plant-based diet has emerged as a resounding anthem for health-conscious individuals seeking a sustainable and compassionate way of nourishing their bodies. With the rise of chronic diseases, concerns about environmental sustainability, and a growing awareness of animal welfare, more and more people are turning to plant-based eating as a powerful solution. It is within this context that this plant-based cookbook takes root, offering a bountiful collection of recipes and insights to inspire and guide you on your journey to vibrant well-being.

Imagine a plate filled with a vibrant array of vegetables, glistening fruits bursting with natural sweetness, hearty whole grains that satisfy and energize, and the subtle richness of plant-based fats. This is the essence of a plant-based diet—a harmonious symphony of colors, flavors, and textures that not only tantalizes the taste buds but also nourishes the body from within. Whether you are a committed vegan, a curious flexitarian, or simply someone seeking to incorporate more plant-based meals into your routine, this cookbook serves as your compass, pointing the way toward a world of culinary possibilities that are both delicious and nourishing.

The health benefits of a plant-based diet are undeniable. Fruits, vegetables, whole grains, legumes, nuts, and seeds form the foundation of this way of eating, providing an abundant array of essential nutrients, antioxidants, and fiber that promote overall well-being. Scientific research consistently highlights the potential of a plant-based diet in reducing the risk of chronic diseases such as heart disease, diabetes, and certain types of cancer. By embracing a plant-based lifestyle, you take a proactive step toward better health, empowering yourself with the knowledge that the food on your plate can be a powerful ally in disease prevention and management.

But the benefits extend beyond personal health. Our collective consciousness is awakening to the environmental impact of our dietary choices. Animal agriculture, with its significant water usage, greenhouse gas emissions, and deforestation, poses a strain on our planet's resources. By shifting towards plant-based eating, we can significantly reduce our carbon footprint and contribute to a more sustainable future. Embracing a plant-based diet becomes an act of environmental stewardship, a way to honor the interconnectedness of all life on Earth.

Embarking on a plant-based journey may seem daunting at first, but rest assured, this cookbook is here to guide you every step of the way. Whether you're a seasoned cook or a novice in the kitchen, the pages ahead offer a wealth of information, tips, and techniques to help you navigate this exciting culinary adventure. From pantry staples and kitchen essentials to creative ingredient substitutions and cooking methods, you'll find a treasure trove of knowledge to support your plant-based endeavors.

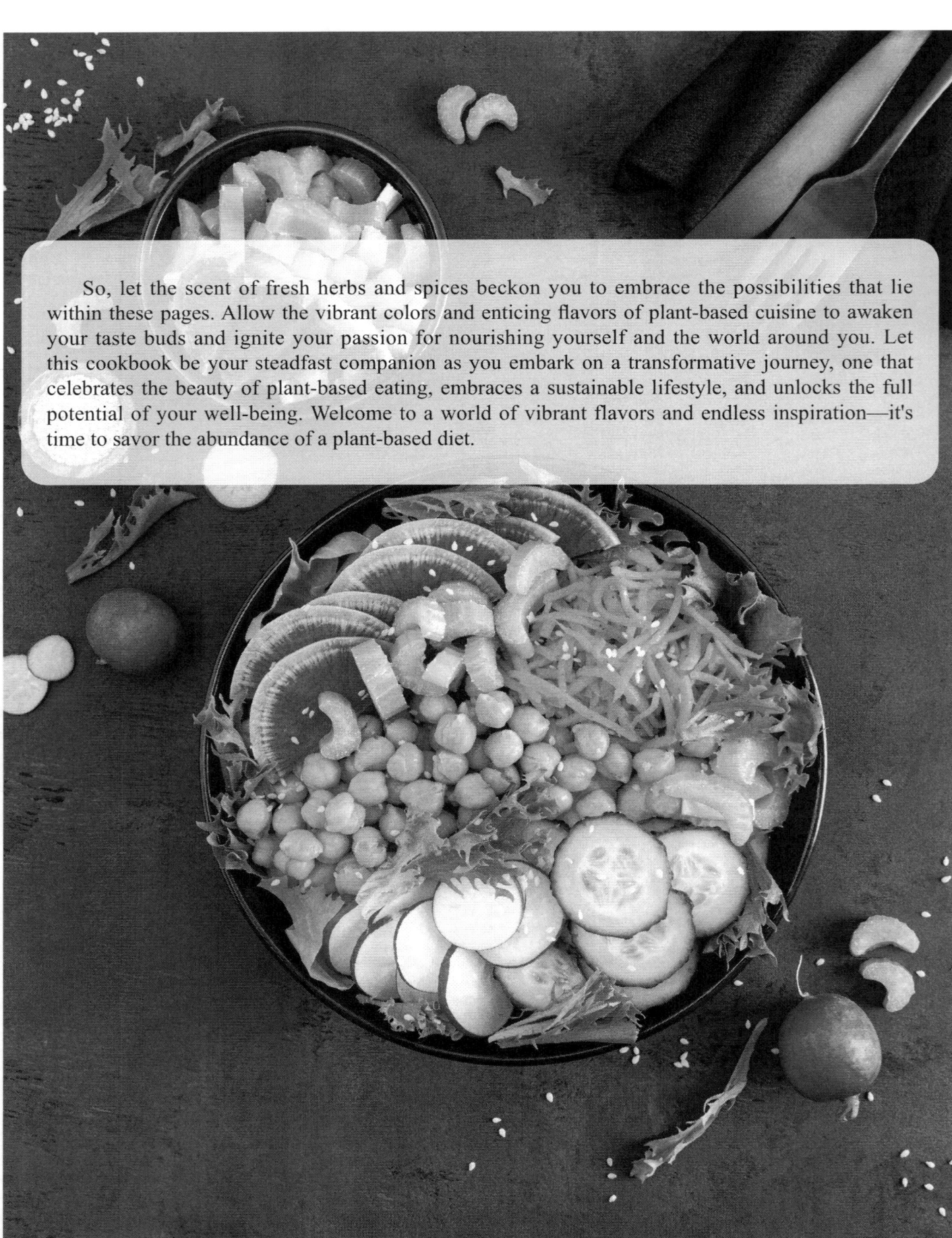

So, let the scent of fresh herbs and spices beckon you to embrace the possibilities that lie within these pages. Allow the vibrant colors and enticing flavors of plant-based cuisine to awaken your taste buds and ignite your passion for nourishing yourself and the world around you. Let this cookbook be your steadfast companion as you embark on a transformative journey, one that celebrates the beauty of plant-based eating, embraces a sustainable lifestyle, and unlocks the full potential of your well-being. Welcome to a world of vibrant flavors and endless inspiration—it's time to savor the abundance of a plant-based diet.

Chapter 1 Plant-Based Diet: a Healthy Way to Eat

Understanding Plant-Based Diet

Definition of a Plant-Based Diet

A plant-based diet is a nutritional approach that centers around the consumption of predominantly plant-derived foods while minimizing or eliminating the intake of animal products. At its core, this dietary pattern emphasizes the inclusion of a wide variety of whole, unprocessed plant foods such as fruits, vegetables, whole grains, legumes, nuts, and seeds.

The defining characteristic of a plant-based diet is the focus on plant foods as the foundation of meals. Fruits and vegetables are celebrated for their vibrant colors, flavors, and array of essential vitamins, minerals, and antioxidants that support overall health and well-being. Whole grains like quinoa, brown rice, and oats

provide a rich source of complex carbohydrates, dietary fiber, and important micronutrients. Legumes, including beans, lentils, and chickpeas, offer a plant-based protein source, along with valuable fiber and essential minerals.

Nuts and seeds, such as almonds, walnuts, chia seeds, and flaxseeds, are nutrient-dense powerhouses, packed with healthy fats, protein, and a range of vitamins and minerals. These ingredients provide satiety and contribute to the overall balance and variety of a plant-based diet. Additionally, plant-based fats like avocado, olive oil, and coconut oil can be used in moderation to enhance flavor and provide necessary dietary fats.

While a plant-based diet prioritizes plant foods, it does not necessarily exclude all animal products. Some individuals may choose to incorporate small amounts of animal products, such as dairy, eggs, or fish, into their plant-based eating approach. However, the emphasis is on reducing or eliminating these animal products and instead focusing on plant-based alternatives.

It is important to note that a plant-based diet is not synonymous with being vegan or vegetarian, which entail complete avoidance of animal products. Instead, it encompasses a spectrum of dietary choices and can be adapted to suit individual preferences and needs. This flexibility allows individuals to embrace a plant-based diet in a way that aligns with their health goals, ethical considerations, and cultural practices.

The appeal of a plant-based diet lies in its potential health benefits. By consuming a wide variety of plant foods, individuals can access a broad spectrum of essential nutrients, including vitamins, minerals, antioxidants, and dietary fiber. Plant-based diets have been associated with a reduced risk of chronic diseases such as heart disease, obesity, type 2 diabetes, and certain types of cancer. They can also support weight management, improve digestion, and promote overall vitality.

Beyond personal health, a plant-based diet has gained recognition for its positive environmental impact. Animal agriculture is a significant contributor to greenhouse gas emissions, deforestation, and water pollution. By adopting a plant-based diet, individuals can reduce their carbon footprint, conserve natural resources, and contribute to a more sustainable future for the planet.

In summary, a plant-based diet emphasizes the consumption of whole, unprocessed plant foods while minimizing or eliminating animal products. It offers a diverse array of fruits, vegetables, whole grains, legumes, nuts, and seeds, providing a wealth of essential nutrients and health benefits. By embracing a plant-based diet, individuals can nourish their bodies, support environmental sustainability, and align their dietary choices with their values.

The Rising Popularity of Plant-Based Diets

The rising popularity of plant-based diets is a global phenomenon that has gained significant traction in recent years. People from all walks of life are increasingly embracing this dietary approach, driven by a variety of factors that contribute to its growing appeal.

♦ Health Consciousness: As individuals become more aware of the importance of nutrition and its impact on overall health, many are turning to plant-based diets as a means to improve their well-being. Numerous scientific studies have highlighted the potential health benefits of plant-based eating, including reduced risks of chronic diseases such as heart disease, diabetes, certain cancers, and obesity. The abundance of essential nutrients, antioxidants, and dietary fiber found in plant-based foods supports optimal health and contributes to a balanced and nourishing diet.

♦ Environmental Sustainability: Concerns about the environmental impact of food production have spurred the rise of plant-based diets. Animal agriculture is a significant contributor to greenhouse gas emissions, deforestation, water pollution, and other environmental issues. Plant-based diets, with their emphasis on plant foods, require fewer resources and have a lower carbon footprint. Choosing plant-based options can help individuals reduce their environmental impact and promote sustainability.

♦ Ethical Considerations: The ethical treatment of animals is another significant factor driving the popularity of plant-based diets. Many individuals are increasingly concerned about animal welfare and choose to reduce or eliminate the consumption of animal products from their diets. Plant-based eating allows for a more compassionate approach to food choices, supporting a lifestyle that aligns with one's values and respect for animal life.

♦ Celebrity and Influencer Endorsement: The endorsement of plant-based diets by celebrities, athletes, and social media influencers has played a crucial role in increasing their popularity. Prominent figures in entertainment, sports, and wellness have publicly shared their positive experiences with plant-based eating, attracting attention and inspiring others to explore this dietary approach. Their influence has helped to normalize plant-based diets and make them more accessible to a broader audience.

♦ Availability of Plant-Based Options: The growing demand for plant-based products has led to an increase in the availability and variety of plant-based alternatives in the market. Supermarkets, restaurants, and food companies have responded to this demand by introducing a wide range of plant-based options, including meat substitutes, dairy alternatives, and plant-based convenience foods. This increased accessibility has made it easier for individuals to adopt and maintain a plant-based lifestyle.

♦ Social Awareness and Media Coverage: Plant-based diets have gained significant media coverage and social awareness in recent years. Documentaries, books, and online platforms have highlighted the benefits of plant-based eating, raising awareness and educating the public about the potential impact of dietary choices on personal health, the environment, and animal welfare. This increased exposure has led to a broader understanding and acceptance of plant-based diets as a viable and appealing option.

The rising popularity of plant-based diets reflects a global shift in dietary patterns towards more sustainable, health-conscious, and ethical choices. With an increasing wealth of information and resources available, individuals are empowered to embrace plant-based eating as a way to enhance their well-being, reduce their environmental impact, and make a positive contribution to the world around them.

Health Benefits of a Plant-Based Diet

A plant-based diet offers a myriad of health benefits that contribute to overall well-being and vitality. By prioritizing plant foods and minimizing or eliminating animal products, individuals can access a wide range of essential nutrients, antioxidants, and dietary fiber, which promote optimal health and reduce the risk of chronic diseases. Here are some of the key health benefits associated with a plant-based diet:

♦ Reduced Risk of Chronic Diseases: Scientific research consistently links plant-based eating patterns with a lower risk of chronic diseases such as heart disease, stroke, type 2 diabetes, certain types of cancer, and obesity. The abundant array of vitamins, minerals, and phytonutrients found in plant-based foods helps support cardiovascular health, maintain healthy blood pressure levels, regulate blood sugar, and promote healthy weight management.

♦ Heart Health: Plant-based diets have been shown to be beneficial for heart health. They are typically low in saturated fats and cholesterol, both of which contribute to cardiovascular disease. Additionally, plant-based diets are rich in dietary fiber, antioxidants, and heart-healthy fats, such as monounsaturated and polyunsaturated fats found in nuts, seeds, and oils. These components help lower cholesterol levels, reduce inflammation, improve blood lipid profiles, and support overall heart health.

♦ Weight Management: Plant-based diets are often associated with weight management and weight loss. The high fiber content of plant-based foods promotes satiety, helping individuals feel fuller for longer and potentially reducing overall calorie intake. Additionally, plant-based diets tend to be lower in calorie density compared to diets that include animal products, making it easier to maintain a healthy weight.

♦ Digestive Health: The fiber content in plant-based foods is crucial for maintaining a healthy digestive system. Dietary fiber aids in promoting regular bowel movements, preventing constipation, and supporting a healthy gut microbiome. Additionally, a plant-based diet can help reduce the risk of developing gastrointestinal conditions such as diverticulosis, hemorrhoids, and colorectal cancer.

♦ Nutritional Adequacy: When properly planned, a plant-based diet can meet all nutritional requirements. By consuming a diverse range of plant foods, individuals can obtain essential vitamins, minerals, and nutrients such as vitamin C, vitamin E, folate, potassium, magnesium, and phytonutrients. Plant-based sources of protein, such as legumes, tofu, tempeh, and quinoa, can provide adequate protein intake.

♦ Anti-inflammatory Effects: Plant-based diets are typically rich in anti-inflammatory foods, such as fruits, vegetables, nuts, and seeds, which contain bioactive compounds with anti-inflammatory properties. These compounds help reduce chronic inflammation in the body, which is linked to various diseases, including heart disease, diabetes, and certain types of cancer.

♦ Improved Gut Health: Plant-based diets, particularly those rich in fiber, can positively impact gut health by promoting the growth of beneficial gut bacteria. A healthy gut microbiome is associated with improved digestion, enhanced nutrient absorption, strengthened immune function, and a reduced risk of certain diseases, including autoimmune conditions and gastrointestinal disorders.

It is important to note that while a plant-based diet offers numerous health benefits, individual nutrient needs may vary based on factors such as age, sex, activity level, and overall health status. It is recommended to consult with a healthcare professional or registered dietitian to ensure a well-balanced and nutrient-dense plant-based diet that meets individual needs.

Environmental Sustainability

Embracing a plant-based diet has significant positive implications for environmental sustainability. The environmental impact of food production and consumption is a growing concern, and transitioning to a plant-based diet can help mitigate some of the most pressing environmental challenges we face today. Here are some key aspects highlighting the environmental sustainability benefits of a plant-based diet:

♦ Reduced Greenhouse Gas Emissions: Animal agriculture is a major contributor to greenhouse gas emissions, including carbon dioxide (CO_2), methane (CH_4), and nitrous oxide (N_2O). Livestock farming, particularly intensive animal farming, generates substantial amounts of these gases through processes like enteric fermentation, manure management, and deforestation for livestock feed production. By shifting towards plant-based eating, which requires fewer resources and generates fewer emissions, individuals can significantly reduce their carbon footprint and contribute to global efforts to mitigate climate change.

♦ Conservation of Land and Water Resources: Animal agriculture requires vast amounts of land for grazing livestock and growing animal feed crops. This demand for land contributes to deforestation, habitat destruction, and loss of biodiversity. Moreover, animal agriculture consumes large quantities of water for animal drinking, irrigation of feed crops, and processing. By choosing plant-based foods, individuals reduce the demand for land and water resources, allowing for conservation of natural habitats, preservation of biodiversity, and efficient use of water.

♦ Decreased Water Pollution: The runoff of animal waste from industrial farming operations can pollute nearby water bodies, leading to contamination of rivers, lakes, and oceans. The excessive use of fertilizers in animal feed crop cultivation can also contribute to water pollution through nutrient runoff. Plant-based diets, with their reduced reliance on intensive animal farming, help mitigate water pollution risks associated with animal agriculture and promote cleaner water sources.

♦ Preservation of Natural Resources: Producing animal-based food requires significant inputs of resources, including feed crops, water, and energy for farming, transportation, and processing. By adopting a plant-based diet, individuals reduce the strain on natural resources and promote more sustainable resource management. Plant-based foods tend to have a lower ecological footprint and require fewer resources compared to animal-based foods.

♦ Mitigation of Deforestation: The expansion of livestock grazing areas and the cultivation of feed crops, such as soybeans and corn, often contribute to deforestation in regions like the Amazon rainforest. Deforestation not only leads to the loss of valuable ecosystems and biodiversity but also exacerbates climate change by reducing carbon sinks. By opting for plant-based alternatives, individuals help alleviate the demand for feed crops associated with deforestation, contributing to the preservation of vital forest ecosystems.

♦ Sustainable Use of Fisheries: Overfishing and destructive fishing practices pose a significant threat to marine ecosystems and fish populations worldwide. By reducing the demand for fish and seafood, individuals following a plant-based diet can help alleviate pressure on already vulnerable marine ecosystems, promote sustainable fishing practices, and support the long-term health of oceans and aquatic biodiversity.

By adopting a plant-based diet, individuals can play an active role in mitigating environmental degradation, reducing greenhouse gas emissions, conserving natural resources, and protecting vulnerable ecosystems. The collective impact of transitioning to plant-based eating has the potential to contribute to a more sustainable future, fostering a harmonious relationship between humans and the planet we call home.

Getting Started with a Plant-Based Diet

Getting started with a plant-based diet can be an exciting and fulfilling journey towards a healthier, more sustainable lifestyle. Here are some practical steps to help you begin your plant-based eating journey:

♦ Educate Yourself: Take the time to educate yourself about the principles and benefits of a plant-based diet. Read books, watch documentaries, and explore reputable online resources to understand the nutritional aspects, cooking techniques, and recipe ideas that align with a plant-based lifestyle. This knowledge will empower you to make informed choices and ensure a well-balanced diet.

♦ Set Clear Goals: Define your goals and motivations for adopting a plant-based diet. Whether you are driven by health, environmental sustainability, or ethical considerations, having clear goals will help you stay committed and focused on your plant-based journey.

♦ Start Gradually: Transitioning to a plant-based diet doesn't have to be an all-or-nothing approach. Consider starting gradually by incorporating more plant-based meals into your existing diet. Begin by designating certain days of the week as "meatless" or "plant-based" and gradually increase the frequency as you become more comfortable and confident with plant-based cooking.

♦ Emphasize Whole Foods: Focus on consuming whole, unprocessed plant foods. Fill your plate with a variety of fruits, vegetables, whole grains, legumes, nuts, and seeds. These foods are rich in essential nutrients and fiber, and they form the foundation of a healthy plant-based diet.

♦ Experiment with Plant-Based Protein Sources: Explore plant-based protein sources such as legumes (beans, lentils, chickpeas), tofu, tempeh, seitan, edamame, quinoa, and other grains. These ingredients can be versatile and satisfying substitutes for meat and dairy products. Experiment with different recipes and cooking methods to discover your favorite plant-based protein sources.

♦ Explore Plant-Based Recipes: Invest in a plant-based cookbook or explore reliable online recipe sources for inspiration. There is a vast array of delicious plant-based recipes available that can help you create flavorful and satisfying meals. Try incorporating a variety of flavors, herbs, and spices to make your plant-based dishes exciting and enjoyable.

♦ Stock Up on Plant-Based Pantry Staples: Make sure your pantry is well-stocked with plant-based staples like whole grains (quinoa, brown rice, oats), legumes (canned or dried beans, lentils), nuts, seeds, plant-based milk alternatives, spices, and herbs. Having these ingredients on hand will make it easier to prepare nutritious plant-based meals.

♦ Explore Plant-Based Dining Options: When dining out, seek out restaurants or eateries that offer plant-based or vegetarian menu options. Many establishments now cater to the growing demand for plant-based meals, making it easier to find delicious plant-based choices when eating out.

♦ Plan and Prep Ahead: Plan your meals and snacks in advance to ensure you have nutritious plant-based options readily available. Set aside time for meal prepping on weekends or whenever it is convenient for you. This can include washing and chopping vegetables, cooking grains and legumes, and preparing snacks to have on hand throughout the week.

♦ Connect with Others: Join online communities, local meetups, or social media groups focused on plant-based eating. Connecting with like-minded individuals can provide support, inspiration, and opportunities to share experiences, recipes, and tips.

Remember, transitioning to a plant-based diet is a personal journey, and it's important to listen to your body and adapt the approach to suit your needs and preferences. Be patient with yourself and celebrate the small victories along the way. Embracing a plant-based lifestyle has the potential to positively impact your health, the environment, and the well-being of animals.

Cooking Techniques and Tips

Mastering cooking techniques and incorporating useful tips can greatly enhance your experience with plant-based cooking. Here are some cooking techniques and tips to help you make the most of your plant-based culinary adventures:

♦ Embrace Whole Food Cooking: Focus on using whole foods as the foundation of your plant-based meals. Incorporate a variety of vegetables, fruits, whole grains, legumes, nuts, and seeds in your recipes. These ingredients are packed with nutrients and provide a wide range of flavors, textures, and colors to your dishes.

♦ Experiment with Flavorful Herbs and Spices: Herbs and spices are key to adding depth and complexity to plant-based meals. Explore a variety of seasonings, such as basil, oregano, cumin, turmeric, paprika, ginger, garlic, and more. Experiment with different combinations to create unique flavor profiles that suit your taste preferences.

♦ Utilize Different Cooking Methods: Plant-based cooking offers a range of cooking methods to explore. Try techniques like sautéing, roasting, grilling, steaming, baking, stir-frying, or raw preparation. Each method imparts distinct flavors and textures to your ingredients, allowing for a diverse and exciting culinary experience.

♦ Incorporate Plant-Based Protein Sources: Plant-based protein sources, such as legumes, tofu, tempeh, seitan, and quinoa, can be versatile and satisfying additions to your meals. Experiment with marinating, grilling, baking, or sautéing these ingredients to create delicious and protein-rich dishes.

♦ Make Homemade Plant-Based Milks and Cheeses: If you enjoy dairy alternatives, consider making your own plant-based milks and cheeses at home. Nut milks (like almond milk or cashew milk) and plant-based cheeses (such as cashew cheese or tofu-based cheese) can be easily prepared and customized to your taste preferences.

♦ Explore Fermentation: Fermented foods, such as sauerkraut, kimchi, and tempeh, not only add tangy flavors to your dishes but also provide gut-friendly probiotics. Experiment with fermenting vegetables, making your own kombucha, or trying other fermented plant-based products.

♦ Get Creative with Plant-Based Substitutions: Explore plant-based substitutions for traditional ingredients. For example, replace eggs in baking recipes with mashed bananas, applesauce, flaxseed meal, or tofu. Swap dairy products with plant-based alternatives like coconut milk, almond milk, or cashew cream. These substitutions can often be healthier and add unique flavors to your recipes.

♦ Batch Cook and Meal Prep: Consider batch cooking and meal prepping to save time and ensure you always have nutritious plant-based meals on hand. Prepare larger quantities of soups, stews, grains, or roasted vegetables and store them in the refrigerator or freezer for later use. Pre-cut vegetables, cook grains in advance, and assemble salads in containers to simplify meal preparation during busy days.

♦ Blend and Puree for Creamy Textures: Blending or pureeing ingredients can create creamy textures without relying on dairy products. Use blenders, food processors, or immersion blenders to transform cooked vegetables, beans, or soaked nuts into creamy sauces, dips, or dressings.

♦ Embrace Plant-Based Cuisine Diversity: Explore different plant-based cuisines from around the world to expand your culinary repertoire. Discover the flavors of Mediterranean, Asian, Mexican, Indian, Middle Eastern, or African cuisines, which often feature a wide array of plant-based dishes and cooking techniques.

Remember to have fun and be open to trying new ingredients and recipes. Plant-based cooking is an opportunity to be creative, explore new flavors, and develop a deeper appreciation for the abundance of plant-based foods available to you. Enjoy the journey and savor the delicious and nutritious meals you create along the way.

30 Days Plant-Based Diet Meal Plan

DAYS	BREAKFAST	LUNCH	DINNER	SNACK/DESSERT
1	Blueberry Scones	Roasted Balsamic Beets	Orange, Fennel and White Bean Salad	Almond Anise Biscotti
2	Powerhouse Green Juice	Yellow Bell Pepper Boats	Forbidden Black Rice and Edamame Salad	Molasses ginger Oat Cookie Balls
3	Chickpea Country Gravy	Avocado Tartare	Vietnamese Veggie and Rice Noodle Salad	Quinoa Banana Muffins
4	Pan con Tomate	Loaded Frijoles	Quinoa, Corn and Black Bean Salad	Almond Truffles with Toasted Coconut
5	Savory Rosemary–Black Pepper Scones	Chickpea of the Sea Salad	Blueprint: Lifesaving Bowl	Black Sesame–Ginger Quick Bread
6	Nut Butter and Jelly Breakfast Cookies	Zucchini "Parmesan"	Zingy Melon and Mango Salad	Two-Ingredient Peanut Butter Fudge
7	Banana French Toast with Raspberry Syrup	Blackened Sprouts	Classic French Vinaigrette	Walnut Brownies
8	Slow Cooker Apples and Oats	Vegetable Korma Curry	Summer Quinoa Salad	Stone Fruit Compote
9	Plant-Powered Pancakes	Mustard-Roasted Beets and Shallots with Thyme	Lentil, Lemon and Mushroom Salad	Apple Crisp
10	Overnight Chocolate Chia Pudding	Spicy Miso-Roasted Tomatoes and Eggplant	Fiery Couscous Salad	Pumpkin Bread Pudding
11	Best Whole Wheat Pancakes	Portabella Mushroom Gyro	Lemon Garlic Chickpeas Salad	Sweet Potato Spice Cake
12	Banana Zucchini Pancakes	Ginger, Shiitake, Pecan, and Apricot Pilaf	Bulgur Lettuce Cups	Blueberry-Lime Sorbet
13	Savory Oatmeal	Ultimate Veggie Wrap with Kale Pesto	Ancient Grains Salad	Pumpkin Spice Bread
14	Crazy Quinoa Protein Muffins	Roasted Cauliflower with Green Tahini	Taco Tempeh Salad	Golden Banana Bread
15	Congee with Dates and Spices	Spicy Carrots with Coriander	Farro Salad with Italian Vinaigrette	Mango Sticky Rice
16	Stovetop Blueberry Oatmeal	Rosemary-and garlic Beet Salad	Tomato, Corn and Bean Salad	Baked Apples
17	Shiitake Bakin'	Quick Marinated Arame	Garden Salad with Sumac Vinaigrette	Chocolate Microwave Mug Cake
18	Breakfast Tofu	Vegan Goulash	Larb Salad	Pear Chia Pudding

DAYS	BREAKFAST	LUNCH	DINNER	SNACK/DESSERT
19	Chocolate Cherry Oats Bowl	Delicata Squash Boats	Mock Tuna Salad	Almond-Date Energy Bites
20	Chickpea Quiche	Roasted Veggies with Tofu	Purple Potato and Kale Salad	Chocolate Dirt Yogurt Cup
21	Slow-Cooked Steel-Cut Oats	Creamy Mint-Lime Spaghetti Squash	Fava Bean Salad	Chocolate Tahini Muffins
22	Blueberry Tofu Pancakes	Mixed Winter Vegetables with Spicy Poppy Seed Sauce	Creamy Fruit Salad	Coconut Crumble Bars
23	Sunshine Muffins	Roasted Carrots with Ginger Maple Cream	Creamy Chickpea and Avocado Salad	Graham Crackers
24	Zucchini Bread Oatmeal	Mustard-Roasted Broccoli Pâté	Blueprint: Classic Kale Salad	Salted Chocolate Truffles
25	Slow Cooker Maple Breakfast Links	Beet Sushi and Avocado Poke Bowls	Winter Sunshine Salad	Zesty Orange-Cranberry Energy Bites
26	Carrot Cake Oatmeal	Cumin-Citrus Roasted Carrots	Dill Potato Salad	Apple-Oat Crisp
27	Greek Egg and Tomato Scramble	Daikon Beet Pickle with Lime	Strawberry-Pistachio Salad	Peach Cobbler
28	Granola	Baked Spaghetti Squash with Spicy Lentil Sauce	Curried Kale Slaw	Ginger Peach Muffins
29	Avocado Toast	Crispy Maple Mustard Cabbage	Greek Salad in a Jar	Vanilla Nice Cream
30	Cookies for Breakfast	Tangy Cabbage, Apples, and Potatoes	Lentil Salad with Lemon and Fresh Herbs	Chocolate-Peppermint Nice Cream

Chapter 2 Basics

Tempeh Bacon

Prep time: 5 minutes | Cook time: 10 minutes | Serves 4

2 tablespoons soy sauce
1 tablespoon water
1 tablespoon maple syrup (optional)
½ tablespoon liquid smoke
1 (8 ounces / 227 g) package tempeh
1 tablespoon canola oil (optional)

1. In a medium bowl, combine the soy sauce, water, maple syrup (if desired), and liquid smoke. Set aside. 2. Cut the tempeh block in half lengthwise and then slice it as thinly as possible. 3. In a large pan over high heat, heat the oil, if desired. Add the tempeh in a single layer and cook for 2 minutes. Flip and cook for 2 more minutes. 4. While the tempeh is still in the pan, add the liquid mixture and sauté the tempeh for 3 minutes. Flip and cook for 3 more minutes or until the liquid is absorbed. 5. The Tempeh Bacon is best if served immediately.

Per Serving:

calories: 17 | fat: 11g | protein: 11g | carbs: 11g | fiber: 0g

Spicy Cilantro Pesto

Prep time: 10 minutes | Cook time: 0 minutes | Makes about 1 cup

2 cups packed cilantro
¼ cup hulled sunflower seeds, toasted (optional)
1 jalapeño pepper, coarsely chopped (for less heat, remove the seeds)
4 cloves garlic, peeled and chopped
Zest and juice of 1 lime
Salt, to taste (optional)
½ package extra-firm silken tofu (about 6 ounces / 170 g), drained
¼ cup nutritional yeast (optional)

1. In the bowl of a food processor, combine the cilantro, toasted sunflower seeds (if using), jalapeño pepper, garlic, lime zest and juice, salt (if using), tofu, and nutritional yeast (if using). 2. Process the ingredients until smooth and creamy, scraping down the sides of the bowl as needed. 3. Taste and adjust the seasoning by adding more salt if desired. 4. Transfer the spicy cilantro pesto to a jar or container and refrigerate until ready to use.

Per Serving: (¼ cup)

calories: 143 | fat: 8g | protein: 11g | carbs: 10g | fiber: 5g

Easy-Peasy Almond Milk

Prep time: 5 minutes | Cook time: 0 minutes | Makes 2 cups

2 to 3 tablespoons raw almond butter
2 cups water
Pinch sea salt (optional)
1 to 2 dates, or 10 drops pure stevia (or vanilla stevia), or 1 to 2 tablespoons unrefined sugar (optional)
¼ teaspoon pure vanilla extract (optional)

1. In a blender, combine the raw almond butter, water, sea salt (if using), sweetener of choice (dates, stevia, or unrefined sugar), and vanilla extract (if using). 2. Blend the ingredients on high speed until smooth and well combined. 3. If desired, strain the almond milk through a piece of cheesecloth or a fine-mesh sieve to remove any fiber from the almonds. 4. Transfer the almond milk to an airtight container and store it in the refrigerator for up to 5 days.

Per Serving: (1 cup)

calories: 110 | fat: 8g | protein: 3g | carbs: 5g | fiber: 2g

Superfood Salad Topper

Prep time: 5 minutes | Cook time: 0 minutes | Makes 2⅓ cups

½ cup raw cashews
½ cup sprouted or raw pumpkin seeds
1 cup mixed seeds (sunflower, chia, flax, and hemp)
⅓ cup goji berries
2 tablespoons flax oil or extra-virgin olive oil (optional)
1 teaspoon curry powder
1 teaspoon ground turmeric
½ teaspoon ground cinnamon
Pinch of cayenne pepper
Pinch of sea salt (optional)

1. In a large bowl, combine the raw cashews, sprouted or raw pumpkin seeds, mixed seeds (sunflower, chia, flax, and hemp), and goji berries. Toss them together. 2. Add the flax oil or extra-virgin olive oil (if using), curry powder, ground turmeric, ground cinnamon, cayenne pepper, and sea salt (if using). Mix everything well to coat the nuts, seeds, and berries evenly with the spices. 3. Ideally, allow the mixture to marinate for 15 minutes before serving to enhance the flavors. 4. Store the superfood salad topper in an airtight glass container in the refrigerator or freezer. It will remain fresh for several weeks, ready to quickly enhance and nourish your meals.

Per Serving:(2 tablespoons)

calories: 308 | fat: 27g | protein: 10g | carbs: 10g | fiber: 3g

Croutons

Prep time: 5 minutes | Cook time: 15 minutes | Serves 4

½ day-old baguette, sliced
2 tablespoons olive oil (optional)
½ tablespoon garlic salt (optional)

1. Preheat your oven to 350°F (180°C). 2. If desired, brush the baguette slices with olive oil and sprinkle them with garlic salt. 3. Cut the bread slices into cubes and place them on a baking sheet. 4. Bake the cubes in the preheated oven for 10 to 15 minutes, or until they turn golden brown. 5. Allow the croutons to cool before serving. 7. For the best flavor and texture, serve the croutons immediately after baking.

Per Serving:
calories: 94 | fat: 7g | protein: 1g | carbs: 7g | fiber: 0g

Potatoes

Prep time: 0 minutes | Cook time: 5 minutes | Serves 1

1 medium potato

1. Using a fork, poke holes all over the potato to allow ventilation. 2. Place the potato on a microwave-safe plate and microwave it for 2 minutes. 3. Flip the potato over and microwave for an additional 2 minutes. 4. If the potato is not soft yet, continue microwaving in 1-minute increments until it reaches desired softness. 5. Once cooked, store the potato in an airtight container in the refrigerator for up to 4 days.

Per Serving:
calories: 164 | fat: 0g | protein: 4g | carbs: 37g | fiber: 5g

Not-So-Fat Guacamole

Prep time: 15 minutes | Cook time: 13 minutes | Makes 2 cups

1 cup shelled edamame
1 cup broccoli florets
Zest of 1 lime and juice of 2 limes
2 Roma tomatoes, diced
½ small red onion, peeled and diced small
¼ cup finely chopped cilantro
1 clove garlic, peeled and minced (about 1 teaspoon)
Salt, to taste (optional)
1 pinch cayenne pepper, or to taste

1. Place the edamame in a medium saucepan and add enough water to cover. Bring it to a boil and cook for 5 minutes. 2. Drain and rinse the edamame until cooled. 3. Steam the broccoli in a double boiler or steamer basket for about 8 minutes, or until it becomes very tender. Drain and rinse the broccoli until cooled. 4. In a food processor, combine the edamame and broccoli, and purée until smooth and creamy. Add water if needed to achieve a creamy texture. 5. Transfer the puréed mixture to a bowl and add the lime zest and juice, diced tomatoes, diced red onion, finely chopped cilantro, minced garlic, salt (if using), and cayenne pepper. Mix well to combine. 6. Chill the guacamole until ready to serve.

Per Serving: (1 cup)
calories: 136 | fat: 4g | protein: 10g | carbs: 17g | fiber: 6g

Herbed Millet Pizza Crust

Prep time: 5 minutes | Cook time: 40 minutes | Makes 1 large thin-crust pizza crust

½ cup coarsely ground millet
1½ cups water
1 tablespoon mixed dried Italian herbs
¼ teaspoon sea salt (optional)
1 to 2 tablespoons nutritional yeast

1. Preheat your oven to 350°F (180°C). Line an 8-inch-round pie dish or springform pan with parchment paper, allowing you to lift the crust out after it's cooked. Using a nonstick pan will prevent sticking. 2. In a small pot, combine the millet, water, and a pinch of salt. Bring it to a boil, then cover and simmer for 15 to 20 minutes. Stir occasionally to prevent sticking. If desired, you can add the dried herbs while cooking the millet for a more intense flavor, or stir them in after the millet is cooked. 3. Once the millet is cooked, add the salt (if using) and nutritional yeast. Spread the cooked and seasoned millet evenly in your prepared pan, extending it all the way to the edges. 4. Place the crust in the oven and bake for 20 minutes, or until it becomes lightly browned around the edges.

Per Serving: (1 crust)
calories: 378 | fat: 4g | protein: 11g | carbs: 72g | fiber: 8g

Lemon-Thyme Dressing

Prep time: 5 minutes | Cook time: 0 minutes | Serves 6

⅓ cup fresh lemon juice
2 sprigs fresh thyme, leaves stripped and chopped, stems discarded
1 garlic clove, sliced in half
1 teaspoon gluten-free tahini
½ teaspoon coconut sugar (optional)
½ teaspoon salt (optional)
Pinch black pepper
¼ cup plain gluten-free hummus

1. In a jar with a tight-fitting lid, combine the fresh lemon juice, chopped thyme leaves, sliced garlic, tahini, coconut sugar (if desired), salt (if desired), and black pepper. 2. Add the plain gluten-free hummus to the jar in a slow, steady stream while stirring or shaking to incorporate it into the dressing. 3. Taste the dressing and adjust the seasoning if needed. 4. Refrigerate the dressing for up to 5 days. Before serving, remove the garlic clove.

Per Serving:
calories: 7 | fat: 0g | protein: 0g | carbs: 2g | fiber: 0g

Tomato Sauce

Prep time: 10 minutes | Cook time: 40 minutes | Makes 4 cups

1 medium yellow onion, peeled and diced small
6 cloves garlic, peeled and minced
6 tablespoons minced basil
2 tablespoons minced oregano
1 (28 ounces / 794 g) can diced tomatoes, puréed
Salt, to taste (optional)

1. In a large saucepan, place the diced yellow onion and sauté it over medium heat for 10 minutes. If needed, add water, 1 to 2 tablespoons at a time, to prevent the onion from sticking to the pan. 2. Add the minced garlic, minced basil, and minced oregano to the saucepan and cook for another 3 minutes. 3. Pour in the puréed tomatoes and add salt to taste (if desired). Stir well to combine all the ingredients. 4. Cover the saucepan and cook the tomato sauce over medium-low heat for 25 minutes, allowing the flavors to meld together.

Per Serving: (1 cup)

calories: 48 | fat: 0g | protein: 2g | carbs: 10g | fiber: 4g

Tahini Dressing

Prep time: 5 minutes | Cook time: 0 minutes | Makes ½ cup

¼ cup tahini
1 teaspoon minced garlic
3 tablespoons lemon juice
1 tablespoon maple syrup (optional)
1 teaspoon soy sauce
1 teaspoon ground cumin
1 tablespoon olive oil (optional)
1 tablespoon hot water
Pinch of salt and pepper (optional)

1. In a small bowl, whisk together the tahini, minced garlic, lemon juice, maple syrup (if using), soy sauce, ground cumin, olive oil (if using), hot water, and a pinch of salt and pepper until well combined. 2. Adjust the consistency by adding more hot water if desired, to achieve your preferred thickness. 3. Store the tahini dressing in an airtight container in the refrigerator for up to 7 days.

Per Serving: (½ cup)

calories: 283 | fat: 24g | protein: 6g | carbs: 16g | fiber: 3g

Creamy Herbed Hemp Dressing

Prep time: 10 minutes | Cook time: 0 minutes | Serves 6

½ cup hemp seeds
¼ cup chopped flat-leaf parsley
2 tablespoons raw cashews
1 scallion, sliced
1 tablespoon apple cider vinegar
1 tablespoon fresh lemon juice
2 teaspoons capers, drained
1 teaspoon nutritional yeast
½ teaspoon garlic powder
½ teaspoon coconut sugar (optional)
¼ teaspoon dried dill
Salt and black pepper (optional)
1 or 2 tablespoons water (optional)

1. In a high-speed blender, combine the hemp seeds, chopped parsley, raw cashews, sliced scallion, apple cider vinegar, fresh lemon juice, drained capers, nutritional yeast, garlic powder, coconut sugar (if desired), and dried dill. 2. Process the ingredients in the blender until smooth and creamy. 3. Taste the dressing and season with salt and black pepper if desired. Adjust the consistency by adding 1 or 2 tablespoons of water, as needed, to achieve the desired thickness. 4. Transfer the creamy herbed hemp dressing to an airtight container and refrigerate it for up to 5 days.

Per Serving:

calories: 106 | fat: 9g | protein: 4g | carbs: 5g | fiber: 2g

Plant-Based Parmesan

Prep time: 5 minutes | Cook time: 0 minutes | Makes 1 heaping cup

1 cup raw cashews
⅓ cup nutritional yeast
¾ teaspoon garlic powder
½ teaspoon salt (optional)

1. In a blender or food processor, combine the raw cashews, nutritional yeast, garlic powder, and salt (if using). 2. Blend the mixture on medium-high speed until it reaches the texture of grated parmesan cheese. You may need to stop and start the blender or food processor a couple of times to ensure that the nuts are evenly processed and not clumping together at the bottom. 3. Transfer the plant-based parmesan to a glass or plastic container and store it in the refrigerator for up to 1 month.

Per Serving:

calories: 219 | fat: 15g | protein: 11g | carbs: 14g | fiber: 4g

Pure Nut Mylk

Prep time: 2 minutes | Cook time: 0 minutes | Makes 3 cups

1 cup raw, unsalted nuts (almonds, hazelnuts, Brazil nuts, pecans, macadamias, walnuts)
3 cups purified water for blending, plus more if desired

1. Soak the raw nuts overnight in 2 to 3 cups of water. 2. Drain and discard the soaking water. Rinse the nuts well. 3. Place the soaked nuts in a blender along with 3 cups of purified water. 4. Blend on high speed for 2 to 3 minutes or until the mixture becomes smooth and creamy. 5. Strain the blended nut mixture through a cheesecloth or a nut milk bag, squeezing out as much liquid as possible to separate the nut mylk from the pulp. 6. If you prefer a thinner consistency, you can add more purified water to the nut mylk. 7. Pour the pure nut mylk into a glass jar and refrigerate. It will stay fresh for 3 to 4 days in the refrigerator.

Per Serving:

calories: 276 | fat: 23g | protein: 10g | carbs: 10g | fiber: 6g

Green Split Peas

Prep time: 5 minutes | Cook time: 45 minutes | Makes 2 cups

1 cup split peas, rinsed   1½ cups water

1. In a large pot with a lid, combine the split peas and water. 2. Place the pot over high heat and bring the mixture to a boil. 3. Once boiling, cover the pot with the lid and reduce the heat to low. 4. Allow the split peas to simmer for 45 minutes. 5. Once cooked, transfer the split peas to an airtight container and store them in the refrigerator for up to 5 days.

Per Serving: (1 cup)

calories: 347 | fat: 1g | protein: 24g | carbs: 63g | fiber: 25g

Quinoa Mylk

Prep time: 5 minutes | Cook time: 20 minutes | Makes 4 cups

½ cup uncooked quinoa
4 cups purified water, for blending
4 dates

1. Soak the quinoa overnight in 1 cup of water. Drain and rinse until the water runs clear. 2. In a medium saucepan, bring 2 cups of water to a boil. Add the rinsed quinoa and bring to a second boil. Cover and simmer over low heat for 15 minutes. Remove from heat and allow the quinoa to cool. 3. Place the cooled quinoa in a blender with 4 cups of purified water. Blend on high speed for 1 to 3 minutes, or until smooth. 4. Strain the blended quinoa mixture using a cheesecloth or a nut milk bag. Gently squeeze and massage the cloth to strain the milk. 5. Pour the quinoa mylk back into the blender and add the dates. Blend until smooth. 6. Transfer the quinoa mylk to a glass jar with a tight lid and store in the refrigerator for 3 to 4 days.

Per Serving:

calories: 98 | fat: 1g | protein: 3g | carbs: 19g | fiber: 2g

Mango-Orange Dressing

Prep time: 5 minutes | Cook time: 0 minutes | Serves 8

1 cup diced mango
½ cup orange juice
2 tablespoons fresh lime juice
2 tablespoons gluten-free rice vinegar
1 teaspoon coconut sugar (optional)
¼ teaspoon salt (optional)
2 tablespoons chopped cilantro

1. In a blender, combine the diced mango, orange juice, lime juice, rice vinegar, coconut sugar, and salt (if using). Blend until smooth. 2. Stir in the chopped cilantro. 3. Transfer the dressing to an airtight container and refrigerate for up to 2 days.

Per Serving:

calories: 23 | fat: 0g | protein: 0g | carbs: 6g | fiber: 0g

Gut-Healing Sauerkraut

Prep time: 5 minutes | Cook time: 0 minutes | Makes 4 cups

1 medium purple cabbage
1 tablespoon Celtic sea salt (optional)
2 to 4 tablespoons minced fresh ginger, to taste (optional)

1. Peel off and discard any wrinkly, dry or damaged outer leaves from the cabbage. Reserving 1 healthy, pliable leaf for later, cut the cabbage into quarters right through the core. Carefully cut out and discard the tough inner core. Shred the cabbage, using a mandoline, knife or food processor. We prefer using a food processor fitted with the shredding blade. 2. Put the shredded cabbage into a large bowl. Sprinkle the salt (if using) over the cabbage and massage it with your hands until liquid starts to release. Set aside to marinate. 3. Add the minced ginger to the bowl of cabbage. Use your hands to work the ginger through the cabbage evenly, then once again massage the cabbage until it releases plenty of liquid when squeezed in your hands. The released juice will later be used as a brine. 4. Transfer the cabbage to a wide-mouth 1-quart mason jar, packing it down tightly with each handful added to the jar. When the cabbage is tightly packed down, take the cabbage leaf you reserved earlier and gently fold it until it is about the same width all around as the jar. Place the leaf into the jar, on top of the packed cabbage and make sure it covers it completely. 5. Press the cabbage leaf down firmly, then pour enough brine from the mixing bowl to cover all of the cabbage and submerge it in the liquid. The cabbage must be below the water (brine) level, away from oxygen. Be sure to leave an inch of space between the top of liquid and the top of the jar. Doing this allows for expansion. However, do not leave too much room at the top of the jar as too much oxygen could cause your kraut to go bad. 6. Allow the kraut to ferment in a cool, dark place for at least 3 days and up to 10, depending on your desired degree of sourness. Once the kraut has fermented to your liking, seal the jar and transfer it to the refrigerator. Fermenting will continue to take place in the fridge, but this will be very, very slow. The flavors may change over time.

Per Serving:

calories: 45 | fat: 0g | protein: 2g | carbs: 10g | fiber: 3g

Maple-Dijon Dressing

Prep time: 5 minutes | Cook time: 0 minutes | Serves 4

¼ cup apple cider vinegar
2 tablespoons maple syrup
2 teaspoons gluten-free Dijon mustard
¼ teaspoon black pepper
2 tablespoons water
Salt (optional)

1. Combine the vinegar, maple syrup (if desired), mustard, pepper and water in a small jar with a tight-fitting lid. Season with salt to taste, if desired. Refrigerate for up to 5 days.

Per Serving:

calories: 31 | fat: 0g | protein: 0g | carbs: 7g | fiber: 0g

Greener Guacamole

Prep time: 15 minutes | Cook time: 0 minutes |
Makes 1 to 1½ cups

2 ripe avocados, pitted, peeled, and diced
Juice of ½ lime
2 scallions, green and white parts, chopped
1 garlic clove, minced
½ teaspoon ground cumin
½ small bunch cilantro, chopped
Ground black pepper
Salt (optional)

1. In a medium bowl, combine the diced avocados, lime juice, chopped scallions, minced garlic, ground cumin, chopped cilantro, ground black pepper, and salt (if using). 2. Mash the ingredients together with a fork until you reach your desired guacamole consistency. 3. Transfer the guacamole to a serving bowl and chill in the refrigerator until ready to serve.

Per Serving:

calories: 40 | fat: 4g | protein: 1g | carbs: 3g | fiber: 2g

Date Syrup

Prep time: 30 minutes | Cook time: 0 minutes |
Makes 1⅓ cups

1 cup Medjool dates, pitted (about 10 large dates)
1¼ cups purified water, for blending
1½ teaspoons fresh lemon juice

1. In a small bowl, cover the pitted Medjool dates with warm water and let them sit for 30 minutes. 2. Drain and rinse the dates to remove any excess water. 3. Place the soaked and rinsed dates in a high-speed blender along with the purified water and fresh lemon juice. 4. Blend the mixture on high speed for 45 to 60 seconds, or until smooth and well combined. 5. Transfer the date syrup to an airtight container and store it in the refrigerator for up to 2 weeks.

Per Serving:

calories: 111 | fat: 0g | protein: 1g | carbs: 30g | fiber: 2g

Easy DIY Pizza Crust

Prep time: 5 minutes | Cook time: 10 to 15 minutes |
Makes 2 medium pizza crusts

1 cup whole grain flour
1 tablespoon dry active yeast
1 teaspoon unrefined sugar (optional)
½ teaspoon sea salt (optional)
1 tablespoon olive oil (optional)
1 cup water

1. Preheat the oven to 400°F (205°C). Sprinkle some coarsely ground millet or corn flour on 1 large or 2 small baking sheets. 2. Combine the flour, yeast, sugar, and salt (if using) in a large bowl. Make a well in the center and add the oil (if using), then the water. Stir the dough together with a spoon until it's too dry to stir, then bring it together with your hands. Add more water or flour as necessary to make a soft dough that doesn't stick to your fingers. 3. Knead for 5 minutes on a lightly floured board. Press or roll out into two pizza crusts. 4. Lay the crusts on the baking sheets, and put them in the oven for 10 minutes, or until they start to get a light color around the edges.

Per Serving: (1 crust)

calories: 288 | fat: 8g | protein: 10g | carbs: 47g | fiber: 8g

Chili Powder

Prep time: 15 minutes | Cook time: 0 minutes |
Makes about ½ cup

3 arbol chiles
5 guajillo chiles
5 California chiles
2 tablespoons cumin seeds (not ground)
2 tablespoons garlic powder
1 tablespoon dried oregano
1 tablespoon onion powder

1. Heat a cast-iron skillet over high heat. While the skillet heats up, remove and discard the stems and seeds from the arbol, guajillo, and California chiles. 2. Place the chiles in the hot, dry skillet and roast them for 3 to 5 minutes, turning occasionally, until their color slightly changes and they become softer. Transfer the roasted chiles to a blender or food processor. 3. In the same hot skillet, add the cumin seeds and toast them until they begin popping. Immediately transfer the toasted cumin seeds to the blender, along with the garlic powder, dried oregano, and onion powder. 4. Cover the blender tightly and blend the ingredients until they form a fine powder. Allow the powder to settle for 2 to 3 minutes before removing the lid. 5. Transfer the homemade chili powder to a cool, dry container and store it in a cool, dry location for up to 6 months.

Per Serving:

calories: 7 | fat: 0g | protein: 0g | carbs: 1g | fiber: 0g

Pineapple Chutney

Prep time: 25 minutes | Cook time: 15 minutes |
Makes 1½ cups

½ medium yellow onion, peeled and diced small
1 tablespoon grated ginger
2 jalapeño peppers, seeded and minced
½ tablespoon cumin seeds, toasted and ground
½ fresh pineapple, peeled, cored, and diced
½ cup finely chopped cilantro
Salt, to taste (optional)

1. In a large skillet or saucepan, sauté the diced onion over medium heat for 7 to 8 minutes. Add water, 1 to 2 tablespoons at a time, if needed, to prevent sticking. 2. Add the grated ginger, minced jalapeño peppers, and ground cumin seeds to the skillet. Cook for an additional 4 minutes. 3. Add the diced pineapple to the skillet and remove it from the heat. 4. Stir in the finely chopped cilantro and season with salt, if desired.

Per Serving: (½ cup)

calories: 98 | fat: 0g | protein: 2g | carbs: 24g | fiber: 3g

Peanut Milk

Prep time: 5 minutes | Cook time: 0 minutes | Makes 3 cups

1 cup unsalted roasted peanuts
¼ cup raisins
3 cups water

1. In a blender pitcher, soak the peanuts and raisins in the water. Let the mixture sit overnight or for at least 6 hours. 2. Blend the water, peanuts, and raisins together on high for 1 to 2 minutes. 3. Using cheesecloth or a mesh nut-milk bag, strain the milk into a pitcher, separating out the liquid from the solids. 4. Store in an airtight container in the fridge for up to 5 days.

Per Serving: (1 cup)
calories: 284 | fat: 24g | protein: 14g | carbs: 9g | fiber: 4g

Buckwheat Sesame Milk

Prep time: 5 minutes | Cook time: 0 minutes | Makes 4 cups

1 cup cooked buckwheat
1 tablespoon tahini, or other nut or seed butter
1 teaspoon pure vanilla extract (optional)
2 to 3 dates, or 15 drops pure stevia (or vanilla stevia), or 2 to 3 tablespoons unrefined sugar (optional)
3 cups water

1. Put everything in a blender, and purée until smooth. 2. Strain the fiber through a piece of cheesecloth or a fine-mesh sieve. 3. Keep in an airtight container in the fridge for up to 5 days.

Per Serving: (1 cup)
calories: 76 | fat: 2g | protein: 2g | carbs: 12g | fiber: 1g

Mayonnaise

Prep time: 5 minutes | Cook time: 0 minutes | Makes 1½ cups

1 (12 ounces / 340 g) package extra-firm silken tofu, drained
1 teaspoon dry mustard
½ teaspoon onion powder
½ teaspoon garlic powder
½ teaspoon salt, or to taste (optional)
3 tablespoons red wine vinegar

1. Combine all ingredients in the bowl of a food processor. Purée until smooth and creamy.

Per Serving: (½ cup)
calories: 110 | fat: 6g | protein: 11g | carbs: 3g | fiber: 0g

Lemon-Tahini Dressing

Prep time: 5 minutes | Cook time: 0 minutes | Serves 8

¼ cup fresh lemon juice
1 teaspoon maple syrup (optional)
1 small garlic clove, chopped
½ cup gluten-free tahini
¼ teaspoon salt (optional)
⅛ teaspoon black pepper
¼ to ½ cup water

1. Pulse the lemon juice, sugar, garlic, tahini, salt (if desired), and pepper in a high-speed blender to combine. Slowly add the water, starting with ¼ cup, until it reaches the desired consistency. Refrigerate in an airtight container for up to 5 days.

Per Serving:
calories: 94 | fat: 8g | protein: 3g | carbs: 4g | fiber: 1g

Mama Mia Marinara Sauce

Prep time: 10 minutes | Cook time: 2 to 3 hours | Makes about 7 cups

1 medium onion, diced
5 garlic cloves, minced
2 (28 ounces / 794 g) cans no-salt-added crushed tomatoes
½ cup red wine
2 tablespoons Italian seasoning, or 1 tablespoon each dried basil and dried oregano
Ground black pepper
Salt (optional)

1. Put the onion, garlic, and tomatoes in the slow cooker. Swirl the wine in the empty tomato cans and pour everything into the slow cooker. Add the Italian seasoning, pepper, and salt (if using). Stir to combine. 2. Cover and cook on High for 2 to 3 hours or on Low for 4 to 5 hours.

Per Serving:
calories: 30 | fat: 0g | protein: 1g | carbs: 4g | fiber: 1g

Roasted Red Pepper Spread

Prep time: 15 minutes | Cook time: 0 minutes | Makes 2 cups

2 cups cooked great northern beans, or 1 (15 ounces / 425 g) can, drained and rinsed

1 red bell pepper, roasted, seeded, and coarsely chopped
3 cloves garlic, peeled and minced
3 tablespoons finely chopped dill
Zest and juice of 1 lemon
Salt, to taste (optional)
Pinch cayenne pepper

1. Combine all ingredients in the bowl of a food processor and purée until smooth and creamy.

Per Serving:
calories: 230 | fat: 0g | protein: 15g | carbs: 42g | fiber: 13g

Chapter 3 Breakfasts

Blueberry Scones

Prep time: 10 minutes | Cook time: 20 minutes | Makes 8 scones

1 cup whole wheat flour
¾ cup old-fashioned rolled oats
½ teaspoon baking powder
½ teaspoon salt (optional)
1 cup frozen blueberries, thawed and drained
3 tablespoons cold coconut butter
¾ cup almond milk
1 tablespoon fresh lemon juice
2 teaspoons coconut sugar (optional)

1. Preheat the oven to 475ºF (245ºC). Lightly grease a baking sheet or line it with parchment paper. 2. In a medium bowl, mix together the whole wheat flour, rolled oats, baking powder, and salt (if using). 3. Add the cold coconut butter to the dry ingredients and use a pastry cutter, two forks, or your fingers to cut the butter into the mixture until well combined. 4. Gently fold in the thawed and drained blueberries. 5. In a separate small bowl, combine the almond milk and fresh lemon juice. Stir to combine. 6. Pour the almond milk mixture into the dry ingredients and mix with a fork until it forms a shaggy ball of dough. Be careful not to overmix. 7. Split the dough into two equal parts. Shape each part into a circle about 1 inch thick on the prepared baking sheet, leaving space between them. 8. Sprinkle one teaspoon of coconut sugar (if using) over each circle of dough. 9. Use a knife to cut each circle into 4 wedges, creating a total of 8 scones. 10. Bake in the preheated oven for 20 minutes, or until a toothpick inserted in the middle comes out clean and the scones are golden brown. 11. Allow the scones to cool slightly before serving. They are best served warm. Toast any leftovers before serving.

Per Serving: (2 scones)
calories: 250 | fat: 8g | protein: 8g | carbs: 45g | fiber: 7g

Savory Rosemary–Black Pepper Scones

Prep time: 10 minutes | Cook time: 20 minutes | Makes 8 scones

1 cup whole wheat flour
¾ cup old-fashioned rolled oats
2 tablespoons minced fresh rosemary
½ teaspoon baking powder
½ teaspoon freshly ground black pepper
½ teaspoon salt (optional)
3 tablespoons puréed white beans or tahini
¾ cup almond milk
1 tablespoon fresh lemon juice

1. Preheat the oven to 475ºF (245ºC). Lightly grease a baking sheet or use parchment paper. 2. In a medium bowl, mix together the whole wheat flour, rolled oats, minced fresh rosemary, baking powder, black pepper, and salt (if desired). 3. Add the puréed white beans or tahini to the dry ingredients. Use a pastry cutter, two forks, or your fingers to mix until well combined. 4. In a separate small bowl, combine the almond milk and fresh lemon juice. Stir to combine. 5. Add the almond milk mixture to the dry ingredients. Mix with a fork until the dough comes together into a shaggy ball; avoid overmixing. 6. Split the dough into two equal balls. Place one ball of dough onto one end of the prepared baking sheet and press it into a circle about 1 inch thick. Repeat with the second ball of dough on the other end of the baking sheet. 7. Use a knife to cut each circle of dough into 4 wedges, creating a total of 8 scones. 8. Bake the scones in the preheated oven for 20 minutes, or until a toothpick inserted in the middle comes out clean and the scones are golden brown. 9. Serve the scones warm. If there are any leftovers, toast them before serving for optimal taste and texture.

Per Serving: (2 scones)
calories: 237 | fat: 9g | protein: 10g | carbs: 41g | fiber: 7g

Banana Zucchini Pancakes

Prep time: 10 minutes | Cook time: 10 minutes | Makes 8 pancakes

1 cup whole wheat or all-purpose flour
2 teaspoons baking powder
½ teaspoon salt (optional)
2 tablespoons canola oil, plus more for greasing (optional)
1 mashed banana
¼ cup grated zucchini
1 cup plant-based milk
1½ teaspoons vanilla extract
1 tablespoon maple syrup (optional)

1. Preheat a nonstick pan over medium-high heat. If you're not using a nonstick pan or if it needs some extra greasing, you can lightly oil the pan. 2. In a medium bowl, mix together the flour, baking powder, salt (if using), canola oil, mashed banana, grated zucchini, plant-based milk, vanilla extract, and maple syrup (if using). Gently mix until the batter is smooth, but it's okay to have some lumps remaining. 3. Scoop out the batter with a ¼-cup measuring cup and pour it onto the preheated pan. Cook the pancake until bubbles begin to form in the center, then flip it over and cook the other side until light brown. 4. Remove the pancake from the heat and repeat the process with the remaining batter. 5. Serve the banana zucchini pancakes warm with your favorite toppings such as fresh fruit, a drizzle of maple syrup, or a dollop of yogurt.

Per Serving: (1 pancake)
calories: 130 | fat: 5g | protein: 3g | carbs: 19g | fiber: 1g

Savory Oatmeal

Prep time: 10 minutes | Cook time: 10 minutes | Makes 2 bowls

- 1 cup gluten-free old-fashioned rolled oats
- 1 carrot, peeled and shredded
- 1½ cups water
- 1 cup stemmed and chopped kale
- ¼ cup salsa or marinara sauce
- 2 tablespoons nutritional yeast
- ½ chopped avocado
- 2 tablespoons roasted pumpkin seeds
- Smoked paprika or crushed red pepper (optional)
- Salt and black pepper (optional)

1. In a small saucepan, combine the oats and shredded carrot. Add the water (adjust the amount to achieve your preferred oatmeal consistency; 1½ cups water will yield a fairly thick oatmeal). 2. Place the saucepan over medium heat and bring the mixture to a simmer. Cook, stirring often, until the oats and carrots are tender, which should take about 5 minutes. 3. Stir in the chopped kale, salsa or marinara sauce, and nutritional yeast. Allow the mixture to cook for another minute or until the kale wilts. 4. Pour the savory oatmeal into bowls and top each bowl with chopped avocado and roasted pumpkin seeds. 5. Sprinkle with smoked paprika or crushed red pepper if desired, and season with salt and black pepper to taste. 6. Serve the savory oatmeal hot and enjoy!

Per Serving: (½ bowl)
calories: 153 | fat: 7g | protein: 9g | carbs: 24g | fiber: 7g

Nut Butter and Jelly Breakfast Cookies

Prep time: 10 minutes | Cook time: 20 minutes | Makes 12 cookies

- ¾ cup nut butter
- ½ cup berries or 1 small banana, mashed with a fork
- ¼ cup plus 2 tablespoons fruit preserves
- 1 to 1¼ cups whole wheat flour
- ¾ teaspoon baking powder
- ⅛ teaspoon salt (optional)

1. Preheat the oven to 350°F (180°C). Line two baking sheets with parchment paper. 2. In a food processor, combine the nut butter, berries or mashed banana, and fruit preserves. Pulse until thoroughly combined. 3. Add 1 cup of the whole wheat flour, baking powder, and salt (if desired) to the food processor. Continue to pulse until the ingredients are well combined. If the dough is too sticky, gradually add more flour, up to an additional ¼ cup, until a thick dough forms. The dough should be smooth and glossy, with no visible flour. If needed, transfer the dough to a bowl and knead it until the flour is fully incorporated. 4. Divide the dough into 12 equal pieces. Roll each piece into a ball, then flatten it to form a cookie shape. If desired, create hashmarks on the cookies using a fork, resembling traditional peanut butter cookies. 5. Place the cookies on the prepared baking sheets and bake for 17 to 20 minutes, or until the tops are golden brown. 6. Allow the cookies to cool completely on the baking sheets before serving. 7. Store the cookies in an airtight container at room temperature for up to 5 days.

Per Serving: (1 cookie)
calories: 141 | fat: 9g | protein: 5g | carbs: 13g | fiber: 3g

Strawberry, Banana, and Granola Yogurt Bowls

Prep time: 10 minutes | Cook time: 0 minutes | Serves 2

- 2 cups plain plant-based yogurt
- 1 cup granola
- 2 tablespoons maple syrup (optional)
- 1 cup sliced strawberries
- 1 medium banana, sliced

1. Divide the plain plant-based yogurt between two serving bowls, ensuring an even amount in each bowl. 2. Top each bowl with ½ cup of granola, spreading it evenly over the yogurt. 3. Drizzle 1 tablespoon of maple syrup (if desired) over each bowl for added sweetness. You can adjust the amount of maple syrup based on your preference. 4. Add sliced strawberries and banana slices to each bowl, distributing them evenly. 5. Serve the strawberry, banana, and granola yogurt bowls immediately and enjoy!

Per Serving:
calories: 391 | fat: 8g | protein: 12g | carbs: 66g | fiber: 9g

Crazy Quinoa Protein Muffins

Prep time: 15 minutes | Cook time: 35 minutes | Serves 6

- ½ cup quinoa
- 2 tablespoons ground chia seeds
- ¼ cup almond flour
- 3 tablespoons vanilla protein powder
- ½ teaspoon salt (optional)
- ½ cup dates, chopped small
- 2 tablespoons coconut oil (optional)
- 3 tablespoons maple syrup (optional)
- 1 teaspoon vanilla extract
- ¼ cup unsweetened shredded coconut
- ½ cup raisins

1. Rinse the quinoa and place it in a small saucepan with a lid. Add ½ cup of water, cover, and bring to a boil over medium-high heat. Reduce the heat to low and let it simmer for 20 minutes. Remove from heat, uncover, and allow it to cool. 2. Preheat the oven to 450°F (235°C). Line six muffin cups with paper liners. 3. In a small bowl, mix the ground chia seeds with ¼ cup plus 2 tablespoons of water. Set aside to thicken. 4. In a separate small bowl, combine the almond flour, protein powder, and salt (if desired). Add the chopped dates and mix well to coat the dates with the flour mixture. Set aside. 5. If using coconut oil, place it in a medium bowl and microwave for 10 to 20 seconds to melt it. Remove from the microwave and add the maple syrup (if desired). Stir well. Allow it to cool, and then add the chia seed mixture, vanilla extract, shredded coconut, almond flour mixture, cooked quinoa, and raisins. Mix everything together until well combined. 6. Divide the batter evenly among the prepared muffin cups. Bake in the preheated oven for 12 to 15 minutes, or until a toothpick inserted into the center of a muffin comes out clean. 7. Remove the muffins from the oven and let them cool in the pan for a few minutes. Transfer them to a wire rack to cool completely before serving.

Per Serving: (1 muffin)
calories: 179 | fat: 6g | protein: 7g | carbs: 26g | fiber: 5g

Slow Cooker Apples and Oats

Prep time: 15 minutes | Cook time: 3 hours | Serves 2

- 1½ cups peeled and sliced apples
- 1 cup old-fashioned oats
- ½ cup melted dairy-free butter
- ½ cup coconut sugar (optional)
- 2 tablespoons lemon juice
- 2 tablespoons hempseed, toasted in shell
- 1 teaspoon ground cinnamon
- 1 cup chopped pecans

1. Place all the ingredients in the slow cooker and stir to combine. 2. Set the slow cooker to high heat and cook for 2 to 3 hours, depending on your preferred level of doneness. The oats should be tender and the apples softened. 3. Once cooked, serve the slow cooker apples and oats hot, warm, or cooled, according to your preference.

Per Serving:

calories: 587 | fat: 37g | protein: 15g | carbs: 49g | fiber: 15g

Pan con Tomate

Prep time: 5 minutes | Cook time: 0 minutes | Makes 2 slices

- 2 large slices toast
- 1 garlic clove, halved
- 1 Roma tomato, halved
- Salt (optional)
- Nutritional yeast (optional)

1. Take the garlic clove and cut it in half. 2. Take the halved Roma tomato. 3. Rub each slice of toast with the cut side of the garlic clove, gently pressing it onto the bread to release its flavor. 4. Rub each slice of toast with the cut side of the Roma tomato, allowing the tomato juices to soak into the bread. 5. If desired, sprinkle a pinch of salt over each slice of toast for added flavor. 6. Optional: Sprinkle some nutritional yeast over the top of each slice of toast for extra taste and texture. 7. Serve the Pan con Tomate immediately and enjoy!

Per Serving: (1 slice)

calories: 90 | fat: 1g | protein: 3g | carbs: 17g | fiber: 2g

Zucchini Bread Oatmeal

Prep time: 5 minutes | Cook time: 20 minutes | Serves 4

- 2 cups rolled oats
- 1 medium zucchini, grated
- 4 cups water
- ½ cup unsweetened plant-based milk
- 1 tablespoon ground cinnamon
- ½ cup raisins
- 1 tablespoon maple syrup (optional)
- Pinch of salt (optional)
- 2 medium bananas, sliced
- 4 tablespoons chopped walnuts (optional)

1. In a medium saucepan over medium-high heat, combine the rolled oats, grated zucchini, and water. Bring to a boil. 2. Reduce the heat to medium-low and simmer, stirring often, until the oats are soft and creamy, about 15 minutes. 3. Remove the saucepan from the heat. Add the plant-based milk, ground cinnamon, raisins, maple syrup (if using), and salt (if using). Stir well to combine. 4. Divide the oatmeal among 4 bowls. 5. Top each portion with half a sliced banana and 1 tablespoon of chopped walnuts (if using).

Per Serving:

calories: 301 | fat: 4g | protein: 9g | carbs: 62g | fiber: 8g

Chickpea Country Gravy

Prep time: 10 minutes | Cook time: 10 minutes | Serves 4 to 6

- 8 ounces (227 g) silken tofu
- ½ cup unsweetened soy milk
- 2 tablespoons chickpea flour
- 1 (15 ounces / 425 g) can chickpeas, drained and rinsed
- 1 tablespoon dried sage
- 2 teaspoons liquid aminos
- 1 teaspoon freshly ground black pepper
- ½ teaspoon ground fennel

1. In a blender, combine the silken tofu, unsweetened soy milk, and chickpea flour. Blend until the mixture becomes smooth and creamy. 2. In a sauté pan or skillet, add the tofu mixture, drained and rinsed chickpeas, dried sage, liquid aminos, freshly ground black pepper, and ground fennel. Stir well to combine. 3. Place the pan over medium heat and bring the mixture to a simmer. Cook for about 5 minutes, stirring occasionally, until the gravy thickens. 4. Once the gravy has thickened, remove it from the heat and it's ready to be served.

Per Serving:

calories: 115 | fat: 3g | protein: 8g | carbs: 14g | fiber: 3g

Powerhouse Green Juice

Prep time: 10 minutes | Cook time: 0 minutes | Serves 1

- 4 ribs celery
- 6 sprigs flat-leaf parsley (leaves and tender stems)
- 2 packed cups spinach leaves
- 6 seasonal green leaves (collard leaves, lettuce leaves, kale, Swiss chard, etc.)
- 3 green apples, cored and chopped
- ½ lemon, peeled
- 1 (1-inch) piece fresh ginger

1. Wash all the vegetables and fruits thoroughly. 2. Prepare the ingredients by cutting the celery ribs into manageable pieces, removing the stems from the parsley sprigs, and chopping the green apples into chunks. 3. Feed all the ingredients, including the celery, parsley, spinach leaves, seasonal green leaves, green apples, lemon, and ginger, through a juicer. Alternate between harder and softer items to ensure optimal juicing. 4. Once all the ingredients have been juiced, give the juice a good stir to combine all the flavors. 5. Serve the Powerhouse Green Juice immediately and enjoy its freshness.

Per Serving:

calories: 216 | fat: 0g | protein: 3g | carbs: 48g | fiber: 7g

Congee with Dates and Spices

Prep time: 10 minutes | Cook time: 20 minutes | Serves 4

4 cups cooked brown rice
½ cup dates, pitted and chopped
½ cup chopped unsulfured apricots
1 large cinnamon stick
¼ teaspoon ground cloves
Salt, to taste (optional)

1. In a large saucepan, bring 2 cups of water to a boil over medium heat. 2. Add the cooked brown rice, chopped dates, chopped apricots, cinnamon stick, and ground cloves to the boiling water. 3. Reduce the heat to medium-low and cook the mixture for 15 minutes, or until it thickens to your desired consistency, stirring occasionally. 4. Season with salt, if desired. Remember to taste and adjust the seasoning according to your preference. 5. Remove the cinnamon stick from the congee before serving. 6. Serve the congee warm in bowls, garnished with additional chopped dates or apricots if desired.

Per Serving:
calories: 307 | fat: 1g | protein: 6g | carbs: 68g | fiber: 6g

Green Banana Smoothie

Prep time: 5 minutes | Cook time: 0 minutes | Makes 2 glasses

2½ to 3 sliced frozen bananas
1½ cups spinach or kale, stems removed
1½ cups plant-based milk

1. In a blender, combine the sliced frozen bananas, spinach or kale, and plant-based milk. 2. Blend all the ingredients on high speed until smooth and creamy. 3. If the consistency is too thick, you can add more plant-based milk to reach your desired consistency. 4. Pour the smoothie into glasses and serve immediately.

Per Serving: (1 glass)
calories: 134 | fat: 4g | protein: 8g | carbs: 16g | fiber: 3g

Chickpea Quiche

Prep time: 10 minutes | Cook time: 45 minutes | Serves 6

2 cups chickpea flour
¼ cup nutritional yeast
1 teaspoon gluten-free baking powder
½ teaspoon salt (optional)
¼ teaspoon ground turmeric
⅛ teaspoon black pepper
2 cups finely chopped greens
3 minced garlic cloves
2 cups water
1 tablespoon olive oil, plus extra for greasing the plates (optional)

1. Preheat the oven to 400°F (205°C). Grease two pie plates with olive oil, if desired. 2. In a large bowl, combine the chickpea flour, nutritional yeast, baking powder, salt (if using), turmeric, and black pepper. 3. Stir in the finely chopped greens and minced garlic. 4. Whisk in the water gradually until a smooth batter with a pancake-like consistency is formed. If preparing the batter in advance, it can be refrigerated overnight. If the batter thickens overnight, add up to ¼ cup more water to thin it out before using. 5. Pour the batter evenly into the prepared pie plates. 6. Bake in the preheated oven for 45 minutes, or until the quiche is cooked through and a toothpick inserted in the middle comes out clean. 7. Remove the quiche from the oven and allow it to cool for 15 minutes. 8. Slice the quiche into wedges and serve. Leftovers can be wrapped in parchment paper and stored in the refrigerator for up to 3 days.

Per Serving:
calories: 167 | fat: 4g | protein: 10g | carbs: 22g | fiber: 5g

Slow-Cooked Steel-Cut Oats

Prep time: 10 minutes | Cook time: 8 hours | Serves 2

1 cup steel-cut oats
2 cups chopped dried apple
1 cup dates, pitted and chopped
1 cinnamon stick

1. In a 2- or 4-quart slow cooker, combine the steel-cut oats, chopped dried apple, dates, cinnamon stick, and 4 cups of water. 2. Cover the slow cooker and cook on low heat for 8 hours, or until the oats are tender and cooked to your desired consistency. 3. Before serving, remove the cinnamon stick from the slow cooker. 4. Stir the oats well before portioning them into serving bowls. 5. Serve the slow-cooked steel-cut oats warm and enjoy!

Per Serving:
calories: 320 | fat: 3g | protein: 10g | carbs: 89g | fiber: 15g

Carrot Cake Oatmeal

Prep time: 10 minutes | Cook time: 15 minutes | Serves 2

¼ cup pecans
1 cup finely shredded carrot
½ cup old-fashioned oats
1¼ cups unsweetened nondairy milk
1 tablespoon pure maple syrup (optional)
1 teaspoon ground cinnamon
1 teaspoon ground ginger
¼ teaspoon ground nutmeg
2 tablespoons chia seeds

1. In a small skillet over medium-high heat, toast the pecans for 3 to 4 minutes, stirring often, until browned and fragrant (watch closely, as they can burn quickly). Pour the pecans onto a cutting board and coarsely chop them. Set aside. 2. In an 8-quart pot over medium-high heat, combine the carrot, oats, milk, maple syrup (if using), cinnamon, ginger, and nutmeg. Bring to a boil, then reduce the heat to medium-low. Cook, uncovered, for 10 minutes, stirring occasionally. 3. Stir in the chopped pecans and chia seeds. Serve immediately.

Per Serving:
calories: 307 | fat: 17g | protein: 7g | carbs: 35g | fiber: 11g

Breakfast Scramble

Prep time: 20 minutes | Cook time: 20 minutes | Serves 6

1 medium red onion, peeled and cut into ½-inch dice
1 medium red bell pepper, seeded and cut into ½-inch dice
1 medium green bell pepper, seeded and cut into ½-inch dice
2 cups sliced mushrooms (from about 8 ounces / 227 g whole mushrooms)
1 large head cauliflower, cut into florets, or 2 (19 ounces / 539 g) cans Jamaican ackee, drained and gently rinsed
Salt, to taste (optional)
½ teaspoon freshly ground black pepper
1½ teaspoons turmeric
¼ teaspoon cayenne pepper, or to taste
3 cloves garlic, peeled and minced
1 to 2 tablespoons low-sodium soy sauce
¼ cup nutritional yeast (optional)

1. Place the onion, red and green peppers, and mushrooms in a medium skillet or saucepan and sauté over medium-high heat for 7 to 8 minutes, or until the onion is translucent. Add water 1 to 2 tablespoons at a time to keep the vegetables from sticking to the pan. 2. Add the cauliflower and cook for 5 to 6 minutes, or until the florets are tender. Add the salt (if using), black pepper, turmeric, cayenne pepper, garlic, soy sauce, and nutritional yeast (if using) to the pan and cook for 5 minutes more, or until hot and fragrant.

Per Serving:
calories: 65 | fat: 0g | protein: 5g | carbs: 11g | fiber: 4g

Loaded Breakfast Burrito

Prep time: 5 minutes | Cook time: 20 minutes | Serves 2

½ block (7 ounces / 198 g) firm tofu
2 medium potatoes, cut into ¼-inch dice
1 cup cooked black beans (see here), drained and rinsed
4 ounces (113 g) sliced mushrooms
1 jalapeño, seeded and diced
2 tablespoons vegetable broth or water
1 tablespoon nutritional yeast
½ teaspoon garlic powder
½ teaspoon onion powder
¼ cup salsa
6 corn tortillas

1. Heat a large skillet over medium-low heat. 2. Drain the tofu, then place it in the pan and mash it down with a fork or mixing spoon. 3. Stir the potatoes, black beans, mushrooms, jalapeño, broth, nutritional yeast, garlic powder, and onion powder into the skillet. Reduce the heat to low, cover, and cook for 10 minutes, or until the potatoes can be easily pierced with a fork. 4. Uncover, and stir in the salsa. Cook for 5 minutes, stirring every other minute. 5. Warm the tortillas in a microwave for 15 to 30 seconds or in a warm oven until soft. 6. Remove the pan from the heat, place one-sixth of the filling in the center of each tortilla, and roll the tortillas into burritos before serving.

Per Serving:
calories: 535 | fat: 8g | protein: 29g | carbs: 95g | fiber: 21g

Cleansing Morning Lemonade

Prep time: 2 minutes | Cook time: 0 minutes | Makes 1 quart

1 large lemon
1 quart warm purified water
Pinch of cayenne pepper, or to taste
1 to 2 teaspoons raw agave nectar (optional)

1. Wash the lemon well and squeeze the juice into a 1-quart glass or mason jar. Add the purified water, cayenne and agave (if using). 2. Stir and drink first thing in the morning on an empty stomach.

Per Serving:
calories: 5 | fat: 0g | protein: 0g | carbs: 1g | fiber: 0g

Plantains with Black Beans and Avocado

Prep time: 5 minutes | Cook time: 10 minutes | Serves 2

2 tablespoons coconut milk
1 large ripe plantain, thinly sliced
1 (15 ounces / 425 g) can black beans, drained and rinsed
½ avocado, peeled, pitted, and cubed
2 tablespoons chopped fresh cilantro

1. In a medium nonstick pan, bring the coconut milk to a boil; then reduce the heat to low. 2. Add the plantain slices to the pan. Cover with a lid and cook on low for 3 minutes. 3. Flip the plantains, add the black beans, and cover with a lid. Cook for 4 minutes more. 4. Serve in bowls and top each serving with avocado and cilantro.

Per Serving:
calories: 393 | fat: 9g | protein: 14g | carbs: 71g | fiber: 17g

Avocado Toast with Tomato and Hemp Hearts

Prep time: 5 minutes | Cook time: 5 minutes | Serves 2

4 slices whole-wheat bread
1 avocado, peeled, pitted, cut into quarters, and thinly sliced
Pinch of salt (optional)
1 medium tomato, thinly sliced
Black pepper
Red pepper flakes
2 teaspoons extra-virgin olive oil (optional)
4 teaspoons hemp hearts

1. Toast the bread slices. 2. On each slice, arrange a quarter of the avocado slices, a pinch of salt (if using), a quarter of the tomato, a pinch of black pepper, and a pinch of red pepper flakes. Drizzle each with ½ teaspoon of olive oil and sprinkle with 1 teaspoon of hemp hearts.

Per Serving:
calories: 379 | fat: 22g | protein:12 g | carbs: 38g | fiber: 11g

Sweet Potato Toasts with Avocado Mash and Tahini

Prep time: 10 minutes | Cook time: 30 minutes | Serves 4

Sweet Potato Toasts:
Olive oil cooking spray
4 medium sweet potatoes
Pinch of salt (optional)
Avocado Mash:
2 medium avocados, pitted and peeled
Juice of ½ lemon
Pinch of salt (optional)
Serve:
2 ounces (57 g) arugula (about 2 cups)
8 teaspoons tahini
8 teaspoons hemp hearts
Pinch red pepper flakes (optional)

1. Make the Sweet Potato Toasts: Preheat the oven to 400°F (205°C). Spray a sheet pan with olive oil cooking spray. 2. Cut the sweet potatoes lengthwise into ½-inch-thick slices (4 per potato). 3. Arrange the sweet potato slices in a single layer on the prepared sheet pan and sprinkle with salt. Bake for 15 minutes. Turn the slices over and continue to bake for another 15 minutes, or until the potatoes are slightly browned and crispy on the outside and soft in the middle. 4. Make the Avocado Mash: In a bowl, mash the avocados with a fork. Add the lemon juice and salt (if using) and stir until combined. 5. Assemble the Toasts: Spread 1 teaspoon of avocado mash over each sweet potato toast. For each, add about 5 arugula leaves, drizzle with ½ teaspoon of tahini, and top with ½ teaspoon of hemp hearts. Add a pinch of red pepper flakes (if using).

Per Serving:
calories: 375 | fat: 23g | protein: 7g | carbs: 38g | fiber: 12g

Shiitake Bakin'

Prep time: 5 minutes | Cook time: 30 minutes | Makes 1 cup

1 (3½ ounces / 99 g) package shiitake mushrooms, stems discarded and sliced thinly
1 teaspoon maple syrup (optional)
1 teaspoon reduced-sodium, gluten-free tamari
¼ teaspoon black pepper
¼ teaspoon garlic powder
¼ teaspoon smoked paprika

1. Preheat the oven to 375°F (190°C) and line a baking sheet with parchment paper. 2. In a medium bowl, combine the sliced shiitake mushrooms, maple syrup (if using), tamari, black pepper, garlic powder, and smoked paprika. Toss well to coat the mushrooms evenly with the seasoning mixture. 3. Spread the seasoned mushrooms in a single layer on the prepared baking sheet. 4. Bake in the preheated oven for 30 minutes, tossing the mushrooms every 10 minutes to ensure even cooking. The mushrooms should start to crisp up during this time. 5. Remove the baking sheet from the oven and allow the shiitake mushrooms to cool on the baking sheet before serving. 6. Once cooled, the shiitake bakin' can be served immediately as a snack or used as a topping for salads, soups, or other dishes. 7. Any leftovers can be stored in an airtight container for up to 3 days.

Per Serving: (1 cup)
calories: 55 | fat: 1g | protein: 2g | carbs: 10g | fiber: 1g

Hemp and Vanilla Bircher Breakfast

Prep time: 15 minutes | Cook time: 0 minutes | Serves 1

⅓ cup certified gluten-free rolled oats
1 tablespoon hulled hemp seeds
1 tablespoon chia seeds
¼ teaspoon vanilla powder or pure vanilla extract
⅛ teaspoon fine sea salt (optional)
1 cup unsweetened almond milk
1 teaspoon pure maple syrup, or to taste (optional)
Serve:
Chopped fresh fruit
Nut or seed butter

1. In a small sealable jar (or other container), combine the oats, hemp seeds, chia seeds, vanilla powder, sea salt, if using, and almond milk. Stir to combine. Place the lid on the container, and refrigerate for at least 4 hours but ideally overnight. 2. Retrieve and uncover the bircher breakfast after it has chilled. Add the maple syrup to the jar and give it a stir to combine. Serve with fresh fruit and a spoonful of nut or seed butter if you like.

Per Serving:
calories: 302 | fat: 12g | protein: 10g | carbs: 33g | fiber: 9g

Stovetop Blueberry Oatmeal

Prep time: 10 minutes | Cook time: 8 minutes | Serves 2

1½ cups plant-based milk
1 cup old-fashioned rolled oats
½ cup fresh or frozen blueberries
Optional Toppings:
1 tablespoon maple syrup (optional)
1 teaspoon cinnamon or pumpkin pie spices
2 tablespoons chopped nuts
2 to 3 tablespoons granola
1 tablespoon coconut shreds
2 tablespoons raw sunflower seeds

1. In a medium saucepan over medium-high heat, bring the plant-based milk to a boil. 2. Stir in the rolled oats and frozen blueberries, then reduce the heat to low. 3. Simmer the mixture for about 5 minutes, stirring occasionally, until the oats are cooked and the blueberries are soft and juicy. 4. Remove the saucepan from the heat and let it sit for a minute or two to cool slightly. 5. Serve the blueberry oatmeal in bowls and add your preferred optional toppings. You can drizzle with maple syrup, sprinkle with cinnamon or pumpkin pie spices, and add chopped nuts, granola, coconut shreds, and sunflower seeds for added flavor and texture. 6. Stir everything together and enjoy the warm and comforting blueberry oatmeal.

Per Serving:
calories: 227 | fat: 7g | protein: 15g | carbs: 44g | fiber: 8g

Strawberries and Cream Overnight Oatmeal

Prep time: 5 minutes | Cook time: 4 to 5 hours | Serves 4 to 6

Nonstick cooking spray (optional)
1¼ cups steel-cut oats
4 cups water
1⅔ cups unsweetened plant-based milk
2 teaspoons vanilla extract
¼ cup maple syrup (optional)
3 tablespoons ground flaxseed
1 pound (454 g) fresh strawberries, stemmed and sliced

1. Coat the inside of the slow cooker with nonstick cooking spray or use a slow cooker liner for easier cleanup (optional). 2. In the slow cooker, combine the steel-cut oats, water, plant-based milk, vanilla extract, and maple syrup (if using). Stir well to combine. 3. Cover the slow cooker and cook on High for 4 to 5 hours or on Low for 8 to 9 hours. The oats will gradually absorb the liquid and become creamy and tender. 4. When the oatmeal is cooked and ready to serve, stir in the ground flaxseed for added nutrition and texture. 5. Portion the oatmeal into bowls and top each serving with 3 to 5 sliced strawberries. 6. Serve the strawberries and cream overnight oatmeal warm and enjoy!

Per Serving:
calories: 320 | fat: 7g | protein: 9g | carbs: 59g | fiber: 9g

Gluten-Free Blueberry Blender Pancakes

Prep time: 5 minutes | Cook time: 10 minutes | Serves 2

1 cup unsweetened plant-based milk
1 teaspoon apple cider vinegar
1 tablespoon extra-virgin olive oil (optional)
3 tablespoons maple syrup, plus more for serving (optional)
1 teaspoon vanilla extract
1 tablespoon baking powder
1 cup gluten-free flour
½ teaspoon salt (optional)
1 tablespoon coconut oil (optional)
½ cup fresh or frozen blueberries

1. In a blender, combine the plant-based milk and apple cider vinegar and let sit for 3 minutes to make a faux buttermilk. 2. Add the olive oil, maple syrup (if using), and vanilla to the "buttermilk" and blend until very smooth. 3. Add the baking powder, flour, and salt (if using) and pulse until just combined. Do not blend long. 4. In a griddle or a large skillet, melt the coconut oil over medium heat. When the griddle is hot, pour the pancake batter on the griddle to make 3-inch pancakes, leaving about 1 inch between them. Drop blueberries onto each pancake as they are cooking. Cook until the pancakes have bubbles in the middle, 3 to 5 minutes. Using a spatula, flip the pancakes and continue to cook until browned, another 3 to 5 minutes. Serve with maple syrup.

Per Serving:
calories: 565 | fat: 20g | protein: 16g | carbs: 87g | fiber: 9g

Basic Baked Granola

Prep time: 5 minutes | Cook time: 50 minutes | Serves 16

8 cups rolled oats
1½ cups pitted and chopped dates
Zest of 2 oranges
1 teaspoon ground cinnamon
1 teaspoon pure vanilla extract
1 teaspoon salt, or to taste (optional)

1. Preheat the oven to 275ºF (135ºC). 2. Add the oats to a large mixing bowl and set aside. Line two 13 × 18-inch baking pans with parchment paper. 3. Place the dates in a medium saucepan with 2 cups of water, bring to a boil, and cook over medium heat for about 10 minutes. Add more water if needed to keep the dates from sticking to the pan. Remove from the heat, add the mixture to a blender with the orange zest, cinnamon, vanilla, and salt (if using), and process until smooth and creamy. 4. Add the date mixture to the oats and mix well. Divide the granola between the two prepared pans and spread it evenly in the pans. Bake for 40 to 50 minutes, stirring every 10 minutes, until the granola is crispy. Remove from the oven and let cool before storing in airtight containers (the cereal will get even crispier as it cools).

Per Serving:
calories: 160 | fat: 3g | protein: 8g | carbs: 42g | fiber: 8g

Applesauce Crumble Muffins

Prep time: 10 minutes | Cook time: 15 to 20 minutes | Makes 12 muffins

1 teaspoon coconut oil, for greasing muffin tins (optional)
2 tablespoons nut butter or seed butter
1½ cups unsweetened applesauce
⅓ cup coconut sugar (optional)
½ cup nondairy milk
2 tablespoons ground flaxseed
1 teaspoon apple cider vinegar
1 teaspoon pure vanilla extract
2 cups whole grain flour
1 teaspoon baking soda
½ teaspoon baking powder
1 teaspoon ground cinnamon
Pinch sea salt (optional)
½ cup walnuts, chopped
Toppings (optional):
¼ cup walnuts
¼ cup coconut sugar (optional)
½ teaspoon ground cinnamon

1. Preheat the oven to 350ºF (180ºC). Prepare two 6-cup muffin tins by rubbing the insides of the cups with coconut oil (if using), or using silicone or paper muffin cups. 2. In a large bowl, mix the nut butter, applesauce, coconut sugar (if using), milk, flaxseed, vinegar, and vanilla until thoroughly combined, or purée in a food processor or blender. 3. In another large bowl, sift together the flour, baking soda, baking powder, cinnamon, salt (if using), and chopped walnuts. 4. Mix the dry ingredients into the wet ingredients until just combined. 5. Spoon about ¼ cup batter into each muffin cup and sprinkle with the topping of your choice (if using). Bake for 15 to 20 minutes, or until a toothpick inserted into the center comes out clean. The applesauce creates a very moist base, so the muffins may take longer, depending on how heavy your muffin tins are.

Per Serving: (1 muffin)
calories: 178 | fat: 6g | protein: 4g | carbs: 28g | fiber: 3g

Chocolate Banana Hemp Smoothie Bowl

Prep time: 10 minutes | Cook time: 0 minutes | Serves 1

Smoothie Bowl:
1 frozen banana, 4 slices reserved for topping
½ cup almond milk or other dairy-free milk
1 tablespoon almond butter
1 tablespoon cocoa powder
1 tablespoon maple syrup (optional)
1 cup spinach
Toppings:
4 banana slices (from above)
1 strawberry, sliced
2 tablespoons dairy-free chocolate chips
2 tablespoons raw shelled hempseed

1. Add the frozen banana (excluding the reserved slices), almond milk, almond butter, cocoa powder, maple syrup (if using), and spinach to a blender. 2. Blend the ingredients until smooth and creamy. 3. Pour the smoothie into a bowl. 4. Arrange the reserved banana slices, sliced strawberry, dairy-free chocolate chips, and hempseed on top of the smoothie. 5. Enjoy the smoothie bowl immediately with a spoon.

Per Serving:

calories: 366 | fat: 11g | protein: 23g | carbs: 36g | fiber: 8g

Avocado Toast

Prep time: 10 minutes | Cook time: 0 minutes | Makes 2 slices

1 ripe avocado, halved, pitted, and sliced
2 large slices toast
Salt (optional)

1. Mash the avocado in a small bowl and spread onto the toast. Sprinkle with salt, if desired.

Per Serving: (1 slice)

calories: 243 | fat: 16g | protein: 5g | carbs: 24g | fiber: 9g

Overnight Pumpkin Spice Chia Pudding

Prep time: 10 minutes | Cook time: 0 minutes | Serves 4

¾ cup chia seeds
2 cups unsweetened plant-based milk
1 (15 ounces / 425 g) can unsweetened pumpkin purée
¼ cup maple syrup (optional)
1 tablespoon pumpkin pie spice blend
1 cup water
½ cup pecans, for serving

1. In a large bowl, whisk together the chia seeds, plant-based milk, pumpkin purée, maple syrup (if using), pumpkin pie spice, and water. 2. Divide the mixture among 4 mason jars or containers with lids. Let sit for 10 minutes. Stir each container to break up any chia clumps. Cover and refrigerate overnight to firm up. To serve, garnish each with some of the pecans.

Per Serving:

calories: 421 | fat: 23g | protein: 12g | carbs: 47g | fiber: 20g

Overnight Chocolate Chia Pudding

Prep time: 2 minutes | Cook time: 0 minutes | Serves 2

¼ cup chia seeds
1 cup unsweetened nondairy milk
2 tablespoons raw cacao powder
1 teaspoon vanilla extract
1 teaspoon pure maple syrup (optional)

1. In a large bowl, combine the chia seeds, unsweetened nondairy milk, raw cacao powder, vanilla extract, and maple syrup (if desired). Stir well to ensure all ingredients are thoroughly mixed. 2. Divide the mixture equally between two ½-pint covered glass jars or containers. 3. Cover the jars or containers and refrigerate them overnight, allowing the chia seeds to absorb the liquid and form a pudding-like consistency. 4. Before serving, give the pudding a good stir to evenly distribute the ingredients. 5. Enjoy the overnight chocolate chia pudding as is or add your favorite toppings such as fresh berries, sliced banana, or a sprinkle of nuts for added texture and flavor.

Per Serving: (1 jar)

calories: 213 | fat: 10g | protein: 9g | carbs: 20g | fiber: 15g

Plant-Powered Pancakes

Prep time: 5 minutes | Cook time: 15 minutes | Makes 8 pancakes

1 cup whole-wheat flour
1 teaspoon baking powder
½ teaspoon ground cinnamon
1 cup plant-based milk
½ cup unsweetened applesauce
¼ cup maple syrup (optional)
1 teaspoon vanilla extract

1. In a large bowl, combine the whole-wheat flour, baking powder, and ground cinnamon. 2. Stir in the plant-based milk, unsweetened applesauce, maple syrup (if desired), and vanilla extract. Mix until there are no dry flour pockets, and the batter is smooth. 3. Heat a large, nonstick skillet or griddle over medium heat. 4. Pour ¼ cup of the batter onto the hot skillet for each pancake. Cook until bubbles start to form on the top surface of the pancake and the sides begin to brown. 5. Flip the pancake and cook for an additional 1 to 2 minutes, or until cooked through and golden brown. 6. Repeat the process with the remaining batter. 7. Serve the pancakes warm and enjoy!

Per Serving: (2 pancakes)

calories: 210 | fat: 2g | protein: 5g | carbs: 44g | fiber: 5g

Steel-Cut Oats with Cranberries and Nuts

Prep time: 5 minutes | Cook time: 30 minutes | Serves 1
1 cup water
¼ cup steel-cut oats, uncooked
¼ cup dried cranberries
1 tablespoon chopped walnuts, toasted
1 tablespoon creamy almond butter
1 teaspoon maple syrup (optional)

1. In a small saucepan, bring the water to a boil. 2. Add the oats and cranberries. Reduce the heat to low and simmer, uncovered, for 20 to 30 minutes, stirring regularly. 3. When the oats have thickened and absorbed the water, remove from the heat and mix in the walnuts. Let the mixture rest for 1 minute. 4. Top with the almond butter and maple syrup (if using). Enjoy warm..

Per Serving:
calories: 290 | fat: 10g | protein: 7g | carbs: 45g | fiber: 5g

Whole-Wheat Blueberry Muffins

Prep time: 5 minutes | Cook time: 25 minutes | Makes 8 muffins

½ cup plant-based milk
½ cup unsweetened applesauce
½ cup maple syrup (optional)
1 teaspoon vanilla extract
2 cups whole-wheat flour
½ teaspoon baking soda
1 cup blueberries

1. Preheat the oven to 375°F (190°C). 2. In a large bowl, mix together the milk, applesauce, maple syrup (if desired), and vanilla. 3. Stir in the flour and baking soda until no dry flour is left and the batter is smooth. 4. Gently fold in the blueberries until they are evenly distributed throughout the batter. 5. In a muffin tin, fill 8 muffin cups three-quarters full of batter. 6. Bake for 25 minutes, or until you can stick a knife into the center of a muffin and it comes out clean. Allow to cool before serving.

Per Serving: (1 muffin)
calories: 200 | fat: 1g | protein: 4g | carbs: 45g | fiber: 2g

Sweet Potato and Black Bean Hash

Prep time: 10 minutes | Cook time: 2 to 3 hours | Serves 4 to 6

1 shallot, diced
2 cups peeled, chopped sweet potatoes (about 1 large or 2 small)
1 medium bell pepper (any color), diced
2 garlic cloves, minced
1 (14½ ounces / 411 g) can black beans, drained and rinsed
1 teaspoon paprika
½ teaspoon onion powder
½ teaspoon garlic powder
¼ cup store-bought low-sodium vegetable broth
4 to 6 tablespoons unsweetened plant-based milk

1. Place the shallot, sweet potatoes, bell pepper, garlic, beans, paprika, onion powder, garlic powder, and broth in the slow cooker. Stir to combine. Cover and cook on Low for 2 to 3 hours, until the potatoes are soft. 2. Remove the lid and add the milk, starting with 4 tablespoons, and stir to combine. You're looking for a creamy sauce to develop. Add more milk as needed and allow to heat through for a few minutes before serving.

Per Serving:
calories: 251 | fat: 1g | protein: 9g | carbs: 53g | fiber: 14g

Fruited Barley

Prep time: 10 minutes | Cook time: 55 minutes | Serves 2

1 to 1½ cups orange juice
1 cup pearled barley
2 tablespoons dried currants
3 to 4 dried unsulfured apricots, chopped
1 small cinnamon stick
⅛ teaspoon ground cloves
Pinch salt, or to taste (optional)

1. Bring 1 cup of water and 1 cup of the orange juice to a boil in a medium saucepan over medium heat. Add the barley, currants, apricots, cinnamon stick, cloves, and salt, if using. Bring the mixture to a boil, cover, reduce the heat to medium-low, and cook for 45 minutes. If the barley is not tender after 45 minutes, add up to an additional ½ cup of orange juice and cook for another 10 minutes. 2. Remove the cinnamon stick before serving.

Per Serving:
calories: 420 | fat: 1g | protein: 10g | carbs: 93g | fiber: 16g

Chocolate Cherry Oats Bowl

Prep time: 5 minutes | Cook time: 5 minutes | Serves 2

½ cup fresh or frozen cherries
2 tangerines
1 cup instant oats
1 scoop soy protein isolate, chocolate flavor
¼ cup almond flakes
2 cups water
Optional Toppings:
Crushed dark chocolate
Mint leaves
Cinnamon

1. In a saucepan, add the water and oats. Place it over medium heat. 2. Bring the mixture to a boil and cook the oats for about 5 minutes, stirring occasionally. 3. Turn off the heat and add the chocolate-flavored soy protein isolate to the cooked oats. Stir thoroughly until well combined. 4. Peel and section the tangerines. 5. Transfer the protein oats to a bowl and garnish with the almond flakes, tangerine sections, and cherries. 6. If desired, add optional toppings such as crushed dark chocolate, mint leaves, or a sprinkle of cinnamon. 7. Serve the oats bowl warm and enjoy! 8. If there are any leftovers, store them in an airtight container in the refrigerator and consume within 2 days. Alternatively, you can store the oats in the freezer for up to 60 days and thaw them at room temperature before eating.

Per Serving:
calories: 349 | fat: 9g | protein: 22g | carbs: 44g | fiber: 7g

Chapter 4 Beans and Grains

Chickpea Caponata

Prep time: 25 minutes | Cook time: 30 minutes | Serves 4

1 medium yellow onion, peeled and diced
2 celery stalks, chopped
1 medium eggplant, stemmed and diced
2 ripe Roma tomatoes, diced
2 cups cooked chickpeas, or 1 (15 ounces / 425 g) can, drained and rinsed
½ cup Kalamata olives, pitted and coarsely chopped
3 tablespoons capers
3 tablespoons red wine vinegar
¼ cup golden raisins
¼ cup pine nuts, toasted (optional)
½ cup chopped basil
Salt and freshly ground black pepper, to taste

1. Place the diced onion and chopped celery in a large saucepan and sauté them over medium heat for 10 minutes. Add 1 to 2 tablespoons of water at a time to prevent the vegetables from sticking to the pan. 2. Add the diced eggplant, tomatoes, and cooked chickpeas to the saucepan. Cook the mixture covered for 15 minutes, or until the vegetables are tender. 3. Stir in the chopped Kalamata olives, capers, red wine vinegar, golden raisins, and toasted pine nuts (if using). Cook for an additional 5 minutes. 4. Remove the saucepan from the heat and stir in the chopped basil. Season with salt and freshly ground black pepper according to your taste.

Per Serving:
calories: 301 | fat: 10g | protein: 11g | carbs: 45g | fiber: 13g

Black and White Bean Chili

Prep time: 10 minutes | Cook time: 20 minutes | Serves 4

1 teaspoon extra-virgin olive oil (optional)
½ yellow onion, diced small
1 large carrot, peeled and diced small
1 red or yellow bell pepper, seeded and diced small
1 small zucchini, diced small
1 (15 ounces / 425 g) can cannellini beans, drained and rinsed
1 (15 ounces / 425 g) can black beans, drained and rinsed
1 (28 ounces / 794 g) can crushed tomatoes
1 cup frozen corn
1 teaspoon chili powder
½ teaspoon salt (optional)
½ teaspoon ground cumin
½ teaspoon garlic powder
1 cup water
2 tablespoons minced fresh cilantro, for garnish
Pinch red pepper flakes, for garnish
1 scallion, white and green parts, thinly sliced, for garnish
1 jalapeño pepper, cut into slices, for garnish (optional)
1 avocado, peeled, pitted, and diced, for garnish
1 lime, cut into wedges, for garnish

1. In a large pot, heat the olive oil over medium heat. If not using oil, you can use a splash of water to sauté the vegetables. Add the diced onion, carrot, bell pepper, and zucchini to the pot. Cook, stirring often, until the vegetables become fragrant and start to become tender, which should take about 10 minutes. 2. Increase the heat to medium-high and add the cannellini beans, black beans, crushed tomatoes, frozen corn, chili powder, salt (if using), ground cumin, garlic powder, and water. Stir well to combine all the ingredients. Bring the mixture to a boil. 3. Once it reaches a boil, reduce the heat to medium-low and let it simmer for about 5 more minutes, allowing the flavors to meld together and the chili to heat through. 4. Spoon the black and white bean chili into bowls. Garnish each bowl with minced fresh cilantro, a pinch of red pepper flakes, thinly sliced scallion, jalapeño slices (if desired), diced avocado, and a lime wedge. 5. Serve and enjoy!

Per Serving:
calories: 329 | fat: 3g | protein: 17g | carbs: 65g | fiber: 20g

Smoky Cajun Bowl

Prep time: 20 minutes | Cook time: 25 minutes | Serves 4

2 cups cooked or canned black beans
1 cup dry quick-cooking brown rice
1 (7 ounces / 198 g) pack smoked tofu, cubed
2 cups canned or fresh tomato cubes
1 tablespoon salt-free Cajun spices
¼ cup water (optional)
Optional Toppings:
peeled slices
Fresh cilantro
Avocado slices

1. If using dry beans, soak and cook 2/3 cup of dry black beans if necessary. Also, cook the quick-cooking brown rice according to the package instructions. 2. In a nonstick deep frying pan over medium-high heat, add the cubed smoked tofu, tomato cubes, and optional 1/4 cup of water. Stir occasionally and cook until everything is heated through. 3. Add the black beans, cooked brown rice, and Cajun spices to the pan. Stir to combine. 4. Turn off the heat and let it sit for about 5 minutes, stirring occasionally to heat everything through. 5. Divide the smoky Cajun beans and rice mixture among 4 bowls. 6. Serve the smoky Cajun bowl with your choice of optional toppings, such as sliced bell peppers, fresh cilantro, and avocado slices. 7. Enjoy!

Per Serving:
calories: 371 | fat: 5g | protein: 20g | carbs: 60g | fiber: 12g

Chickpea Pâté

Prep time: 10 minutes | Cook time: 0 minutes | Serves 4

1 cup whole raw nuts, toasted
2 tablespoons extra-virgin olive oil, plus more for drizzling (optional)
1 (15½ ounces / 439 g) can chickpeas, drained and rinsed well
½ cup filtered water
1 teaspoon fine sea salt, plus more to taste (optional)
½ teaspoon grated or pressed garlic
½ teaspoon raw apple cider vinegar

1. Place the toasted nuts and olive oil in a food processor. Blend until the mixture becomes completely smooth, scraping down the sides as needed. This process may take a few minutes to achieve a runny consistency. 2. Add the drained and rinsed chickpeas, filtered water, sea salt (if using), grated or pressed garlic, and raw apple cider vinegar to the food processor. Continue blending until all the ingredients are well combined and the mixture is completely smooth. This might take a couple of minutes. 3. If needed, adjust the consistency by adding more cooking liquid or water until you achieve your desired texture. 4. Taste the pâté and add more salt if desired. 5. Serve the chickpea pâté drizzled with olive oil, or store it in an airtight container in the refrigerator for up to 4 days.

Per Serving:
calories: 321 | fat: 22g | protein: 11g | carbs: 23g | fiber: 7g

Orzo "Risotto"

Prep time: 10 minutes | Cook time: 15 minutes | Serves 6

4 cups vegetable broth
1 tablespoon olive oil (optional)
1 large shallot or ¼ yellow onion, minced
1 teaspoon dried tarragon or dill
1 pound (454 g) whole wheat orzo
½ cup white wine
Grated zest and juice of 1 lemon
Salt and black pepper (optional)
Chopped flat-leaf parsley (optional)

1. In a medium saucepan, bring the vegetable broth to a boil. Reduce the heat to medium-low and cover to keep it warm. 2. In a large saucepan over medium heat, add the olive oil (if desired). Add the minced shallot and cook, stirring often, until the shallot becomes soft and translucent, about 5 minutes. 3. Stir in the dried tarragon (or dill) and the whole wheat orzo. 4. Add the white wine and stir constantly until the wine is absorbed by the orzo. 5. Continuously stirring, add the warm vegetable broth to the orzo, about 1 cup at a time. Allow the orzo to absorb the broth, which should take approximately 3 to 5 minutes, and the mixture will become creamy. Repeat this step with the remaining broth. 6. Remove the saucepan from the heat and stir in the grated lemon zest and lemon juice. Season with salt and black pepper, if desired. 7. If desired, garnish with chopped flat-leaf parsley before serving.

Per Serving:
calories: 310 | fat: 4g | protein: 8g | carbs: 62g | fiber: 11g

Sweet Potato Tacos

Prep time: 15 minutes | Cook time: 15 minutes | Makes 6 tacos

2 cups cooked or canned black beans
1 (7 ounces / 198 g) pack textured soy mince
3 small cubed sweet potatoes
6 whole wheat taco shells
¼ cup Mexican chorizo seasoning
1 cup water
Optional Toppings:
Red onion
Lemon slices
Jalapeño slices

1. If using dry black beans, soak and cook 1 1/2 cups of dry black beans according to package instructions. Alternatively, use canned black beans and rinse them well. 2. In a medium pot, cook the cubed sweet potatoes covered with water over medium-high heat for about 15 minutes or until they are soft. Drain the excess water and set the cooked sweet potatoes aside. 3. In a nonstick deep frying pan, heat it over medium-high heat and add the textured soy mince, black beans, Mexican chorizo seasoning, and the cup of water. 4. Stir continuously until the soy mince and black beans are cooked and the mixture is well combined. Then, add the cooked sweet potato cubes. 5. Turn off the heat and stir occasionally for about 5 minutes until everything is heated through. 6. Divide the sweet potato mixture among the 6 taco shells. 7. Serve the sweet potato tacos with optional toppings such as sliced red onion, lemon slices, and jalapeño slices. 8. Store the sweet potato mixture in an airtight container in the refrigerator and consume within 3 days. 9. Alternatively, store in the freezer for a maximum of 30 days and thaw at room temperature. Reheat the sweet potato mixture using a microwave, toaster oven, or nonstick frying pan.

Per Serving:
calories: 202 | fat: 3g | protein: 13g | carbs: 29g | fiber: 9g

Butter Bean Pâté

Prep time: 15 minutes | Cook time: 0 minutes | Serves 4

3 cups cooked butter beans or 2 (15½ ounces /439 g) cans beans, drained and well rinsed
¼ cup extra-virgin olive oil (optional)
½ teaspoon finely grated or pressed garlic
½ teaspoon fine sea salt, or more to taste (optional)
Freshly ground black pepper

1. In a food processor, combine the butter beans, extra-virgin olive oil (if using), finely grated or pressed garlic, and fine sea salt (if using). 2. Process the mixture until it becomes completely smooth, with a fluffy whipped texture. This may take a couple of minutes. 3. Taste the pâté and season with more salt and pepper if necessary. 4. Serve the butter bean pâté immediately or store it in an airtight container in the refrigerator for up to 4 days.

Per Serving:
calories: 253 | fat: 15g | protein: 9g | carbs: 23g | fiber: 8g

Nut-Crusted Tofu

Prep time: 10 minutes | Cook time: 20 minutes | Makes 8 slices

½ cup roasted, shelled pistachios
¼ cup whole wheat bread crumbs
1 shallot, minced
1 garlic clove, minced
1 teaspoon grated lemon zest
½ teaspoon dried tarragon
Salt and black pepper (optional)
1 (16 ounces / 454 g) package sprouted or extra-firm tofu, drained and sliced lengthwise into 8 pieces
1 tablespoon Dijon mustard
1 tablespoon lemon juice

1. Preheat the oven to 375ºF (190ºC) and line a baking sheet with parchment paper. 2. Using a food processor or a knife, chop the pistachios until they are about the size of the bread crumbs. In a pie plate, combine the chopped pistachios with the bread crumbs, minced shallot, minced garlic, grated lemon zest, and dried tarragon. Season with salt (if desired) and black pepper. 3. Season the tofu slices with salt and black pepper. 4. In a small bowl, combine the Dijon mustard and lemon juice. 5. Spread the mustard mixture evenly over the top and sides of each tofu slice. Then press each slice into the bread crumb mixture, coating them thoroughly. 6. Place the tofu slices uncoated side down on the prepared baking sheet. Sprinkle any leftover bread crumb mixture evenly on top of the slices. 7. Bake the tofu in the preheated oven for about 20 minutes, or until the tops are browned. 8. Serve the nut-crusted tofu slices.

Per Serving: (1 slice)

calories: 114 | fat: 7g | protein: 8g | carbs: 7g | fiber: 1g

Lucky Black-Eyed Pea Stew

Prep time: 15 minutes | Cook time: 40 minutes | Serves 4

½ cup black-eyed peas, soaked
1 large carrot, peeled and cut into ½-inch pieces (about ¾ cup)
1 large beet, peeled and cut into ½-inch pieces (about ¾ cup)
¼ cup finely chopped parsley
¼ teaspoon cumin seeds, toasted and ground
¼ teaspoon turmeric
¼ teaspoon cayenne pepper
⅛ teaspoon asafetida
¼ teaspoon salt, or to taste (optional)
½ teaspoon fresh lime juice

1. In a pot, combine the soaked black-eyed peas with 3 cups of water and cook over medium heat for 20 to 25 minutes until the peas are tender. 2. Add the carrot and beet to the pot and cook for another 10 minutes. Add more water if the stew gets too thick. 3. Stir in the finely chopped parsley, ground cumin seeds, turmeric, cayenne pepper, and asafetida. Cook for an additional 5 to 7 minutes. 4. Season the stew with salt, if desired. 5. Remove the pot from the heat and stir in the fresh lime juice.

Per Serving:

calories: 106 | fat: 0g | protein: 6g | carbs: 19g | fiber: 7g

Whole grain Corn Muffins

Prep time: 5 minutes | Cook time: 20 minutes | Makes 12 muffins

1½ tablespoons ground flaxseeds
1 cup unsweetened plain almond milk
½ cup unsweetened applesauce
½ cup 100% pure maple syrup (optional)
1 cup cornmeal
1 cup oat flour
1 teaspoon baking soda
1 teaspoon baking powder
½ teaspoon salt (optional)
1 cup corn kernels (from about 2 ears)

1. Preheat the oven to 375ºF (190ºC). Line a 12-cup muffin pan with paper muffin liners or prepare a 12-cup silicone muffin pan. 2. In a small bowl, combine the ground flaxseeds with the almond milk and set it aside for 5 minutes to allow it to gel. 3. In a large mixing bowl, stir together the applesauce and maple syrup (if using). Add the flaxseed-almond milk mixture to the bowl. 4. Sift in the cornmeal, oat flour, baking soda, baking powder, and salt (if using). Stir until well combined, taking care not to overmix. Fold in the corn kernels. 5. Spoon equal portions of the batter into the prepared muffin cups. 6. Bake for 20 minutes, or until a toothpick inserted into the center of a muffin comes out clean. 7. Serve the muffins warm.

Per Serving:

calories: 149 | fat: 1g | protein: 3g | carbs: 30g | fiber: 2g

Red Lentil Pâté

Prep time: 10 minutes | Cook time: 20 minutes | Serves 4

1 cup red lentils
1½ cups filtered water
1 (2-inch) piece kombu
3 large garlic cloves
3 tablespoons extra-virgin olive oil, plus more for serving (optional)
½ teaspoon fine sea salt, or to taste (optional)

1. Rinse the red lentils by placing them in a medium pot, covering them with tap water, swishing them around with your fingers, and then draining. Repeat this rinsing process and return the drained lentils to the pot. 2. Add the filtered water, kombu, and garlic cloves to the pot with the lentils. Bring the mixture to a boil over high heat. 3. Cover the pot, reduce the heat to low, and simmer for 20 minutes, or until the lentils are soft and have absorbed all the water. 4. Remove the pot from the heat and discard the kombu (compost it). 5. Add the extra-virgin olive oil and salt (if desired) to the pot. Stir vigorously until the lentils and garlic become smooth and creamy. 6. Drizzle the pâté with additional olive oil, if desired, and serve it warm or at room temperature. 7. Any leftover pâté can be stored in a jar or airtight container in the refrigerator for up to 4 days.

Per Serving:

calories: 273 | fat: 11g | protein: 12g | carbs: 37g | fiber: 6g

Chana Masala

Prep time: 10 minutes | Cook time: 25 minutes | Serves 2

2 cups cooked or canned chickpeas
1 cup canned or fresh tomato cubes
2 medium onions, minced
2 tablespoons curry spices
¼ cup water
Optional Toppings:
Fresh chili slices
Lime juice
Shredded coconut

1. If using dry chickpeas, soak and cook 2/3 cup of dry chickpeas according to package instructions until tender. Drain and set aside. 2. Place a large pot over medium heat. Add the tomato cubes, minced onions, and water. Cook for a few minutes, stirring occasionally, until the onions are translucent and the tomatoes are cooked. 3. Add the curry spices to the pot and stir thoroughly to combine with the tomato and onion mixture. 4. Add the cooked or canned chickpeas to the pot and mix well, ensuring that all the ingredients are evenly distributed. 5. Cook for a couple more minutes, stirring occasionally to allow the flavors to meld together. 6. Lower the heat to a simmer and let the chana masala curry simmer for about 20 minutes, stirring occasionally. 7. Turn off the heat and let the curry cool down for a minute. 8. Divide the chana masala between two serving bowls. Garnish with optional toppings such as fresh chili slices, a squeeze of lime juice, or shredded coconut. 9. Serve and enjoy your delicious chana masala! If there are leftovers, store the curry in an airtight container in the refrigerator and consume within 2 days. Alternatively, you can freeze the curry for a maximum of 30 days. Thaw the frozen curry at room temperature and reheat in the microwave or a saucepan before serving.

Per Serving:
calories: 401 | fat: 6g | protein: 21g | carbs: 64g | fiber: 20g

Cabbage and Millet Pilaf

Prep time: 15 minutes | Cook time: 45 minutes | Serves 4

2¼ cups vegetable stock, or low-sodium vegetable broth
¾ cup millet
1 medium leek (white and light green parts), diced and rinsed
1 medium carrot, peeled and diced
1 celery stalk, diced
2 cloves garlic, peeled and minced
1 teaspoon minced thyme
1 tablespoon minced dill
3 cups chopped cabbage
Salt and freshly ground black pepper, to taste

1. In a medium saucepan, bring the vegetable stock to a boil over high heat. Add the millet and bring the pot back to a boil. Reduce the heat to medium and cook, covered, for 20 minutes or until the millet is tender and all the vegetable stock is absorbed. 2. In a large saucepan, place the diced leek, carrot, and celery. Sauté over medium heat for 7 to 8 minutes. Add water, 1 to 2 tablespoons at a time, if needed, to prevent sticking. 3. Add the minced garlic, thyme, dill, and chopped cabbage to the saucepan. Cook, stirring frequently, over medium heat until the cabbage is tender, which should take about 10 minutes. 4. Add the cooked millet to the saucepan and cook for an additional 5 minutes, stirring frequently to combine all the flavors. 5. Season the pilaf with salt and freshly ground black pepper to taste. 6. Serve the cabbage and millet pilaf as a side dish or a light main course.

Per Serving:
calories: 193 | fat: 2g | protein: 5g | carbs: 39g | fiber: 6g

Chickpea Tortilla Fajita Stack

Prep time: 20 minutes | Cook time: 0 minutes | Serves 4

Chickpea Tortillas:
1 tablespoon ground chia seeds
1 cup chickpea flour
¼ teaspoon sea salt (optional)
½ teaspoon ground cumin
2 tablespoons extra virgin olive oil (optional)
Filling:
1 tablespoon extra virgin olive oil (optional)
½ cup diced white onion
1 yellow bell pepper, diced
8 ounces (227 g) white mushrooms, diced
½ cup diced tomatoes
2 teaspoons fajita seasoning
½ teaspoon salt (optional)
¼ teaspoon ground black pepper
1 (15 ounces / 425 g) can pinto beans, drained and rinsed
2 tablespoons raw shelled hempseed
Salsa, for garnish
Avocado, for garnish

Make the Chickpea Tortillas: 1. In a small bowl, mix ground chia seeds with 3 tablespoons of water and set aside. 2. In a medium bowl, combine 1 cup of water, chickpea flour, chia seed mixture, salt (if desired), and ground cumin. Mix until just combined. 3. Heat 2 tablespoons of olive oil (if desired) in an 8-inch skillet over medium-high heat. 4. Pour 1/4 cup of chickpea batter into the skillet and tilt the pan in a circular motion to spread the batter evenly and cover the bottom of the pan like a crepe. 5. Cook until golden brown, then flip and cook for another minute. Remove the tortilla to a plate. Repeat until all the batter is used and the tortillas are made.
Make the Filling: 1. Heat 1 tablespoon of olive oil (if desired) in a large skillet over medium-high heat. 2. Add the diced onion, bell pepper, and mushrooms to the skillet. Sauté for 10 to 15 minutes, or until the onion is translucent. 3. Add the diced tomatoes, fajita seasoning, salt (if desired), and ground black pepper. Cook for an additional 5 minutes. 4. Stir in the drained and rinsed pinto beans and raw shelled hempseed. Heat through. Assemble: 6. Start assembling the chickpea tortilla stack by placing one tortilla on a plate. 7. Spoon approximately 1/2 cup of the filling onto the tortilla. 8. Add another tortilla and another 1/2 cup of filling. Repeat until all the filling is used. 9. Top the stack with a final tortilla and garnish with salsa and sliced avocado. 10. Cut the stacked tortillas into quarters, resembling a pie shape, and serve. 11. Enjoy your delicious Chickpea Tortilla Fajita Stack!

Per Serving:
calories: 358 | fat: 12g | protein: 17g | carbs: 48g | fiber: 11g

Kasha Varnishkes (Buckwheat Groats with Bow-Tie Pasta)

Prep time: 20 minutes | Cook time: 35 minutes | Serves 4

2 cups vegetable stock, or low-sodium vegetable broth
1 cup buckwheat groats
1 large yellow onion, peeled and diced small
8 ounces (227 g) button mushrooms, sliced
½ pound (227 g) whole grain farfalle, cooked according to package directions, drained, and kept warm
2 tablespoons finely chopped dill
Salt and freshly ground black pepper, to taste

1. Place the vegetable stock in a medium saucepan and bring to a boil over high heat. Add the buckwheat groats and bring the pot back to a boil over high heat. Reduce the heat to medium and cook, uncovered, until the groats are tender, about 12 to 15 minutes. 2. Place the onion in a large saucepan and sauté over medium heat until well browned, about 15 minutes. Add water 1 to 2 tablespoons at a time to keep the onion from sticking, but use as little water as possible. Add the mushrooms and cook for another 5 minutes. Remove from the heat. Add the cooked pasta, buckwheat groats, and dill. Season with salt and pepper.

Per Serving:
calories: 240 | fat: 1g | protein: 8g | carbs: 51g | fiber: 6g

Bulgur Chickpea Pilaf

Prep time: 15 minutes | Cook time: 35 minutes | Serves 4

1 medium yellow onion, peeled and diced small
3 cloves garlic, peeled and minced
1½ tablespoons grated ginger
1½ cups bulgur
3 cups vegetable stock, or low-sodium vegetable broth
2 cups cooked chickpeas, or 1 (15 ounces / 425 g) can, drained and rinsed
1 Roma tomato, chopped
Zest and juice of 1 lemon
Salt and freshly ground black pepper, to taste
4 green onions (white and green parts), thinly sliced

1. Place the onion in a large saucepan and sauté over medium heat for 10 minutes. Add water 1 to 2 tablespoons at a time to keep the onion from sticking to the pan. Stir in the garlic and ginger and cook for 30 seconds. Add the bulgur and vegetable stock and bring to a boil over high heat. Reduce the heat to medium and cook, covered, until the bulgur is tender, about 15 minutes. 2. Stir in the chickpeas, tomato, and lemon zest and juice and cook for another 5 minutes. Season with salt and pepper and serve garnished with the green onions.

Per Serving:
calories: 344 | fat: 2g | protein: 14g | carbs: 69g | fiber: 13g

Sweet Potato and Cauliflower Rice Pilaf

Prep time: 30 minutes | Cook time: 1 hour 25 minutes | Serves 4

3 to 3½ cups vegetable stock, or low-sodium vegetable broth
1½ cups brown basmati rice
1 large cinnamon stick
2 whole cloves
2 cardamom pods
1 medium yellow onion, peeled and cut into ½-inch dice
1 medium carrot, peeled and cut into ½-inch dice
1 medium sweet potato, peeled and cut into ½-inch dice
½ small head cauliflower, cut into florets
2 cloves garlic, peeled and minced
1 cup peas, thawed if frozen
½ cup chopped cilantro
1 large pinch saffron, soaked in 3 tablespoons hot water
Salt, to taste (optional)

1. Bring 3 cups of the vegetable stock to a boil and add the rice, cinnamon stick, cloves, and cardamom pods. Bring the mixture back to a boil over high heat, then reduce the heat to medium and cook, covered, until the rice is tender, about 45 minutes. Check the rice for tenderness and add more stock, if needed, and cook for another 10 minutes if necessary. Remove the cinnamon stick, cloves, and cardamom pods before serving. 2. Place the onion in a large saucepan and sauté over medium-high heat for 7 to 8 minutes, or until the onion is tender and starting to brown. Add water 1 to 2 tablespoons at a time to keep the onion from sticking to the pan. Add the carrot and sweet potato and cook for 10 minutes. Add the cauliflower and garlic and cook 6 to 7 minutes longer, or until the cauliflower is tender. Add the peas, cilantro, and saffron and its soaking liquid and season with salt (if using). Add the cooked rice and mix well.

Per Serving:
calories: 352 | fat: 2g | protein: 9g | carbs: 64g | fiber: 7g

Quick Panfried Tempeh

Prep time: 5 minutes | Cook time: 10 minutes | Serves 2

2 tablespoons extra-virgin coconut oil, plus more as needed (optional)
½ pound (227 g) tempeh, cut into ¼-inch slices
Flaky or fine sea salt (optional)

1. Warm a large skillet over medium heat. Add the coconut oil and tilt the pan to coat. Add the sliced tempeh in a single layer and cook until golden, 3 to 4 minutes. Turn the tempeh over and cook the other side until golden and crisp, adding more oil if needed. Repeat with any remaining tempeh, adding more oil to the pan before adding the sliced tempeh. Transfer the tempeh to a serving plate and sprinkle with salt; serve warm.

Per Serving:
calories: 336 | fat: 25g | protein: 2g | carbs: 11g | fiber: 0g

Berbere-Spiced Red Lentils

Prep time: 5 minutes | Cook time: 25 minutes | Serves 4

- 1 cup dried red lentils, rinsed
- 3 cups water
- 1 teaspoon extra-virgin olive oil (optional)
- 2 garlic cloves, minced
- ½ medium yellow onion, chopped small
- 3 tomatoes, chopped
- 2 tablespoons Berbere spice
- 1 teaspoon salt (optional)
- 2 teaspoons tomato paste

1. In a large saucepan, combine the lentils and water over high heat and bring to a boil. Lower the heat to medium-low and cook, checking occasionally and adding more water if needed, for 20 minutes. 2. In a medium skillet, heat the olive oil over medium heat. Add the garlic and onion and cook until fragrant, 3 to 5 minutes 3. Add the tomatoes, Berbere spice, salt (if using), and tomato paste and cook, stirring constantly, until the mixture turns a deep red and becomes paste-like, about 5 minutes. Set aside. 4. Add the spiced tomato-and-onion mixture to the lentils and simmer over medium heat until the flavors combine and it's very thick, about 5 minutes. Serve immediately.

Per Serving:

calories: 216 | fat: 3g | protein: 13g | carbs: 38g | fiber: 8g

Black Beans and Rice

Prep time: 25 minutes | Cook time: 20 minutes | Serves 4

- 1 medium yellow onion, peeled and diced
- 1 red bell pepper, seeded and diced
- 2 jalapeño peppers, diced (for less heat, remove the seeds)
- 5 cloves garlic, peeled and minced
- 1 teaspoon cumin seeds, toasted and ground
- 1½ teaspoons oregano, toasted
- 4 cups cooked black beans, or 2 (15 ounces / 425 g) cans, drained and rinsed
- Salt and freshly ground black pepper, to taste
- 3 cups cooked brown rice
- 1 cup chopped cilantro
- 1 lime, quartered

1. Place the onion, red pepper, and jalapeño peppers in a large saucepan and sauté over medium heat for 7 to 8 minutes. Add water 1 to 2 tablespoons at a time to keep the vegetables from sticking to the pan. Add the garlic, cumin, and oregano and cook for 3 minutes. Add the black beans and 1 cup of water. Cook for 10 minutes, adding more water if necessary. Season with salt and pepper. Serve over the brown rice and garnish with the cilantro and lime wedges.

Per Serving:

calories: 406 | fat: 2g | protein: 20g | carbs: 72g | fiber: 19g

Mango Satay Tempeh Bowl

Prep time: 10 minutes | Cook time: 30 minutes | Serves 4

- 1 cup cooked or canned black beans
- ½ cup dry quinoa
- 1 (14 ounces / 397 g) pack tempeh, sliced
- 1 cup peanut butter
- 1 cup fresh or frozen mango cubes
- Optional Toppings:
- Chili flakes
- Shredded coconut

1. When using dry beans, soak and cook ⅓ cup of dry black beans if necessary and cook the quinoa for about 15 minutes. 2. Blend the mango into a smooth purée using a blender or food processor or blender, and set it aside. 3. Add the tempeh slices and the peanut butter to an airtight container. 4. Close the lid and shake well until the tempeh slices are evenly covered with the peanut butter. 5. Preheat the oven to 375°F (190°C) and line a baking sheet with parchment paper. 6. Transfer the peanut butter tempeh slices onto the baking sheet and bake for about 15 minutes or until the tempeh is browned and crispy. 7. Divide the black beans, quinoa, mango purée and tempeh slices between two bowls, serve with the optional toppings and enjoy! 8. Store the mango tempeh bowl in an airtight container in the fridge, and consume within 2 days. Alternatively, store in the freezer for a maximum of 30 days and thaw at room temperature. Serve cold It's not necessary to reheat the tempeh and beans.

Per Serving:

calories: 536 | fat: 24g | protein: 30g | carbs: 55g | fiber: 7g

Wild Rice, Cabbage and Chickpea Pilaf

Prep time: 20 minutes | Cook time: 1 hour 20 minutes | Serves 4

- ½ cup wild rice
- 1 medium onion, peeled and diced small
- 1 medium carrot, peeled and grated
- 1 small red bell pepper, seeded and diced small
- 3 cloves garlic, peeled and minced
- 1 tablespoon grated ginger
- 1½ cups chopped green cabbage
- 1 cup cooked chickpeas
- 1 bunch green onions (white and green parts), thinly sliced
- 3 tablespoons chopped cilantro
- Salt and freshly ground black pepper, to taste

1. Bring 2 cups of water to a boil in a large saucepan. Add the wild rice and bring the water back to a boil over high heat. Reduce the heat to medium and cook, covered, for 55 to 60 minutes. Drain off any excess water and set aside. 2. Heat a large skillet over medium heat. Add the onion, carrot, and red pepper and sauté the vegetables for 10 minutes. Add water 1 to 2 tablespoons at a time to keep the vegetables from sticking to the pan. Add the garlic and ginger and cook for another minute. Add the cabbage and cook for 10 to 12 minutes, or until the cabbage is tender. Add the chickpeas, green onions, and cilantro. Season with salt and pepper and cook for another minute to heat the chickpeas. Remove from the heat, add the cooked wild rice and mix well.

Per Serving:

calories: 171 | fat: 1g | protein: 7g | carbs: 33g | fiber: 6g

Chickpea Masala

Prep time: 10 minutes | Cook time: 15 minutes | Serves 4

¼ cup canned coconut milk
½ medium sweet onion, chopped
1 medium jalapeño pepper, seeded, ribs removed, and diced
2 garlic cloves, minced
1 tablespoon minced fresh ginger
1 (15 ounces / 425 g) can crushed tomatoes
1 (15 ounces / 425 g) can chickpeas, rinsed and drained
1 teaspoon ground cinnamon
1 teaspoon ground coriander
1 teaspoon ground turmeric
½ teaspoon ground cloves
½ teaspoon ground cumin

1. In a small pot, combine the coconut milk, onion, jalapeño pepper, garlic, and ginger. Cook on medium heat for 2 minutes. 2. Add the tomatoes with their juices, the chickpeas, cinnamon, coriander, turmeric, cloves, and cumin. Reduce the heat to low and cook for 10 minutes more. 3. Serve warm.

Per Serving:

calories: 149 | fat: 5g | protein: 6g | carbs: 23g | fiber: 7g

Mushroom Barley Risotto

Prep time: 20 minutes | Cook time: 55 minutes | Serves 3 to 4

1 ounce (28 g) dried porcini mushrooms, soaked for 30 minutes in 1 cup of water that has just been boiled
3 large shallots, peeled and finely diced
8 ounces (227 g) cremini mushrooms, sliced
2 sage leaves, minced
3 cloves garlic, peeled and minced
1½ cups pearled barley
½ cup dry white wine
3 to 4 cups vegetable stock, or low-sodium vegetable broth
¼ cup nutritional yeast (optional)
Salt and freshly ground black pepper, to taste

1. Drain the soaked porcini mushrooms, reserving the liquid. Finely chop the mushrooms and set them aside. 2. In a 2-quart saucepan, sauté the shallots over medium heat for 4 to 5 minutes. Add water, 1 to 2 tablespoons at a time, to prevent sticking. 3. Add the cremini mushrooms to the saucepan and cook for another 5 minutes, allowing them to brown with minimal added water. 4. Stir in the minced sage, minced garlic, pearled barley, and white wine. Cook for 1 minute. 5. Add 2 cups of vegetable stock and the 1 cup of reserved porcini soaking liquid to the saucepan. Increase the heat to high and bring the mixture to a boil. 6. Reduce the heat to medium and cover the saucepan. Let it cook for 25 minutes. 7. If needed, add more vegetable stock during the cooking process and continue cooking for another 15 to 20 minutes, or until the barley is tender and creamy. 8. Stir in the chopped porcini mushrooms and nutritional yeast (if using). Season with salt and pepper to taste. Serve the mushroom barley risotto immediately.

Per Serving:

calories: 354 | fat: 2g | protein: 15g | carbs: 74g | fiber: 16g

BLAT (Bacon, Lettuce, Avocado and Tomato) Pitas

Prep time: 10 minutes | Cook time: 5 minutes | Makes 4 sandwiches

2 teaspoons coconut oil (optional)
½ cup dulse, picked through and separated
Few drops liquid smoke
Salt and black pepper (optional)
2 avocados, sliced
¼ cup chopped cilantro
2 sliced scallions
2 tablespoons lime juice
4 8-inch whole wheat pitas
4 cups greens
4 sliced plum tomatoes

1. Place a large cast-iron skillet over medium heat. Once it's warm, add the coconut oil (if desired), then the dulse and liquid smoke. Toss to combine. Cook, stirring often, until the dulse is crispy, about 5 minutes. Remove from the heat and season with pepper to taste. 2. Mash the avocado with the cilantro, scallions, and lime juice. Season with salt and pepper to taste, if desired. 3. Slice the pitas in half and toast lightly. Gently open them, and divide the avocado mixture evenly into all 8 halves. Divide the greens, tomatoes, and dulse evenly among the pitas and serve.

Per Serving: (1 sandwich)

calories: 381 | fat: 19g | protein: 10g | carbs: 50g | fiber: 14g

Green Chile Rice with Black Beans

Prep time: 20 minutes | Cook time: 1 hour | Serves 4

1 poblano chile pepper, seeded and diced small
1 (4 ounces / 113 g) can mild green chiles
1 cup coarsely chopped cilantro
½ cup spinach
4 cups vegetable stock, or low-sodium vegetable broth
1½ cups medium grain brown rice
1 medium yellow onion, peeled and diced small
1 teaspoon ground cumin
1 jalapeño pepper, seeded and minced
2 cups cooked black beans, or 1 (15 ounces / 425 g) can, drained and rinsed
Zest of 1 lime
Salt, to taste (optional)

1. In a blender, combine the poblano pepper, green chiles, cilantro, and spinach. Blend until smooth, adding some vegetable stock as needed to achieve a smooth consistency. 2. Transfer the mixture to a medium saucepan and add the remaining vegetable stock. Stir in the brown rice and bring to a boil over high heat. Reduce the heat to medium, cover the saucepan, and cook for 45 to 50 minutes or until the rice is tender. 3. Meanwhile, in a large saucepan, sauté the diced onion over medium heat for 7 to 8 minutes. Add water, 1 to 2 tablespoons at a time, if needed, to prevent sticking. 4. Stir in the ground cumin, minced jalapeño pepper, and black beans. Cook for an additional 5 minutes. 5. Once the rice is cooked, fold it into the onion and black bean mixture in the saucepan. Add the lime zest and season with salt, if desired. 6. Serve the green chile rice with black beans as a delicious and flavorful main dish or side dish.

Per Serving:

calories: 403 | fat: 2g | protein: 13g | carbs: 71g | fiber: 11g

Fried Rice with Tofu Scramble

Prep time: 15 minutes | Cook time: 35 minutes | Serves 2

4 cups cooked quick-cooking brown rice
1 cup cooked or canned green peas
1 (7 ounces / 198 g) pack extra-firm tofu, scrambled
1 cup julienned carrots
¼ cup curry spices
1 cup water
Optional Toppings:
Lemon slices
Sauerkraut
Fresh cilantro

1. Cook 1 1/2 cups of brown rice according to package instructions, usually for about 25 minutes. 2. Heat a large nonstick frying pan over medium heat and add 1/2 cup of water and the scrambled tofu. 3. Stir in the curry spices and cook for about 5 minutes, stirring occasionally to prevent sticking, until the tofu is heated through and most of the water has evaporated. 4. Add the julienned carrots, cooked brown rice, and green peas to the pan along with the remaining 1/2 cup of water. Stir-fry for another 5 minutes or until the water has evaporated. 5. Turn off the heat and divide the fried rice between 2 bowls. Serve with optional toppings such as lemon slices, sauerkraut, and fresh cilantro. 6. Store any leftover fried rice in an airtight container in the refrigerator and consume within 3 days. Alternatively, you can store it in the freezer for a maximum of 30 days. Thaw at room temperature and reheat in a nonstick frying pan or microwave before serving.

Per Serving:
calories: 286 | fat: 10g | protein: 18g | carbs: 30g | fiber: 8g

Red Lentil Dal

Prep time: 15 minutes | Cook time: 35 minutes | Serves 4

1 large yellow onion, peeled and diced
2 cloves garlic, peeled and minced
1 bay leaf
1 tablespoon grated ginger
1 teaspoon turmeric
1 tablespoon cumin seeds, toasted and ground
1 tablespoon coriander seeds, toasted and ground
½ teaspoon crushed red pepper flakes
2 cup red lentils, rinsed
Salt, to taste (optional)
Zest of 1 lemon

1. Place the onion in a large saucepan and sauté over medium heat for 10 minutes. Add water 1 to 2 tablespoons at a time to keep the onion from sticking to the pan. Add the garlic, bay leaf, ginger, turmeric, cumin, coriander, and crushed red pepper flakes and cook for another minute. 2. Add the lentils and 4 cups of water and bring the pot to a boil over high heat. Reduce the heat to medium and cook, covered, for 20 to 25 minutes, or until the lentils are tender and have started to break down. Remove from the heat. Season with salt (if using) and add the lemon zest.

Per Serving:
calories: 379 | fat: 2g | protein: 24g | carbs: 68g | fiber: 12g

Farro Tabbouleh

Prep time: 15 minutes | Cook time: 30 minutes | Serves 6

2½ cups water or vegetable broth
1 cup farro, soaked overnight and drained
3 scallions, sliced thin
1 English cucumber, diced
1 red or yellow bell pepper, finely diced
1 bunch flat-leaf parsley leaves, chopped
Handful mint leaves, chopped
Grated zest and juice of 2 lemons
¼ cup vegetable broth
¼ teaspoon salt (optional)
⅛ teaspoon black pepper

1. Combine the water and farro in a medium saucepan. Bring to a boil, then reduce the heat to low, cover, and cook, stirring occasionally, until the farro is al dente, about 25 minutes. 2. Allow to cool for 10 minutes, then transfer to a large bowl along with the remaining ingredients. Toss to combine and serve. (The tabbouleh can be refrigerated for up to 2 days, though the herbs will discolor.).

Per Serving:
calories: 115 | fat: 1g | protein: 4g | carbs: 26g | fiber: 5g

Mushroom Risotto

Prep time: 10 minutes | Cook time: 55 minutes | Serves 4

1 yellow onion, chopped
3 garlic cloves, minced
½ celery stalk, minced
1 tablespoon water, plus more as needed
9 ounces (255 g) baby portabella mushrooms, coarsely chopped
4 ounces (113 g) shiitake mushrooms, coarsely chopped
1 tablespoon apple cider vinegar
1½ cups Arborio rice
6 cups no-sodium vegetable broth, divided
1 (15 ounces /425 g) can red kidney beans, drained and rinsed
Scallions, green parts only, cut into chiffonade, for serving

1. In an 8-quart pot over high heat, combine the onion, garlic, and celery. Sauté for 2 to 3 minutes, adding water 1 tablespoon at a time to prevent burning. Add the baby portabella and shiitake mushrooms and sauté for 3 to 4 minutes, stirring, until the liquid from the mushrooms evaporates. 2. Sprinkle the vinegar over the vegetables, stir, and cook for 1 minute. Stir in the rice and sauté for 1 minute more. 3. Add 3 cups of vegetable broth and bring to a simmer. Reduce the heat to low and cover the pot. Cook, undisturbed, for 20 minutes. 4. Add 1½ cups of vegetable broth, stir, cover the pot, and cook for 10 minutes more. 5. Add the remaining 1½ cups of vegetable broth. Cook, stirring continuously but lightly, for 5 to 10 minutes more, or until the liquid has been mostly absorbed. 6. Stir in the red kidney beans. Serve warm, topped with scallions.

Per Serving:
calories: 382 | fat: 1g | protein: 14g | carbs: 80g | fiber: 7g

Chapter 5 Vegetables and Sides

Creamy Curried Potatoes and Peas

Prep time: 15 minutes | Cook time: 30 minutes | Serves 4

1 tablespoon extra-virgin olive oil (optional)
8 small red potatoes (about 1 pound / 454 g), diced small
3 garlic cloves, minced
1 (2-inch) piece fresh ginger, peeled and minced
1 small yellow onion, cut into ¼-inch pieces
3 teaspoons curry powder
2 cups water
1 cup frozen peas
3 tablespoons tomato paste
1 teaspoon salt, plus more as needed (optional)
Black pepper
Red pepper flakes (optional)
¼ cup chopped fresh cilantro, for garnish

1. In a large saucepan or wok, heat the oil over medium heat (optional). Add the diced potatoes and cook, stirring often, until they start to brown, about 10 minutes. 2. Push the potatoes to one side of the pan, then add the minced garlic, minced ginger, and chopped onion. Cook, stirring occasionally, until very fragrant, about 5 minutes. 3. Stir the onion mixture with the potatoes until well combined. 4. Add the curry powder and water to the pan, stirring until well combined. Raise the heat to high and bring the mixture to a boil. 5. Lower the heat to medium and cook, stirring occasionally, until the potatoes are fork-tender, approximately 10 to 15 minutes. 6. Stir in the frozen peas, tomato paste, and salt (if using). Continue cooking, stirring occasionally, until the liquid reduces to a creamy sauce, about 4 to 5 minutes. 7. Taste and season with salt (if using) and black pepper to your liking. Sprinkle with red pepper flakes (if using) and chopped fresh cilantro. 8. Serve the creamy curried potatoes and peas hot.

Per Serving:
calories: 323 | fat: 4g | protein: 9g | carbs: 65g | fiber: 9g

Vegetable Spring Rolls with Spicy Peanut Dipping Sauce

Prep time: 15 minutes | Cook time: 10 minutes | Serves 2

Spicy Peanut Dipping Sauce:
2 tablespoons defatted peanut powder
1 tablespoon maple syrup (optional)
1 tablespoon rice vinegar
½ teaspoon onion powder
½ teaspoon garlic powder
½ teaspoon red pepper flakes
Spring Rolls:
6 rice paper wraps
6 large lettuce leaves
1½ cups cooked brown rice
1 cup shredded carrots
1 bunch fresh cilantro
1 bunch fresh mint
1 bunch fresh basil

Make the Spicy Peanut Dipping Sauce: 1. In a small saucepan over medium heat, combine the peanut powder, maple syrup (if desired), rice vinegar, onion powder, garlic powder, and red pepper flakes. 2. Cook for 10 minutes, stirring occasionally. 3. Remove the sauce from the heat and set it aside to cool. Make the Spring Rolls: 1. Fill a shallow bowl or pan with warm water. Dip a rice paper wrap into the water for 10 to 15 seconds, until it becomes soft and pliable. 2. Remove the rice paper wrap and place it on a cutting board or other clean, smooth surface. 3. Lay a lettuce leaf flat on the rice paper wrap. 4. Add ¼ cup of brown rice, 2 to 3 tablespoons of shredded carrots, and a few leaves each of cilantro, mint, and basil on top of the lettuce leaf. 5. Wrap the sides of the rice paper halfway into the center, then roll the wrap from the bottom to the top to form a tight roll. 6. Repeat the process for the remaining spring rolls. 7. Serve the vegetable spring rolls with the Spicy Peanut Dipping Sauce in a dipping bowl on the side.

Per Serving:
calories: 263 | fat: 3g | protein: 11g | carbs: 46g | fiber: 5g

Roasted Balsamic Beets

Prep time: 5 minutes | Cook time: 50 minutes | Serves 6

6 medium beets, scrubbed
¼ cup plus 2 tablespoons balsamic vinegar, divided
2 teaspoons pure maple syrup (optional)
1½ tablespoons virgin olive oil (optional)
Salt and pepper, to taste (optional)

1. Preheat the oven to 400°F (205°C). 2. Trim both ends of the beets and peel them. Cut the beets into ½-inch dices. 3. Arrange the diced beets in a single layer in a large glass baking dish. 4. Drizzle the diced beets with ¼ cup of balsamic vinegar. If desired, add the maple syrup and olive oil. Season with salt and pepper to taste, and gently toss the beets until they are evenly coated. 5. Cover the baking dish with foil and place it in the preheated oven. 6. Roast the covered beets for 25 minutes. Then, remove them from the oven and add the remaining 2 tablespoons of balsamic vinegar. Carefully toss the beets to coat. 7. Roast the beets uncovered for another 25 minutes or until they are fork-tender. 8. Serve the roasted balsamic beets immediately, or allow them to cool thoroughly on the counter. The beets can be stored in a sealed container in the refrigerator for up to 5 days.

Per Serving:
calories: 84 | fat: 4g | protein: 1g | carbs: 12g | fiber: 2g

Spring Steamed Vegetables with Savory Goji Berry Cream

Prep time: 15 minutes | Cook time: 10 minutes | Serves 6

Savory Goji Berry Cream:
¼ cup dried goji berries
1 tablespoon apple cider vinegar
1 tablespoon mellow or light miso
1 tablespoon fresh lemon juice
1 (1-inch) piece of fresh ginger, peeled and chopped
1 teaspoon pure maple syrup (optional)
3 tablespoons virgin olive oil
(optional)
Salt and pepper, to taste (optional)
Vegetables:
1½ pounds (680 g) trimmed spring vegetables
Salt and pepper, to taste (optional)
Garnishes:
Scant ¼ cup walnut halves, toasted and chopped
1 green onion, thinly sliced

1. Make the Savory Goji Berry Cream: Place the goji berries in a small bowl and cover them with boiling water. Let the berries sit for 5 minutes or until they've plumped and softened. Spoon the goji berries into a blender, reserving the soaking water. 2. Add the apple cider vinegar, miso, lemon juice, ginger, maple syrup, olive oil, salt, and pepper, if using, to the blender. Add 3 tablespoons of the goji soaking water, and then whiz the mixture on high until creamy and smooth. Set aside. 3. Make the Vegetables: After you've trimmed the vegetables, set a large pot with about 1 inch of water on the stove. Bring the water to a simmer. Arrange the vegetables in a steamer basket and set them into the pot. Cover and steam until all the vegetables are just tender, about 8 minutes. 4. Arrange the steamed vegetables on your serving platter and top with the Savory Goji Berry Cream. Garnish with the chopped walnuts and sliced green onions.

Per Serving:
calories: 136 | fat: 9g | protein: 5g | carbs: 17g | fiber: 5g

Beet Sushi and Avocado Poke Bowls

Prep time: 20 minutes | Cook time: 20 minutes | Serves 2

2 red beets, trimmed and peeled
3 cups water
2 teaspoons low-sodium soy sauce or gluten-free tamari
½ teaspoon wasabi paste (optional)
1 tablespoon maple syrup (optional)
1 teaspoon sesame oil (optional)
1 teaspoon rice vinegar
1 cup frozen shelled edamame
1 cup cooked brown rice
1 cucumber, peeled and cut into matchsticks
2 carrots, cut into matchsticks
1 avocado, peeled, pitted, and sliced
1 scallion, green and white parts, chopped small, for garnish
2 tablespoons sesame seeds, for garnish (optional)

1. In a medium saucepan, combine the beets and water and bring to a boil over high heat. Lower the heat to medium and cook until they are tender but not mushy, about 15 minutes. Drain, rinse, and set aside to cool. 2. In a small bowl, make the dressing by mixing together the soy sauce, wasabi (if using), maple syrup, sesame oil, and rice vinegar and set aside. 3. When the beets are cooled, slide off the skins. Using a sharp knife, cut the beets into very thin slices to resemble tuna sashimi. Put the beet slices in a small bowl and top with 1 teaspoon of the dressing. Set aside to marinate. 4. Put the edamame in a microwave-safe bowl, add water to cover, and cook in the microwave for 1 minute. Drain and set aside. 5. To assemble the bowls, divide the rice between 2 bowls. Top each bowl with the sliced beets, rice, cucumbers, carrots, edamame, and avocado and drizzle with the remaining dressing. Garnish with the scallions and sesame seeds (if using).

Per Serving:
calories: 488 | fat: 22g | protein: 16g | carbs: 63g | fiber: 18g

Mustard-Roasted Broccoli Pâté

Prep time: 15 minutes | Cook time: 20 minutes | Makes 2 cups

3 cups broccoli florets
1 leek, white and light green parts only, rough-chopped
⅓ cup plus 2 tablespoons virgin olive oil, divided (optional)
1½ tablespoons grainy mustard, divided
2 teaspoons fresh thyme leaves
Salt and pepper, to taste (optional)
2 teaspoons lemon zest
1½ tablespoons fresh lemon juice
2 tablespoons nutritional yeast
Flaky sea salt, to taste (optional)
Serve:
Sliced bread
Olives
Pickles
Vegetables

1. Preheat the oven to 400°F (205°C). Line a baking sheet with parchment paper. 2. Toss the broccoli florets and leeks with 1 tablespoon of the olive oil, 1 tablespoon of the grainy mustard, and the thyme leaves, salt, and pepper, if using. After everything is coated, spread the mixture out on the lined baking sheet. Roast the vegetables until lightly browned and tender, about 15 to 18 minutes. 3. When they have slightly cooled, transfer the roasted vegetables to a food processor. Pulse the mixture until the broccoli is somewhat chopped. Set aside a spoonful of the chopped broccoli for garnish. 4. To the food processor, add the remaining ½ tablespoon of the grainy mustard and the lemon zest, lemon juice, salt, pepper, and nutritional yeast. Pulse until everything is combined. With the food processor running on low, drizzle in ⅓ cup of the olive oil through the feed tube. Continue to mix until you have a smooth, lightly chunky paste. Remove the bowl from the food processor, check the seasoning, and adjust if necessary. 5. Scrape the pâté mixture into a 2-cup nonreactive serving vessel, and scatter the reserved chopped broccoli over the top. Pour the remaining 1 tablespoon of the olive oil on top. Cover and place the pâté in the fridge for at least 2 hours or until the top oil layer has solidified a little bit. 6. Sprinkle the flaky sea salt, if using, over the pâté before you serve it with sliced bread, olives, pickles, and vegetables.

Per Serving: (½ cup)
calories: 200 | fat: 18g | protein: 4g | carbs: 7g | fiber: 2g

Chickpea of the Sea Salad

Prep time: 15 minutes | Cook time: 4 hours | Serves 3 to 4

- 1 (1-pound / 454 g) bag dried chickpeas, rinsed and sorted to remove small stones and debris
- 7 cups water
- ¼ teaspoon baking soda
- 5 tablespoons plant-based mayonnaise
- 1 tablespoon yellow mustard
- ¼ cup diced dill pickles
- ¼ cup finely diced onions
- 1 celery stalk, diced
- 2 tablespoons rice vinegar
- ½ teaspoon kelp powder
- Ground black pepper
- Salt (optional)

1. Put the rinsed and sorted chickpeas, water, and baking soda in a slow cooker. Cover and cook on High for 4 hours or on Low for 8 to 9 hours. 2. Once cooked, strain and discard the cooking liquid. Transfer 2 cups of the cooked chickpeas to a food processor and pulse 5 to 10 times to break them up, but not turn them into mush. Transfer the pulsed chickpeas to a medium bowl. Save the remaining cooked chickpeas for another recipe. 3. To the pulsed chickpeas, add the mayonnaise, mustard, diced dill pickles, finely diced onions, diced celery, rice vinegar, kelp powder, and ground black pepper. Stir well to combine and form a salad-like mixture. 4. Taste and season with salt, if desired. 5. Chill the Chickpea of the Sea Salad in the refrigerator until ready to serve.

Per Serving:

calories: 313 | fat: 21g | protein: 8g | carbs: 25g | fiber: 7g

Zucchini "Parmesan"

Prep time: 10 minutes | Cook time: 20 minutes | Serves 4

- 4 zucchini, sliced into ½-inch rounds
- ½ cup almond milk
- 1 teaspoon arrowroot powder
- 1 teaspoon fresh lemon juice
- ½ teaspoon salt (optional)
- ½ cup whole wheat bread crumbs
- ¼ cup hemp seeds
- ¼ cup nutritional yeast
- ½ teaspoon garlic powder
- ¼ teaspoon black pepper
- ¼ teaspoon crushed red pepper

1. Preheat the oven to 375°F (190°C). Line two baking sheets with parchment paper. 2. In a medium bowl, combine the sliced zucchini, almond milk, arrowroot powder, lemon juice, and ¼ teaspoon of salt (if using). Stir well to combine. 3. In a large bowl with a lid, combine the whole wheat bread crumbs, hemp seeds, nutritional yeast, garlic powder, black pepper, and crushed red pepper. 4. Take the zucchini slices from the almond milk mixture in batches and add them to the bowl with the breadcrumb mixture. Put the lid on the bowl and shake it to evenly coat the zucchini slices with the breadcrumb mixture. 5. Place the coated zucchini slices in a single layer on the prepared baking sheets. 6. Bake the zucchini slices in the preheated oven for about 20 minutes, or until they turn golden brown. 7. Serve the zucchini "Parmesan" slices.

Per Serving:

calories: 191 | fat: 6g | protein: 11g | carbs: 25g | fiber: 5g

Sweet and Savory Root Veggies and Butternut Squash

Prep time: 20 minutes | Cook time: 3½ to 5 hours | Serves 4 to 6

- 1 large sweet potato (about ½ pound / 227 g), peeled and cut into 1½-inch chunks
- 2 red or yellow potatoes (about ⅔ pound / 272 g), unpeeled and cut into 1½-inch chunks
- 1 medium yam (about ⅓ pound / 136 g), scrubbed, peeled, and cut into 1½-inch chunks
- 1 small butternut squash (about 1 pound / 454 g), peeled and cut into 1½-inch chunks
- 1 medium onion, diced
- 4 carrots, cut into 1-inch rounds
- 2 apples, any variety, peeled and cut into 1-inch chunks
- ½ cup golden raisins
- ½ cup pitted dates, quartered
- ¼ cup maple syrup or date syrup (optional)
- Juice from 2 oranges (about 1 cup)
- Zest from 1 orange
- 1 cup store-bought low-sodium vegetable broth
- 2 teaspoons ground cinnamon
- 1 teaspoon ground ginger

1. Place the sweet potato, potatoes, yam, butternut squash, onion, carrots, apples, golden raisins, dates, maple syrup (if using), orange juice, orange zest, vegetable broth, cinnamon, and ginger in the slow cooker. 2. Cover the slow cooker and cook on High for 3½ to 5 hours or on Low for 8 to 10 hours until the vegetables are tender and cooked through. 3. Stir the mixture gently to combine all the flavors and serve hot.

Per Serving:

calories: 460 | fat: 1g | protein: 7g | carbs: 116g | fiber: 15g

Blackened Sprouts

Prep time: 10 minutes | Cook time: 20 minutes | Serves 4

- 1 pound (454 g) fresh Brussels sprouts, trimmed and halved
- 2 tablespoons avocado oil (optional)
- Sea salt and ground black pepper, to taste
- 1 cup walnut halves
- 1 tablespoon pure maple syrup (optional)

1. Preheat the oven to 425°F (220°C). Line a baking sheet with parchment paper or grease it well. 2. In a medium bowl, toss the Brussels sprouts with avocado oil (if using). Season well with sea salt and ground black pepper to taste. 3. Arrange the seasoned Brussels sprouts in a single layer on the prepared baking sheet. 4. Roast the Brussels sprouts in the preheated oven for 20 minutes, or until the edges start to blacken. 5. Meanwhile, place the walnut halves in a bowl and drizzle them with pure maple syrup (if using). Toss until well coated. 6. During the last 3 minutes of the roasting time for the Brussels sprouts, place the coated walnut halves on the same baking sheet. This will allow them to toast and caramelize. 7. Remove the baking sheet from the oven and let the blackened sprouts and caramelized walnuts cool slightly before serving.

Per Serving:

calories: 254 | fat: 20g | protein: 6g | carbs: 16g | fiber: 5g

Ginger, Shiitake, Pecan, and Apricot Pilaf

Prep time: 15 minutes | **Cook time:** 3 hours | **Serves 4 to 6**

1 small onion, diced
2 celery stalks, diced
2 carrots, diced
1 cup wild rice
2 cups brown rice
1 (1-inch) piece fresh ginger, peeled and minced, or 1 teaspoon ground ginger
1 teaspoon garlic powder
6 cups store-bought low-sodium vegetable broth
1 tablespoon low-sodium soy sauce, tamari, or coconut aminos
4 ounces (113 g) shiitake mushrooms, stemmed
1 cup chopped pecans
½ cup chopped dried apricots
½ bunch flat-leaf parsley, coarsely chopped

1. Place the diced onion, celery, and carrots in the slow cooker. 2. Add the wild rice, brown rice, minced ginger (or ground ginger), garlic powder, vegetable broth, and soy sauce to the slow cooker. Stir to combine. 3. Add the sliced shiitake mushrooms to the slow cooker and stir again. 4. Cover the slow cooker and cook on High for 3 hours or on Low for 5 to 6 hours, until all the liquid is absorbed and the rice is cooked. 5. Once cooked, fluff the pilaf with a fork. 6. Serve the pilaf hot and top it with chopped pecans, dried apricots, and coarsely chopped flat-leaf parsley.

Per Serving:
calories: 757 | fat: 24g | protein: 19g | carbs: 126g | fiber: 15g

Tangy Cabbage, Apples, and Potatoes

Prep time: 15 minutes | **Cook time:** 3 to 4 hours | **Serves 4 to 6**

6 red or yellow potatoes (about 2 pounds / 907 g), unpeeled and cut into 1½-inch chunks
½ medium onion, diced
2 apples, peeled, cored, and diced
½ teaspoon ground cinnamon
½ medium head green cabbage, sliced
1 cup store-bought low-sodium vegetable broth
½ cup apple juice, apple cider, or hard apple cider
2 tablespoons apple cider vinegar
2 teaspoons ground mustard, or 1 tablespoon spicy brown mustard
1 teaspoon fennel seeds
1 bay leaf
Ground black pepper
Salt (optional)

1. In the slow cooker, layer the potatoes, onion, and apples, in that order. Sprinkle the cinnamon over the apples. Top with the cabbage. 2. In a small bowl, whisk together the broth, apple juice, vinegar, mustard, fennel, bay leaf, pepper, and salt (if using). Pour over the cabbage. 3. Cover and cook on High for 3 to 4 hours or on Low for 6 to 8 hours. Remove and discard the bay leaf and serve.

Per Serving:
calories: 266 | fat: 1g | protein: 7g | carbs: 62g | fiber: 10g

Spicy Carrots with Coriander

Prep time: 15 minutes | **Cook time:** 0 minutes | **Serves 2**

3 cups shredded carrots
4 garlic cloves, minced
¼ cup rice vinegar
1 tablespoon maple syrup (optional)
1 tablespoon ground coriander
1 teaspoon red pepper flakes
½ teaspoon freshly ground black pepper
¼ tablespoon cayenne pepper
1 teaspoon dried dill (optional)
1 teaspoon dried parsley (optional)

1. In a large mixing bowl, combine the shredded carrots, minced garlic, rice vinegar, maple syrup (if using), red pepper flakes, ground coriander, black pepper, and cayenne pepper. 2. If desired, add the dried dill and dried parsley to the mixture. 3. Let the mixture sit for at least 10 minutes to allow the flavors to meld together. 4. Serve and enjoy the spicy carrots with coriander as a side dish or a crunchy snack.

Per Serving:
calories: 101 | fat: 0g | protein: 2g | carbs: 23g | fiber: 4g

Ultimate Veggie Wrap with Kale Pesto

Prep time: 20 minutes | **Cook time:** 10 minutes | **Serves 2**

Kale Pesto:
¼ cup raw cashews, soaked at least 2 hours
1 cup kale, de-stemmed and coarsely chopped
1 clove garlic
½ teaspoon salt (optional)
2 tablespoons nutritional yeast
3 tablespoons extra virgin olive oil (optional)
Wrap:
½ cup broccoli florets
2 spinach tortillas
¼ cup grated carrots
¼ cup diced red onion
½ yellow bell pepper, diced
6 ounces (170 g) spinach
2 tablespoons raw shelled hempseed
2 tablespoons sunflower seed kernels

Make Kale Pesto: 1. Place the soaked cashews, kale, garlic, and salt (if using) in a small food processor. Process for about 30 seconds until well combined. 2. Add nutritional yeast and olive oil (if using) to the food processor and process for a few more seconds until the pesto is well blended. Set aside.
Assemble the Wrap: 3. Fill a medium saucepan with water and place a steamer insert in it. Bring the water to a boil. Add the broccoli florets to the steamer and steam for 10 minutes until tender. Remove from the steamer and set aside. 4. Lay out the spinach tortillas. Divide the kale pesto evenly between the tortillas, leaving about 1 inch around all edges. 5. Divide the remaining ingredients in half and arrange them in a line next to each other and along the length of each tortilla. 6. Roll up the tortillas snugly without tearing them. Cut each tortilla in half and serve.

Per Serving:
calories: 554 | fat: 36g | protein: 24g | carbs: 34g | fiber: 8g

Stir-Fried Vegetables with Miso and Sake

Prep time: 25 minutes | Cook time: 10 minutes | Serves 4

¼ cup mellow white miso
½ cup vegetable stock, or low-sodium vegetable broth
¼ cup sake
1 medium yellow onion, peeled and thinly sliced
1 large carrot, peeled, cut in half lengthwise, and then cut into half-moons on the diagonal
1 medium red bell pepper, seeded and cut into ½-inch strips
1 large head broccoli, cut into florets
½ pound (227 g) snow peas, trimmed
2 cloves garlic, peeled and minced
½ cup chopped cilantro (optional)
Salt and freshly ground black pepper, to taste

1. In a small bowl, whisk together the mellow white miso, vegetable stock, and sake. Set aside. 2. Heat a large skillet over high heat. Add the onion, carrot, red bell pepper, and broccoli. Stir-fry for 4 to 5 minutes, adding water 1 to 2 tablespoons at a time to prevent sticking. 3. Add the snow peas and continue to stir-fry for another 4 minutes. 4. Add the minced garlic and cook for 30 seconds. 5. Pour in the miso mixture and cook until heated through. 6. Remove the skillet from the heat and stir in the chopped cilantro, if using. Season with salt and freshly ground black pepper.

Per Serving:
calories: 135 | fat: 1g | protein: 7g | carbs: 24g | fiber: 7g

Loaded Frijoles

Prep time: 10 minutes | Cook time: 20 minutes | Serves 6

1 tablespoon avocado oil (optional)
1 yellow onion, finely chopped
3 garlic cloves, minced
2 teaspoons chili powder
1 teaspoon ground cumin
2 (15 ounces / 425 g) cans pinto beans, undrained
¼ cup tomato sauce
Sea salt, to taste (optional)

1. In a 4-quart pan, warm the avocado oil (if using) over medium-high heat. Add the finely chopped onion and sauté for 5 minutes until it becomes translucent. 2. Add the minced garlic and cook for 30 seconds. Then, add the chili powder and ground cumin and cook for an additional 30 seconds, stirring continuously. 3. Stir in the pinto beans (including the liquid from the cans) and tomato sauce. Taste and add salt (if using), adjusting according to your preference. 4. Mash the beans with a potato masher or purée them using an immersion blender until you reach the desired consistency. Cook the beans over medium-low heat for 15 minutes or until they thicken. If the beans become too thick, you can add a little water to achieve the desired consistency. 5. Serve the loaded frijoles hot with your favorite toppings such as shredded cheese, diced avocado, chopped cilantro, sliced jalapeños, or sour cream.

Per Serving:
calories: 142 | fat: 3g | protein: 7g | carbs: 22g | fiber: 6g

Crispy Maple Mustard Cabbage

Prep time: 5 minutes | Cook time: 40 minutes | Serves 6

2 tablespoons virgin olive oil (optional)
1 tablespoon grainy mustard
1½ teaspoons pure maple syrup (optional)
½ head large cabbage or 1 small whole cabbage
Salt and pepper, to taste (optional)

1. Preheat the oven to 400ºF (205ºC). 2. In a small bowl, whisk together the olive oil, grainy mustard, and maple syrup, if using. 3. Cut the cabbage into 1-inch wedges. Once you have the wedges, remove most of the core, leaving a thin strip intact so that the wedge holds together through the roasting process. 4. Lay the wedges on a large baking sheet. Brush the side facing up with the olive oil mixture. Season with salt and pepper, if using. Slide the baking sheet into the oven, and roast for 20 minutes. 5. Remove the baking sheet from the oven, and carefully flip the wedges over with a spatula. Brush with the remaining olive oil mixture. Slide the baking sheet back into the oven, and roast for another 20 minutes or until the cabbage wedges are quite browned and have crispy edges. Serve the cabbage warm.

Per Serving:
calories: 75 | fat: 5g | protein: 2g | carbs: 8g | fiber: 2g

Maple glazed Butternut Squash and Brussels Sprouts

Prep time: 15 minutes | Cook time: 2 to 2½ hours | Serves 4 to 6

1 medium butternut squash (about 2 to 3 pounds / 907 g to 1.4 kg), peeled, seeded, and cut into 1-inch cubes
¾ pound (340 g) Brussels sprouts, halved
¼ cup apple cider vinegar
2 tablespoons maple syrup (optional)
½ teaspoon ground cinnamon
Ground black pepper
Salt (optional)
1 cup chopped pecans
4 to 5 Medjool dates, pitted and chopped

1. Place the cubed butternut squash and halved Brussels sprouts in a slow cooker. 2. Cover and cook on High for 2 to 2½ hours or on Low for 4 to 6 hours. Check for doneness periodically, as the cooking time may vary. The squash should be tender but not mushy, and the Brussels sprouts should still have some texture. 3. In a measuring cup or medium bowl, stir together the apple cider vinegar, maple syrup (if using), and ground cinnamon to make the glaze. 4. Pour the glaze mixture over the cooked vegetables in the slow cooker and gently toss to coat them. 5. Season with ground black pepper and salt, if desired. 6. Add the chopped pecans and dates to the mixture and give it a final gentle toss. 7. Serve the maple glazed butternut squash and Brussels sprouts immediately.

Per Serving:
calories: 372 | fat: 20g | protein: 7g | carbs: 50g | fiber: 12g

Cumin-Citrus Roasted Carrots

Prep time: 10 minutes | Cook time: 30 minutes | Serves 6

8 large carrots, sliced into ½-inch rounds
¼ cup orange juice
¼ cup vegetable broth
1 teaspoon ground cumin
¼ teaspoon ground turmeric
Salt and black pepper (optional)
1 tablespoon fresh lime juice
Chopped flat-leaf parsley (optional)

1. Preheat the oven to 400ºF (205ºC). 2. Place the carrots in a large baking dish, then add the orange juice, broth, cumin, and turmeric. Season with salt and pepper, if desired. 3. Bake, uncovered, until the carrots are lightly browned and the juices have reduced slightly, about 30 minutes, stirring halfway through. Drizzle with the lime juice and parsley, if desired, and serve.

Per Serving:
calories: 47 | fat: 0g | protein: 1g | carbs: 11g | fiber: 3g

Roasted Veggies with Tofu

Prep time: 10 minutes | Cook time: 30 minutes | Serves 4

1½ pounds (680 g) mixed vegetables
1 pound (454 g) extra-firm tofu or tempeh
¼ cup vegetable broth
2 tablespoons spice blend
Salt and black pepper (optional)

1. Preheat the oven to 400ºF (205ºC). Line two baking sheets with parchment paper. 2. Chop the vegetables into equal-size pieces. Cube the tofu. 3. Divide the vegetables and tofu between the prepared baking sheets. Drizzle with the broth, and sprinkle the spices evenly over the baking sheets. Toss to thoroughly coat, and season with salt (if desired) and pepper. 4. Bake, uncovered, until the vegetables are cooked through and starting to brown, about 30 minutes. (Rotate the baking sheets halfway through if necessary for even cooking.) Serve.

Per Serving:
calories: 218 | fat: 7g | protein: 16g | carbs: 25g | fiber: 8g

Quick Marinated Arame

Prep time: 10 minutes | Cook time: 0 minutes | Makes 2 cups

1½ cups dried arame
4 cups boiling filtered water
1 tablespoon extra-virgin olive oil (optional)
1 tablespoon tamari
1 tablespoon brown rice vinegar
1 tablespoon mirin
Fine sea salt (optional)
2 tablespoons (½ ounce / 14 g) raw unhulled sesame seeds, toasted
Thinly sliced scallions to serve

1. Put the arame in a medium bowl, cover with the boiling water, and set aside for 20 minutes to hydrate and soften. 2. Thoroughly drain the arame in a sieve set over a bowl. Transfer to a bowl and add the oil, tamari, vinegar, and mirin. Taste and season with a pinch of salt if needed. Stir in the sesame seeds. The arame can be stored in a jar in the fridge for up to 1 week. Serve sprinkled with scallions.

Per Serving: (1 cup)
calories: 169 | fat: 12g | protein: 4g | carbs: 14g | fiber: 2g

Baby Potatoes with Dill, Chives, and Garlic

Prep time: 5 minutes | Cook time: 20 minutes | Serves 2

2 cups water
12 baby potatoes
2 garlic cloves, minced
2 tablespoons chopped fresh dill
2 tablespoons chopped fresh chives
Pinch freshly ground black pepper (optional)

1. In a medium saucepan, combine the water and baby potatoes. Bring to a boil over medium-high heat and cook for about 20 minutes or until the potatoes are soft when pierced with a fork. 2. Drain the liquid from the saucepan and add the minced garlic to the cooked potatoes. Mix well to evenly distribute the garlic. 3. Serve the baby potatoes warm and top each portion with 1 tablespoon of chopped fresh dill, 1 tablespoon of chopped fresh chives, and a pinch of freshly ground black pepper if desired.

Per Serving:
calories: 155 | fat: 1g | protein: 4g | carbs: 34g | fiber: 6g

Sautéed Root Vegetables with Parsley, Poppy Seeds, and Lemon

Prep time: 10 minutes | Cook time: 10 minutes | Serves 4

2 tablespoons extra-virgin coconut oil (optional)
2 large garlic cloves, finely chopped
1 pound (454 g) root vegetables, grated
1 teaspoon fine sea salt, plus more to taste (optional)
1 tablespoon poppy seeds
Grated zest of 1 small lemon
1 tablespoon freshly squeezed lemon juice
1½ cups fresh flat-leaf parsley leaves, coarsely chopped

1. Warm the oil in a large skillet over medium heat. Add the garlic and sauté for 1 minute, or until golden. Stir in the grated vegetables and salt, if using, and cook for 8 minutes, or until the vegetables are softened. Remove from the heat and stir in the poppy seeds, lemon zest, lemon juice, and parsley. Season to taste with more salt and serve warm or at room temperature. Any leftovers can be stored in an airtight container in the fridge for up to 3 days.

Per Serving:
calories: 130 | fat: 8g | protein: 2g | carbs: 14g | fiber: 4g

Roasted Cauliflower with Green Tahini

Prep time: 15 minutes | Cook time: 25 minutes | Serves 4

5 cups small cauliflower florets
1 cup cooked chickpeas
1 tablespoon virgin olive oil (optional)
2 teaspoons fresh lemon juice
2 teaspoons za'atar spice
Salt and pepper, to taste (optional)
Green Tahini:
⅓ cup tahini
2 tablespoons fresh lemon juice
2 teaspoons apple cider vinegar
2 tablespoons filtered water, plus extra if necessary
1 tablespoon raw agave nectar or pure maple syrup (optional)
½ cup fresh basil leaves
4 green onions, chopped
1 clove garlic, chopped
Salt and pepper, to taste (optional)
Serve:
Fresh lemon wedges (optional)

1. Preheat the oven to 400ºF (205ºC). Line a baking sheet with parchment paper. 2. Place the cauliflower florets and chickpeas on the prepared baking sheet. Drizzle with olive oil (if using) and lemon juice. Sprinkle with za'atar spice, salt, and pepper (if using). Toss the vegetables and chickpeas to coat them evenly. 3. Roast in the preheated oven for 20 to 25 minutes, tossing the vegetables and chickpeas occasionally, until the cauliflower is browned and the chickpeas are crisp. 4. While the vegetables are roasting, prepare the green tahini. In a blender, combine tahini, lemon juice, apple cider vinegar, filtered water, agave nectar (if using), basil leaves, green onions, garlic, salt, and pepper (if using). Blend on high speed until smooth and creamy. Adjust the consistency by adding more filtered water if necessary. Taste and adjust the seasonings. 5. Serve the roasted cauliflower and chickpeas hot, drizzled with the green tahini sauce. Serve with fresh lemon wedges on the side if desired.

Per Serving:
calories: 272 | fat: 16g | protein: 10g | carbs: 28g | fiber: 8g

Portabella Mushroom Gyro

Prep time: 15 minutes | Cook time: 15 minutes | Serves 2

Vegetables:
2 large portabella mushroom caps
2 tablespoons vegan Worcestershire sauce
1 teaspoon ground cumin
1 teaspoon maple syrup (optional)
½ teaspoon dried oregano
1 tablespoon coconut oil (optional)
¼ cup diced red onion
½ red bell pepper, diced large
Fresh White Sauce:
½ cup vegan mayonnaise
¼ cup raw shelled hempseeds
1 tablespoon lemon juice
¼ teaspoon dried mint
¼ teaspoon dill weed
Assemble:
2 pita flatbreads
1 ounce (28 g) baby spinach

Make the Vegetables: 1. Remove the stems from the portabella mushroom caps and use a spoon to scrape and remove the gills. Discard the stems and gills. Slice the mushroom caps into thick strips. 2. In a medium bowl, mix together the vegan Worcestershire sauce, ground cumin, maple syrup (if using), and dried oregano. Place the mushroom slices in the marinade and let them marinate for 10 minutes. 3. If using, heat the coconut oil in a large skillet over medium-high heat. Add the diced red onion and red bell pepper and sauté for 10 minutes until they are softened and slightly caramelized. Add the marinated mushroom slices to the skillet and sauté for an additional 5 minutes. Remove from heat and let the mixture cool.
Make the Fresh White Sauce: 1. In a small bowl, mix together the vegan mayonnaise, raw shelled hemp seeds, lemon juice, dried mint, and dill weed. Set the sauce aside. Assemble: 2. Lay out a layer of baby spinach leaves on each pita flatbread. Spoon the Fresh White Sauce down the center of each flatbread. 3. Place the sautéed mushroom and bell pepper mixture on top of the Fresh White Sauce. 4. Fold each flatbread to overlap the filling and secure it with decorative picks or toothpicks. 5. Serve the portabella mushroom gyros immediately and enjoy!

Per Serving:
calories: 374 | fat: 26g | protein: 16g | carbs: 27g | fiber: 4g

Roasted Carrots with Ginger Maple Cream

Prep time: 10 minutes | Cook time: 25 minutes | Serves 6

Carrots:
1 pound (454 g) medium carrots, cut into ½-inch batons
1 teaspoon minced fresh thyme leaves
2 teaspoons virgin olive oil (optional)
Salt and pepper, to taste (optional)
Ginger Maple Cream:
2 tablespoons raw cashew butter
1½ tablespoons filtered water
1 tablespoon pure maple syrup (optional)
1½ teaspoons fresh lemon juice
1 piece of fresh ginger, peeled and finely grated
Salt, to taste (optional)

1. Preheat the oven to 400ºF (205ºC). Line a baking sheet with parchment paper. 2. Make the Carrots: Place the carrots on the baking sheet. Toss them with the thyme, olive oil, salt, and pepper, if using. Arrange the carrots in a single layer, and slide the baking sheet into the oven. Roast the carrots until just tender, about 25 minutes. Flip and toss the carrots at the halfway mark. 3. Make the Ginger Maple Cream: In a medium bowl, stir the cashew butter with the water until no big chunks of cashew butter remain. Press the cashew butter on the side of the bowl and slowly work it into the water. Whisk in the maple syrup, lemon juice, and grated ginger. Season the cream with salt, if using. 4. Arrange the carrots on a serving platter. Drizzle the Ginger Maple Cream over the carrots, and serve warm.

Per Serving:
calories: 85 | fat: 4g | protein: 2g | carbs: 11g | fiber: 2g

Steamed Kabocha Squash with Nori and Scallions

Prep time: 10 minutes | Cook time: 15 minutes | Serves 4

½ medium kabocha squash with skin left on, seeded, and cut into wedges
1 sheet nori, toasted and crushed
2 scallions, thinly sliced, plus more for garnish
2 tablespoons tamari
1 tablespoon mirin
2 tablespoons raw unhulled sesame seeds, toasted

1. Set up a steamer and fill the pot with about 2 inches of filtered water. Bring to a boil over high heat and set the steamer basket in place. Arrange the kabocha wedges skin side down in the basket in a single layer and steam for 12 to 15 minutes, until the flesh is soft when pierced with a paring knife. 2. Meanwhile, combine the nori, scallions, tamari, and mirin in a small bowl; set aside. 3. When the squash is cooked, transfer to a serving platter and drizzle the nori mixture over the top. Sprinkle with the sesame seeds and scallions and serve. (Any leftovers can be stored in the fridge for 2 to 3 days.)

Per Serving:
calories: 37 | fat: 3g | protein: 2g | carbs: 7g | fiber: 1g

Avocado Tartare

Prep time: 15 minutes | Cook time: 0 minutes | Makes 2 cups

¼ cup finely diced red onion
2 tablespoons capers, drained and minced
¼ cup minced fresh flat-leaf parsley, plus extra for garnish
1 teaspoon Dijon mustard
2 teaspoons fresh lemon juice
½ teaspoon gluten-free tamari soy sauce
1 teaspoon virgin olive oil (optional)
Salt and pepper, to taste (optional)
1 medium just-ripe avocado
4 to 5 drops of hot sauce (optional)
Crackers and crostini, for serving

1. In a medium bowl, combine the diced red onion, capers, minced parsley, Dijon mustard, lemon juice, tamari soy sauce, olive oil (if using), salt, and pepper (if using). 2. Cut the avocado in half and remove the pit. Carefully peel the skin off the avocado, preserving the flesh's integrity. Dice the avocado flesh into small pieces and add it to the medium bowl. Toss everything gently to combine. 3. Add the hot sauce (if using) and toss again. Taste the avocado tartare and adjust the seasoning as desired. 4. Garnish the avocado tartare with extra chopped parsley. Serve it immediately with crackers or crostini.

Per Serving: (1 cup)
calories: 211 | fat: 18g | protein: 3g | carbs: 13g | fiber: 8g

Daikon Beet Pickle with Lime

Prep time: 5 minutes | Cook time: 0 minutes | Serves 6

1 medium-large daikon radish, peeled
2 small beets, peeled
¼ cup freshly squeezed lime juice, or more to taste
1 teaspoon fine sea salt, or more to taste (optional)

1. Thinly shave the daikon and beets on a mandoline, or slice paper-thin with a sharp knife. Transfer to a medium bowl, add the lime juice and salt, if using, and mix well to combine. Add more lime juice or salt to taste if necessary. Serve immediately, or store in a jar in the fridge for up to 2 weeks.

Per Serving:
calories: 15 | fat: 0g | protein: 0g | carbs: 4g | fiber: 1g

Baked Spaghetti Squash with Spicy Lentil Sauce

Prep time: 15 minutes | Cook time: 55 minutes | Serves 4

2 small spaghetti squash (about 1 pound / 454 g each), halved
Salt and freshly ground black pepper, to taste
1 medium yellow onion, peeled and diced small
3 cloves garlic, peeled and minced
2 teaspoons crushed red pepper flakes, or to taste
¼ cup tomato paste
1 cup cooked green lentils
1 cup vegetable stock, or low-sodium vegetable broth, plus more as needed
Chopped parsley

1. Preheat the oven to 350ºF (180ºC). 2. Season the cut sides of the squash with salt and pepper. Place the squash halves, cut side down, on a baking sheet, and bake them for 45 to 55 minutes, or until the squash is very tender (it is done when it can be easily pierced with a knife). 3. While the squash bakes, place the onion in a large saucepan and sauté over medium heat for 5 minutes. Add water 1 to 2 tablespoons at a time to keep the onion from sticking to the pan. Add the garlic, crushed red pepper flakes, tomato paste, and ½ cup of water and cook for 5 minutes. Add the lentils to the pan and cook until heated through. Season with additional salt. Purée the lentil mixture using an immersion blender or in a blender with a tight-fitting lid, covered with a towel, until smooth and creamy. Add some of the vegetable stock, as needed, to make a creamy sauce. 4. To serve, scoop the flesh from the spaghetti squash (it should come away looking like noodles) and divide it among 4 plates. Top with some of the lentil sauce and garnish with the parsley.

Per Serving:
calories: 94 | fat: 0g | protein: 6g | carbs: 18g | fiber: 5g

Chapter 6 Stews and Soups

Black-Eyed Pea and Collard Stew with Spicy Tahini

Prep time: 20 minutes | Cook time: 40 minutes | Serves 6

Stew:
2 tablespoons olive oil (optional)
1 large yellow onion, chopped
1 large green bell pepper, chopped
2 small carrots, chopped
1 large celery rib, chopped
1 teaspoon dried thyme
1 bay leaf
¼ teaspoon cayenne pepper or crushed red pepper
3 garlic cloves, minced
1 (14½ ounces / 411 g) can fire-roasted tomatoes with juice
1 cup pearled barley, soaked
1 teaspoon reduced-sodium tamari
2 cups water
1 cup vegetable broth
1 bunch collard greens, stemmed and chopped
2 cups cooked black-eyed peas
1 tablespoon fresh lemon juice
Salt and black pepper (optional)
Spicy Tahini:
2 tablespoons nutritional yeast
1 to 2 tablespoons Sriracha sauce
1 teaspoon fresh lemon juice
1 teaspoon maple syrup (optional)
¼ teaspoon liquid smoke
¼ cup tahini
¼ to ½ cup water
Sliced scallions

1. Heat olive oil (if using) in a Dutch oven over medium-high heat. Add the chopped onion, bell pepper, carrots, and celery. Stir to thoroughly coat the vegetables. Cook for 2 minutes, then reduce the heat to medium and cover. Gently cook the vegetables for 5 minutes, stirring occasionally. 2. Add the dried thyme, bay leaf, and cayenne pepper (or crushed red pepper). Stir in the minced garlic and cook for an additional 2 minutes. 3. Add the fire-roasted tomatoes with their juice, soaked pearled barley, and reduced-sodium tamari. Cook, stirring often, until the moisture has evaporated, approximately 3 minutes. 4. Pour in the water and vegetable broth, then add the chopped collard greens. Increase the heat to high and bring the mixture to a boil. Reduce the heat to medium-low, cover the pot, and simmer for 15 minutes. 5. Stir in the cooked black-eyed peas. Remove the pot from the heat and let the stew sit for 15 minutes. Discard the bay leaf. Stir in the fresh lemon juice and season with salt and black pepper, if desired. 6. While the stew is resting, prepare the spicy tahini sauce. In a jar with a tight-fitting lid, combine the nutritional yeast, Sriracha sauce, fresh lemon juice, maple syrup (if using), liquid smoke, and tahini. Add water, 1 tablespoon at a time, and shake the jar to mix until the sauce reaches a pourable consistency that will stick to a spoon. Refrigerate the sauce until ready to serve. 7. To serve, ladle the stew into bowls and top each serving with a drizzle of the spicy tahini sauce. Garnish with sliced scallions.

Per Serving:
calories: 354 | fat: 11g | protein: 14g | carbs: 54g | fiber: 15g

Chilean Bean Stew

Prep time: 20 minutes | Cook time: 35 minutes | Serves 4

1 large yellow onion, peeled and diced small
4 cloves garlic, peeled and minced
1 medium butternut squash (about 1 pound / 454 g), peeled, halved, seeded, and cut into ½-inch pieces
2 cups cooked pinto beans, or 1 (15 ounces / 425 g) can, drained and rinsed
6 ears corn, kernels removed (about 3½ cups)
Salt and freshly ground black pepper, to taste
1 cup finely chopped basil

1. Place the onion in a large saucepan and sauté over medium heat for 10 minutes. Add water 1 to 2 tablespoons at a time to keep the onion from sticking to the pan. 2. Add the garlic, squash, beans, corn, and 2 cups of water and cook for 25 minutes, or until the squash is tender. Season with salt and pepper and stir in the basil.

Per Serving:
calories: 305 | fat: 2g | protein: 15g | carbs: 65g | fiber: 14g

Savory Squash Soup

Prep time: 20 minutes | Cook time: 27 minutes | Serves 4

2½ cups butternut squash, peeled, halved, seeded, and diced (from about 1 medium)
1 large russet potato, diced (about 1 cup)
1 medium yellow onion, peeled and chopped (about ½ cup)
1 clove garlic, peeled and chopped
¼ teaspoon dried Italian herb mix, or a pinch each of oregano, basil, rosemary, and thyme
Pinch freshly ground black pepper, or to taste
¼ cup green peas
¼ teaspoon fresh lime juice
Finely chopped parsley

1. Bring 3 cups of water to boil in a large pot over high heat. Add the squash, potato, onion, garlic, herb mix, and pepper. Reduce the heat to medium and cook, covered, for 20 minutes, or until the vegetables are tender. 2. Purée the soup using an immersion blender or in a blender with a tight-fitting lid, covered with a towel. Return the soup to the pot and add the green peas and lime juice. Cook for an additional 5 to 7 minutes, or until the peas are tender. Serve hot, garnished with the parsley.

Per Serving:
calories: 137 | fat: 0g | protein: 4g | carbs: 32g | fiber: 4g

Vegetable Goulash

Prep time: 5 minutes | Cook time: 25 minutes | Serves 4 to 6

4 cups vegetable broth
4 cups diced (½-inch) yellow potatoes
2 cups frozen carrots
2 tablespoons tomato paste
½ cup chopped water-packed roasted red pepper
¼ cup sweet paprika
1 teaspoon whole caraway seeds
3 strips dried porcini mushrooms, chopped (about 2 tablespoons)
1 tablespoon onion powder
½ teaspoon garlic powder
2 teaspoons dried parsley
½ teaspoon smoked paprika
1 bay leaf

1. In a large Dutch oven or saucepan, combine the broth, potatoes, carrots, tomato paste, roasted red pepper, sweet paprika, caraway, mushrooms, onion powder, garlic powder, parsley, smoked paprika, and bay leaf. Bring to a boil over high heat. 2. Reduce the heat to low. Cover, and simmer for 15 to 20 minutes, or until the potatoes are tender and a knife slides in easily. Remove from the heat. 3. Remove the bay leaf, and serve.

Per Serving:
calories: 295 | fat: 2g | protein: 14g | carbs: 55g | fiber: 10g

Winter Squash Soup

Prep time: 15 minutes | Cook time: 30 minutes | Makes 2½ quarts

2 tablespoons extra-virgin coconut oil (optional)
1 medium yellow onion, diced
3 large garlic cloves, finely chopped
2 teaspoons fine sea salt, plus more to taste (optional)
1 large winter squash, halved, seeded, peeled, and cut into 1-inch cubes
5 cups filtered water
Freshly ground black pepper
Tamari (optional)

1. Warm the oil in a large pot over medium-high heat. Add the onion and cook for 6 to 8 minutes, until beginning to brown. Stir in the garlic and salt, if using, and cook for 3 to 4 minutes, until the garlic is golden and fragrant. Add the squash and water (the water should come almost to the top of the chopped squash), raise the heat, and bring to a boil; then cover the pot, reduce the heat to low, and simmer for 12 to 15 minutes, until the squash is tender. Test by pressing a piece of squash against the side of the pot; it should crush easily with a little pressure. Remove from the heat, season with pepper to taste, and set aside to cool slightly. 2. Working in batches, scoop the soup into an upright blender (filling it no more than two-thirds full) and puree on high speed until smooth and velvety, then pour into a large bowl or another large pot. Season to taste with more salt and pepper, and with tamari, if using, and serve warm. Store leftover soup in jars in the fridge for up to 5 days, or freeze for up to 3 months.

Per Serving: (½ quart)
calories: 93 | fat: 6g | protein: 1g | carbs: 12g | fiber: 2g

Fall Harvest Vegetable Chowder

Prep time: 30 minutes | Cook time: 55 minutes | Serves 6

1 medium yellow onion, peeled and diced (about 1 cup)
3 celery stalks, diced (about 1 cup)
2 medium carrots, peeled and diced (about 1 cup)
6 cups vegetable stock, or low-sodium vegetable broth
2 small zucchini, diced
2 small yams, peeled and diced
4 bay leaves
2 tablespoons thyme
3 to 4 ears corn, kernels removed (about 2 cups)
4 cups packed spinach leaves

1. Place the onion, celery, carrots, and ½ cup of vegetable stock in a large soup pot and sauté over medium-high heat for 6 to 8 minutes, or until the onion is translucent. 2. Add the zucchini, yams, bay leaves, thyme, and the remaining broth and bring to a boil over high heat. Reduce the heat to medium-low and simmer for 20 to 30 minutes, or until the vegetables are tender. 3. Add half the corn and cook for 10 to 15 more minutes. Remove the bay leaves. 4. Purée the soup using an immersion blender or in batches in a blender with a tight-fitting lid, covered with a towel. Return the soup to the pot and add the remaining corn and spinach leaves. Cook for 5 more minutes, or until the spinach is wilted. Stir well and serve hot.

Per Serving:
calories: 150 | fat: 1g | protein: 3g | carbs: 32g | fiber: 5g

Fennel and Ginger Butternut Squash Soup

Prep time: 15 minutes | Cook time: 25 minutes | Serves 4

1 small yellow onion, diced
2 garlic cloves, minced
½ fennel bulb, cut into slices
1 tablespoon water, plus more as needed
2 tablespoons grated peeled fresh ginger
½ butternut squash, peeled and diced into ½-inch pieces
½ cauliflower head, cut into florets
4 to 6 cups no-sodium vegetable broth
¼ teaspoon freshly ground black pepper

1. In a large pot over medium-high heat, combine the onion, garlic, and fennel. Cook, stirring occasionally, for 5 minutes, or until the onion is translucent but not browned. Add water, 1 tablespoon at a time, if it seems like the onion and garlic are cooking too quickly. 2. Add the ginger and cook, stirring, for 30 seconds. 3. Add the butternut squash, cauliflower, and just enough vegetable broth to cover the vegetables. Bring the liquid to a simmer, cover the pot, reduce the heat to medium-low, and cook for 15 minutes, or until the butternut squash can be easily pierced with a fork. 4. Using an immersion blender, purée the soup until smooth. Add more broth if you desire a thinner consistency. 5. Season with pepper and serve.

Per Serving:
calories: 91 | fat: 1g | protein: 4g | carbs: 21g | fiber: 6g

Carrot Ginger Soup

Prep time: 15 minutes | **Cook time:** 25 minutes | **Serves 6**

- 3 tablespoons water
- 1 cup diced red, white, or yellow onion
- 1 teaspoon minced garlic
- 2 tablespoons minced ginger
- 3 cups chopped carrots
- 2 cups chopped russet potatoes
- 4 cups vegetable broth
- Salt and pepper, to taste (optional)

1. In a large pot, heat the water over medium-high heat. 2. Add the diced onion, minced garlic, and minced ginger to the pot. Sauté for 2 to 3 minutes, or until the onion becomes translucent and tender. 3. Add the chopped carrots, chopped russet potatoes, and vegetable broth to the pot. Stir well to combine. 4. Bring the mixture to a boil, then reduce the heat to low and simmer for 20 minutes, or until the carrots and potatoes are tender. 5. Remove the pot from the heat. Using an immersion blender, purée the soup until smooth and creamy. Alternatively, you can transfer the soup to a regular blender and blend it in batches until smooth. 6. Taste the soup and season with salt and pepper, if desired. 7. Serve the Carrot Ginger Soup hot in bowls.

Per Serving:
calories: 80 | fat: 0g | protein: 2g | carbs: 18g | fiber: 3g

Zucchini Bisque

Prep time: 20 minutes | **Cook time:** 25 minutes | **Serves 4**

- 1 medium yellow onion, peeled and finely chopped
- 4 medium zucchini, finely chopped
- 2 cups vegetable stock, or low-sodium vegetable broth
- ½ teaspoon minced thyme
- ¼ teaspoon ground nutmeg
- ½ teaspoon lemon zest
- ½ to 1 cup unsweetened plain almond milk
- Salt and freshly ground black pepper, to taste

1. In a large saucepan, place the chopped onion over medium heat. Sauté for 7 to 8 minutes, or until the onion becomes tender. Add 1 to 2 tablespoons of water at a time to prevent sticking. 2. Add the finely chopped zucchini, vegetable stock, minced thyme, ground nutmeg, and lemon zest to the saucepan. Cook for about 15 minutes, or until the zucchini is tender. 3. Using an immersion blender or in batches in a blender with a tight-fitting lid (covered with a towel), purée the soup until smooth. 4. Return the soup to the pot and add the almond milk. Stir well. Season with salt and freshly ground black pepper according to your taste. Cook until the soup is heated through. 5. Serve the Zucchini Bisque hot in bowls.

Per Serving:
calories: 31 | fat: 0g | protein: 1g | carbs: 6g | fiber: 0g

Miso Noodle Soup with Shiitake Mushrooms

Prep time: 5 minutes | **Cook time:** 25 minutes | **Serves 4 to 6**

- 1 (8 ounces / 227 g) package brown rice noodles
- 4 cups vegetable broth
- 2 cups water
- 1 (5 ounces / 142 g) package shiitake mushrooms, cut into ¼-inch-thick slices
- 3 scallions, green and white parts, thinly sliced on a bias (about ½ cup)
- 3 garlic cloves, sliced
- 3 or 4 (¼-inch) slices unpeeled fresh ginger
- 8 ounces (227 g) bok choy
- 2 tablespoons red miso paste
- 1 tablespoon soy sauce

1. Cook the brown rice noodles according to the package instructions, usually for about 5 minutes. Drain and set aside. 2. In a large Dutch oven or saucepan, combine the vegetable broth, water, sliced shiitake mushrooms, scallions, garlic, and ginger. Cover the pot and bring the mixture to a boil over high heat. 3. Reduce the heat to low, cover the pot, and simmer for 15 minutes to allow the flavors to meld together. 4. Uncover the pot and increase the heat to medium. Add the bok choy to the simmering broth and cook for 3 minutes, or until the bok choy is crisp-tender. 5. Add the cooked brown rice noodles to the soup and heat through. 6. Remove the pot from the heat. Add the red miso paste and soy sauce to the soup, and stir until the miso has dissolved. 7. Remove the slices of ginger from the soup, as they were added for flavoring. 8. Serve the Miso Noodle Soup with Shiitake Mushrooms hot in bowls.

Per Serving:
calories: 396 | fat: 3g | protein: 13g | carbs: 80g | fiber: 8g

Anti-Inflammatory Miso Soup

Prep time: 15 minutes | **Cook time:** 25 minutes | **Serves 6**

- 2¼ cup vegetable broth
- 4 carrots, sliced into rounds
- 1 large yellow onion, chopped
- 1 ounce (28 g) dried shiitake mushrooms, broken or chopped into bite-size pieces
- 4 garlic cloves, minced
- 2 teaspoons ground turmeric
- 3 cups water
- ½ cup quinoa, rinsed and drained
- ¼ teaspoon black pepper
- 1 bunch bok choy, chopped
- 1 cup finely chopped red cabbage
- ¼ cup gluten-free red miso
- 1 red or yellow bell pepper, chopped fine
- 3 scallions, sliced thin

1. In a large Dutch oven or heavy-bottomed pot, place ½ cup of vegetable broth over medium heat. Add the carrots and onion to the hot broth and sauté, stirring often, until the vegetables are tender, about 5 minutes. 2. Add the dried shiitake mushrooms, minced garlic, and ground turmeric to the pot. Stir to combine. 3. Pour in the water, 2 cups of vegetable broth, quinoa, and black pepper. Increase the heat to medium-high, cover the pot, and allow it to simmer for 15 minutes. 4. Add the chopped bok choy and red cabbage to the pot. Reduce the heat to medium, cover the pot again, and cook until the vegetables are slightly tender, about 3 minutes. 5. Remove the lid and whisk in the gluten-free red miso. Remove the pot from the heat. Add the chopped bell pepper and sliced scallions. 6. Serve the Anti-Inflammatory Miso Soup hot in bowls.

Per Serving:
calories: 139 | fat: 2g | protein: 7g | carbs: 26g | fiber: 5g

Kale and White Bean Soup

Prep time: 10 minutes | Cook time: 2 to 3 hours | Serves 4 to 6

2 medium shallots, finely diced
3 garlic cloves, minced
2 (14½ ounces / 411 g) cans white beans, drained and rinsed
1 pound (454 g) fresh Tuscan or curly kale (about 5 large stalks), chopped
6 cups store-bought low-sodium vegetable broth
Ground black pepper
Salt (optional)
½ bunch fresh flat-leaf parsley, chopped

1. In a slow cooker, combine the finely diced shallots, minced garlic, white beans, chopped kale, vegetable broth, ground black pepper, and salt (if using). 2. Cover the slow cooker and cook on High for 2 to 3 hours or on Low for 4 to 5 hours until the flavors meld together and the kale is tender. 3. Just before serving, stir in the chopped fresh flat-leaf parsley. 4. Taste and adjust the seasoning, adding salt if desired.

Per Serving:

calories: 233 | fat: 2g | protein: 13g | carbs: 42g | fiber: 12g

Spanish Chickpea Stew

Prep time: 30 minutes | Cook time: 40 minutes | Serves 4

1 medium onion, peeled and diced small
1 green bell pepper, seeded and diced small
2 cloves garlic, peeled and minced
1 teaspoon cumin seeds, toasted and ground
1 teaspoon sweet paprika
½ teaspoon smoked paprika
1 bay leaf
1 large tomato, diced small
3 medium Yukon Gold potatoes (about 1 pound / 454 g), cut into ½-inch dice
5 cups vegetable stock, or low-sodium vegetable broth
2 cups cooked chickpeas, or 1 (15 ounces / 425 g) can, drained and rinsed
1 medium bunch Swiss chard, ribs removed, chopped
Salt and freshly ground black pepper, to taste

1. In a large pot, place the diced onion and bell pepper and sauté over medium heat for 10 minutes. Add 1 to 2 tablespoons of water at a time to prevent the vegetables from sticking to the pot. 2. Add the minced garlic, ground cumin seeds, sweet paprika, smoked paprika, and bay leaf. Cook for 1 minute, stirring continuously. 3. Stir in the diced tomato and cook for an additional 3 minutes. 4. Add the diced potatoes, vegetable stock, and chickpeas to the pot. Bring the mixture to a boil over high heat. 5. Reduce the heat to medium and cover the pot. Let it simmer for 20 minutes or until the potatoes are tender. 6. Add the chopped Swiss chard to the pot. Season with salt and freshly ground black pepper. Cook, covered, until the Swiss chard wilts, approximately 5 minutes. 7. Remove the bay leaf before serving.

Per Serving:

calories: 304 | fat: 2g | protein: 12g | carbs: 60g | fiber: 11g

Tuscan Bean Stew

Prep time: 25 minutes | Cook time: 40 minutes | Serves 6

3 large leeks (white and light green parts), diced and rinsed
2 celery stalks, diced
2 medium carrots, peeled and diced
2 cups chopped green cabbage
1 large russet potato, peeled and diced
6 cloves garlic, peeled and minced
3 cups cooked cannellini beans
6 cups vegetable stock, or low-sodium vegetable broth
½ cup chopped basil
Salt and freshly ground black pepper, to taste

1. In a large saucepan, place the diced leeks, celery, and carrots. Sauté the vegetables over medium heat for about 10 minutes, adding water 1 to 2 tablespoons at a time to prevent sticking. 2. Add the chopped cabbage, diced potato, minced garlic, cooked cannellini beans, and vegetable stock or low-sodium vegetable broth to the pot. Bring the stew to a boil over high heat. 3. Reduce the heat to medium and cook the stew, uncovered, for 30 minutes or until the potatoes are tender. 4. Stir in the chopped basil and season the Tuscan bean stew with salt and freshly ground black pepper according to your taste preferences. 5. Serve the stew hot in bowls.

Per Serving:

calories: 128 | fat: 0g | protein: 3g | carbs: 29g | fiber: 4g

Weeknight Chickpea Tomato Soup

Prep time: 10 minutes | Cook time: 25 minutes | Serves 2

1 to 2 teaspoons olive oil or vegetable broth
½ cup chopped onion
3 garlic cloves, minced
1 cup mushrooms, chopped
⅛ to ¼ teaspoon sea salt, divided (optional)
1 tablespoon dried basil
½ tablespoon dried oregano
1 to 2 tablespoons balsamic vinegar or red wine
1 (19 ounces / 539 g) can diced tomatoes
1 (14 ounces / 397 g) can chickpeas, drained and rinsed, or 1½ cups cooked
2 cups water
1 to 2 cups chopped kale

1. In a large pot, heat the olive oil (or vegetable broth) over medium heat. Add the chopped onion, minced garlic, and chopped mushrooms. Sauté until the vegetables have softened, about 7 to 8 minutes. If desired, add a pinch of sea salt while sautéing. 2. Stir in the dried basil and dried oregano, mixing well. Add the balsamic vinegar (or red wine) to deglaze the pan, using a wooden spoon to scrape up any browned bits from the bottom. 3. Add the diced tomatoes and chickpeas to the pot. Stir to combine. Adjust the consistency by adding enough water to achieve your desired thickness. 4. Add the chopped kale and the remaining salt (if desired). Cover the pot and simmer the soup for 5 to 15 minutes, or until the kale is cooked to your preferred tenderness. 5. Serve the Weeknight Chickpea Tomato Soup hot in bowls.

Per Serving:

calories: 272 | fat: 6g | protein: 13g | carbs: 45g | fiber: 14g

Bloody Caesar Gazpacho

Prep time: 20 minutes | Cook time: 0 minutes | Serves 6

6 cups chopped ripe tomatoes
1 small red onion, chopped
1 English cucumber, chopped
2 stalks celery, chopped
2 cloves garlic, chopped
Fresh chili pepper, chopped, to taste (optional)
2 teaspoons celery salt (optional)
⅓ cup raw almonds, soaked for at least 6 hours
2 tablespoons red wine vinegar
⅓ cup virgin olive oil (optional)
Vegan gluten-free worcestershire sauce or gluten-free tamari soy sauce, to taste
Hot sauce, to taste
Freshly ground black pepper, to taste
Garnishes:
Thinly sliced celery
Thinly sliced red onion
Lime wedges
Pitted green olives
Additional hot sauce

1. In a large bowl, toss together the chopped tomatoes, red onions, cucumber, celery, garlic, chili (if using), and celery salt (if using). Cover the bowl with plastic wrap and let it sit at room temperature for 1 hour. 2. Uncover the vegetables and transfer them to the bowl of a food processor. Pour all the marinating liquid from the bowl into the food processor as well. Drain the soaked almonds and add them to the food processor. Process on high speed until the vegetables and almonds are pureed. 3. Reduce the speed of the food processor to low, and drizzle in the red wine vinegar and olive oil (if using). Stop the machine when you have a smooth mixture. 4. Pass the gazpacho through a fine strainer into a large bowl to remove any solids. Season the gazpacho with vegan gluten-free Worcestershire sauce or gluten-free tamari soy sauce, hot sauce, and freshly ground black pepper. Adjust the seasonings according to your taste preferences. 5. Store the gazpacho covered in the refrigerator until ready to serve. It can be refrigerated for up to 5 days. 6. Serve the Bloody Caesar Gazpacho chilled and garnish with thinly sliced celery, red onion, lime wedges, pitted green olives, and additional hot sauce, if desired.

Per Serving:

calories: 140 | fat: 10g | protein: 4g | carbs: 12g | fiber: 4g

Weeknight Root Vegetable Dhal

Prep time: 20 minutes | Cook time: 50 minutes | Serves 4

1 cup red split lentils, rinsed
1 cup finely diced root vegetables of your choice
1 small yellow onion, finely diced
1 cup cherry or grape tomatoes, halved
4 cloves garlic, minced
1 (2-inch) piece of fresh ginger, peeled and minced
1 teaspoon ground turmeric
Pinch of dried chili flakes
3½ cups filtered water
Salt and pepper, to taste (optional)
2 tablespoons virgin coconut oil (optional)
½ teaspoon cumin seeds
½ teaspoon coriander seeds
½ teaspoon mustard seeds
⅓ cup chopped fresh cilantro leaves, for garnish
Lemon wedges, for serving

1. In a medium soup pot, combine the rinsed lentils, diced root vegetables, diced onion, halved tomatoes, minced garlic, minced ginger, ground turmeric, and dried chili flakes. Pour the filtered water into the pot and give everything a stir. 2. Place the pot on the stove over medium heat. Bring the mixture to a boil and then reduce the heat to simmer. Let it cook for about 40 minutes, whisking the dal often. Towards the end of cooking, the lentils should be completely broken down. In the last 10 minutes, whisk the dal vigorously to encourage the lentils to break down further. The consistency should be soupy. Season the dal with salt and pepper, if desired. Keep it warm. 3. Heat the coconut oil (if using) in a small sauté pan over medium-high heat. Add the cumin seeds, coriander seeds, and mustard seeds. Once the seeds become fragrant and start popping, remove the pan from the heat. 4. Gently spoon the toasted spice oil with the whole spices on top of the dal. You can lightly stir it in if you prefer. Alternatively, you can portion out the dal first and then spoon the spice oil on top. Garnish the dal with the chopped cilantro. 5. Serve the Weeknight Root Vegetable Dhal hot with lemon wedges.

Per Serving: (1 cup)

calories: 270 | fat: 8g | protein: 13g | carbs: 40g | fiber: 8g

Millet Stew

Prep time: 25 minutes | Cook time: 45 minutes | Serves 4 to 6

5 to 6 cups vegetable stock, or low-sodium vegetable broth
2 (1-inch) pieces cinnamon stick
2 tablespoons grated ginger
1 bay leaf
1 large onion, peeled and cut into ¾-inch pieces
2 large carrots, peeled and cut into ½-inch slices
2 cloves garlic, peeled and minced
1 cup millet
1 large head cauliflower, cut into large florets
1 (14½ ounces / 411 g) can diced tomatoes
Salt and freshly ground black pepper, to taste
½ cup chopped cilantro

1. In a small pot, combine the vegetable stock, cinnamon sticks, grated ginger, and bay leaf. Cook over medium-high heat for 15 minutes to infuse the flavors. Remove from the heat, discard the spices, and set the vegetable stock aside. 2. Place the onion and carrots in a large saucepan over medium heat. Sauté for 8 to 10 minutes, or until the vegetables are tender and starting to brown. Add 1 to 2 tablespoons of water at a time to prevent sticking. 3. Add the minced garlic to the saucepan and cook for another minute until fragrant. 4. Pour the prepared vegetable stock into the saucepan with the onion, carrots, and garlic. Add the millet, cauliflower florets, and diced tomatoes. Bring the mixture to a boil over high heat. 5. Reduce the heat to medium and cover the saucepan. Simmer for 12 to 15 minutes, or until the cauliflower and millet are tender. 6. Season the stew with salt and freshly ground black pepper to taste. Cook for an additional 5 minutes to allow the flavors to meld. 7. Serve the Millet Stew hot, garnished with chopped cilantro.

Per Serving:

calories: 172 | fat: 1g | protein: 5g | carbs: 34g | fiber: 5g

Brown Lentil Stew with Avocado Salsa

Prep time: 15 minutes | Cook time: 40 minutes | Serves 4

Stew:
1 cup brown lentils, rinsed
½ teaspoon salt, or to taste (optional)
½ teaspoon turmeric
1 medium green bell pepper, seeded and chopped (about ½ cup)
½ cup chopped celery
½ cup chopped tomato
½ teaspoon curry powder
½ teaspoon fresh lime juice
Avocado Salsa:
½ avocado, halved, pitted, peeled and cut into ½-inch cubes (about ½ cup)
½ cup finely diced tomato
½ teaspoon finely chopped cilantro
½ teaspoon fresh lime juice
¼ teaspoon freshly ground black pepper

1. In a large saucepan, combine the rinsed brown lentils, salt (if using), turmeric, and 2 cups of water. Cook uncovered over medium heat for 25 to 30 minutes until the lentils are tender. 2. Add the chopped green bell pepper, celery, chopped tomato, and curry powder to the saucepan. Cook for an additional 10 minutes. 3. Just before serving, stir in the fresh lime juice. 4. In a medium bowl, combine the diced avocado, finely diced tomato, chopped cilantro, fresh lime juice, and freshly ground black pepper. Mix well to combine. 5. Serve the hot lentil stew in bowls and top with the avocado salsa.

Per Serving:
calories: 226 | fat: 4g | protein: 13g | carbs: 36g | fiber: 8g

Cozy Lentil Soup

Prep time: 15 minutes | Cook time: 40 minutes | Serves 10

3 tablespoons virgin olive oil (optional)
1 medium yellow onion, small diced
2 teaspoons minced fresh thyme leaves
½ teaspoon smoked paprika
½ teaspoon dried tarragon
2 medium carrots, small diced
2 stalks celery, small diced
Salt and pepper, to taste
4 cloves garlic, minced
1 cup French lentils, rinsed
1 can (14 ounces / 397 g) crushed tomatoes
1 can (14 ounces / 397 g) diced tomatoes
6 cups vegetable stock

1. In a large, heavy-bottomed pot, heat the olive oil over medium heat. If not using oil, you can use a splash of water to sauté the onions. Add the diced onions to the pot and sauté them until they are completely soft and starting to break down, about 8 minutes. 2. Add the minced thyme, smoked paprika, and dried tarragon to the pot. Stir the spices into the onions and cook for about 1 minute until fragrant. 3. Add the diced carrots and celery to the pot. Season with salt and pepper, if desired. Sauté the carrots and celery for about 2 minutes until they begin to soften. Add the minced garlic and stir for another 30 seconds. 4. Add the rinsed French lentils to the pot and stir to coat them in the oil, spices, and vegetables. Pour in the crushed tomatoes and diced tomatoes, followed by the vegetable stock. Stir to combine all the ingredients. 5. Cover the pot and bring the soup to a boil. Reduce the heat to a simmer and slightly adjust the lid, allowing some steam to escape. Simmer the soup for about 25 minutes, stirring occasionally, until the lentils are tender. 6. Check the soup for seasoning and adjust accordingly with salt and pepper. Serve the Cozy Lentil Soup hot.

Per Serving: (1 cup)
calories: 137 | fat: 5g | protein: 5g | carbs: 20g | fiber: 4g

Hot and Sour Soup

Prep time: 15 minutes | Cook time: 3 to 4 hours | Serves 6 to 8

6 ounces (170 g) shiitake mushrooms, sliced
1 (8 ounces / 227 g) can sliced bamboo shoots
4 garlic cloves, minced
1 (2-inch) piece fresh ginger, peeled and minced
1 (16 ounces / 454 g) package extra-firm tofu, drained and cut into bite-size cubes
8 cups store-bought low-sodium vegetable broth
¼ cup low-sodium soy sauce, tamari, or coconut aminos
¼ cup rice vinegar
½ teaspoon ground white pepper
½ teaspoon red pepper flakes
3 baby bok choy, chopped into bite-size pieces
2 tablespoons cornstarch
¼ cup water
4 scallions, green and white parts, chopped, for serving
½ bunch cilantro, chopped, for serving

1. Put the mushrooms, bamboo shoots, garlic, ginger, tofu, broth, soy sauce, vinegar, white pepper, and red pepper flakes in the slow cooker. Cover and cook on High for 3 to 4 hours or on Low for 7 to 8 hours. 2. In the last 30 minutes of cooking, add the bok choy. In a small bowl, whisk together the cornstarch and water. Add the slurry to the slow cooker and stir well to incorporate. To serve, ladle the soup into bowls and top each with the scallions and cilantro.

Per Serving:
calories: 138 | fat: 5g | protein: 11g | carbs: 14g | fiber: 4g

Italian Lentil Soup

Prep time: 10 minutes | Cook time: 3 to 4 hours | Serves 6 to 8

1 medium onion, diced
3 garlic cloves, minced
2 carrots, diced
2 celery stalks, diced
1 pound (454 g, about 2⅓ cups) dried green or brown lentils, rinsed and sorted
1 (28 ounces / 794 g) can no-salt-added crushed tomatoes
8 cups store-bought low-sodium vegetable broth
1 tablespoon Italian seasoning
Ground black pepper
Salt (optional)

1. Put the onion, garlic, carrots, celery, lentils, tomatoes, broth, Italian seasoning, pepper, and salt (if using) in the slow cooker. 2. Cover and cook on High for 3 to 4 hours or on Low for 7 to 8 hours.

Per Serving:
calories: 354 | fat: 1g | protein: 20g | carbs: 67g | fiber: 34g

Broccoli and "Cheddar" Soup

Prep time: 10 minutes | Cook time: 30 minutes | Serves 4

- 4 cups peeled and diced butternut squash
- 2 sweet potatoes, peeled and diced (about 2 cups)
- 1 small yellow onion, peeled and halved
- 2 garlic cloves, peeled
- 4 cups water
- 2 teaspoons salt (optional)
- 1 (13 ounces / 369 g) can light unsweetened coconut milk
- 1 tablespoon red miso paste
- 3 tablespoons nutritional yeast
- 1 tablespoon tapioca flour
- 3 cups frozen broccoli

1. In a large pot, combine the butternut squash, sweet potatoes, onion, garlic, and water. Bring the mixture to a boil over high heat. Lower the heat to medium-low and cook until the vegetables are fork-tender, about 20 minutes. 2. Transfer the cooked vegetables and liquid to a blender. Puree the mixture until smooth. You may need to do this in batches, depending on the size of your blender. 3. Return the blended soup to the pot and add the salt (if using), coconut milk, red miso paste, nutritional yeast, tapioca flour, and frozen broccoli. Cook the soup over medium heat, stirring often, until the broccoli is heated through and tender, about 10 minutes. 4. Serve the broccoli and "cheddar" soup hot. You can garnish it with additional nutritional yeast or fresh herbs, if desired.

Per Serving:
calories: 353 | fat: 20g | protein: 8g | carbs: 42g | fiber: 9g

Pumpkin and Anasazi Bean Stew

Prep time: 30 minutes | Cook time: 35 minutes | Serves 6 to 8

- 1 large yellow onion, peeled and diced
- 2 large carrots, peeled and diced
- 2 celery stalks, diced
- 2 cloves garlic, peeled and minced
- 2 tablespoons cumin seeds, toasted and ground
- 2 tablespoons tomato paste
- 1 small pumpkin (about 1 pound / 454 g), peeled, seeded, and cut into 1-inch cubes
- 4 cups cooked anasazi beans, or 2 (15 ounces / 425 g) cans, drained and rinsed
- 6 cups vegetable stock, or low-sodium vegetable broth
- Salt and freshly ground black pepper, to taste
- 6 green onions (white and green parts), thinly sliced

1. In a large saucepan, sauté the diced onion, carrots, and celery over medium heat for about 10 minutes. Add water, 1 to 2 tablespoons at a time, if needed, to prevent sticking. 2. Add the minced garlic and cook for another minute. Stir in the ground cumin and tomato paste. 3. Add the cubed pumpkin, cooked anasazi beans, and vegetable stock to the saucepan. Bring the mixture to a boil over high heat, then reduce the heat to medium. Cover the pan and let it simmer for 25 minutes, or until the pumpkin is tender. 4. Season the stew with salt and freshly ground black pepper to taste. 5. Serve the stew garnished with thinly sliced green onions.

Per Serving:
calories: 70 | fat: 0g | protein: 2g | carbs: 15g | fiber: 3g

Tomato and Red Pepper Soup

Prep time: 20 minutes | Cook time: 30 minutes | Serves 4

- 2 medium yellow onions, peeled and coarsely chopped
- 2 large red bell peppers, seeded and coarsely chopped
- 3 large cloves garlic, peeled and minced
- 1 teaspoon thyme leaves
- 1 pound (454 g) fresh tomatoes (about 3 medium), coarsely chopped
- Salt and freshly ground black pepper, to taste
- ¼ cup basil chiffonade

1. Place the onions and red peppers in a large saucepan and sauté over medium heat for 10 minutes. Add water 1 to 2 tablespoons at a time to keep the vegetables from sticking to the pan. 2. Add the garlic and thyme and cook for another minute, then add the tomatoes and cook, covered, for 20 minutes. Purée the soup using an immersion blender or in batches in a blender with a tight-fitting lid, covered with a towel. 3. Season with salt and pepper and serve garnished with the basil

Per Serving:
calories: 55 | fat: 0g | protein: 2g | carbs: 12g | fiber: 2g

Chickpea Vegetable Soup

Prep time: 15 minutes | Cook time: 30 minutes | Serves 4

- 1 yellow onion, coarsely chopped
- 2 carrots, coarsely chopped
- 2 celery stalks, coarsely chopped
- 1 red bell pepper, coarsely chopped
- 3 garlic cloves, minced
- 1 tablespoon water, plus more as needed
- 2 teaspoons grated peeled fresh ginger
- 1 small cauliflower head, cut into small florets
- 1 teaspoon ground turmeric
- 1 teaspoon Hungarian sweet paprika
- 6 cups no-sodium vegetable broth
- 2 cups chopped kale
- 1 (15 ounces /425 g) can chickpeas, rinsed and drained
- Freshly ground black pepper, to taste
- Chopped scallions, green parts only, for garnish

1. In a large pot over medium-high heat, combine the onion, carrots, celery, bell pepper, and garlic. Cook, stirring occasionally, for 5 minutes, or until the onion is translucent but not browned. Add water, 1 tablespoon at a time, if it seems like the onion and garlic are cooking too quickly. 2. Add the grated ginger and cook, stirring, for 30 seconds. 3. Stir in the cauliflower florets, ground turmeric, and Hungarian sweet paprika to coat the cauliflower evenly with the spices. 4. Pour in the vegetable broth and bring the liquid to a simmer. Reduce the heat to medium-low, cover the pot, and cook for 10 minutes. 5. Add the chopped kale and chickpeas to the pot and cook for an additional 5 minutes to soften the kale leaves. Season with freshly ground black pepper. 6. Garnish the soup with chopped scallions (green parts only) before serving.

Per Serving:
calories: 173 | fat: 3g | protein: 8g | carbs: 32g | fiber: 9g

Tom Yum Goong (Thai Hot-and-Sour Soup)

Prep time: 30 minutes | Cook time: 30 minutes | Serves 4

4 cups vegetable stock, or low-sodium vegetable broth	3 shallots, peeled and thinly sliced
4 thin slices fresh ginger	2 Roma tomatoes, chopped
1 stalk lemongrass, cut into 1-inch pieces	1 head baby bok choy, thinly sliced
2 tablespoons Thai red curry paste	1 small carrot, peeled and cut into matchsticks
3 tablespoons low-sodium soy sauce	1 cup mung bean sprouts
Zest and juice of 2 limes	¼ cup chopped Thai basil
1 (14 ounces / 397 g) can lite coconut milk	2 Thai red chiles, sliced into thin rounds
	Cilantro sprigs

1. In a large saucepan, combine the vegetable stock, ginger, lemongrass, Thai red curry paste, soy sauce, lime zest, and lime juice. Bring the pot to a boil over high heat. 2. Stir in the shallots, tomatoes, baby bok choy, and carrot. Reduce the heat to medium-low and simmer the soup for about 25 minutes, or until the vegetables are tender. 3. Remove the slices of ginger and lemongrass from the soup. Add the mung bean sprouts, Thai basil, and Thai red chilies. 4. Serve the Tom Yum Goong soup hot, garnished with cilantro sprigs.

Per Serving:

calories: 332 | fat: 26g | protein: 8g | carbs: 24g | fiber: 8g

Lemony Herbed Lentil Soup

Prep time: 10 minutes | Cook time: 35 minutes | Serves 2

1 cup dried brown or green lentils, rinsed	1 zucchini, diced
4 cups water	1 (15 ounces / 425 g) can crushed tomatoes
1 teaspoon extra-virgin olive oil (optional)	1 teaspoon Italian seasoning
½ small yellow onion, chopped	½ teaspoon smoked paprika
2 garlic cloves, minced	2 cups baby spinach
1 celery stalk, minced	Juice of 1 lemon
2 carrots, sliced	1 teaspoon salt, plus more as needed (optional)
1 potato, peeled and diced	

1. In a large saucepan, combine the lentils and water and bring them to a boil over high heat. Reduce the heat to medium and simmer until the lentils are soft, about 25 minutes. 2. Meanwhile, in a large skillet, heat the olive oil (if using) over medium heat. Add the chopped onion and minced garlic and sauté until fragrant, about 5 minutes. Then add the minced celery, sliced carrots, and diced potato. Cook for an additional 5 minutes. 3. Transfer the cooked vegetable mixture to the saucepan with the lentils and stir until well combined. 4. To the lentil and vegetable mixture, add the diced zucchini, crushed tomatoes, Italian seasoning, and smoked paprika. Bring the soup to a boil over medium-high heat, then reduce the heat to medium and simmer for about 10 minutes to allow the flavors to meld. 5. Stir in the baby spinach and continue cooking until it wilts. 6. Remove the soup from heat and add the freshly squeezed lemon juice. Season with salt to taste, if desired. 7. Serve the Lemony Herbed Lentil Soup hot, garnished with fresh herbs or a sprinkle of lemon zest, if desired.

Per Serving:

calories: 546 | fat: 5g | protein: 31g | carbs: 102g | fiber: 21g

Lime-Mint Soup

Prep time: 5 minutes | Cook time: 20 minutes | Serves 4

4 cups vegetable broth	and green parts
¼ cup fresh mint leaves, roughly chopped	3 minced garlic cloves cloves
¼ cup chopped scallions, white	3 tablespoons freshly squeezed lime juice

1. In a large stockpot, combine the broth, mint, scallions, garlic, and lime juice. Bring to a boil over medium-high heat. 2. Cover, reduce the heat to low, simmer for 15 minutes, and serve.

Per Serving:

calories: 55 | fat: 2g | protein: 5g | carbs: 5g | fiber: 1g

Corn Chowder

Prep time: 25 minutes | Cook time: 40 minutes | Serves 6

2 medium yellow onions, peeled and diced small	and diced
2 red bell peppers, seeded and finely chopped	1½ pounds (680 g) tomatoes (4 to 5 medium), diced
3 ears corn, kernels removed (about 2 cups)	6 cups vegetable stock, or low-sodium vegetable broth
3 cloves garlic, peeled and minced	¾ cup finely chopped basil
2 large russet potatoes, peeled	Salt and freshly ground black pepper, to taste

1. Place the onions and peppers in a large saucepan and sauté over medium heat for 10 minutes. Add water 1 to 2 tablespoons at a time to keep the vegetables from sticking to the pan. Add the corn and garlic, and sauté for 5 more minutes. Add the potatoes, tomatoes, peppers, and vegetable stock. Bring the mixture to a boil over high heat. Reduce the heat to medium and cook, uncovered, for 25 minutes, or until the potatoes are tender. 2. Purée half of the soup in batches in a blender with a tight-fitting lid, covered with a towel. Return the puréed soup to the pot. Add the basil and season with salt and pepper.

Per Serving:

calories: 209 | fat: 0g | protein: 6g | carbs: 48g | fiber: 5g

Chipotle Black Bean Soup

Prep time: 30 minutes | Cook time: 35 minutes | Serves 4

1 large yellow onion, peeled and diced
1 large green bell pepper, seeded and diced
3 cloves garlic, peeled and minced
1 tablespoon cumin seeds, toasted and ground
1 teaspoon dried Mexican oregano, toasted
1 teaspoon coriander seeds, toasted and ground
1 dried chipotle pepper, halved, toasted in a dry skillet for 2 to 3 minutes, soaked in cool water for 15 minutes, and chopped
1 cup orange juice
Zest of 1 orange
4 cups cooked black beans, or 2 (15 ounces / 425 g) cans, drained and rinsed
Salt and freshly ground black pepper, to taste

1. Place the diced onion and green bell pepper in a large pan and sauté over medium heat for 7 to 8 minutes. Add 1 to 2 tablespoons of water at a time to prevent the vegetables from sticking to the pan. 2. Add the minced garlic, ground cumin seeds, dried Mexican oregano, ground coriander seeds, and chopped chipotle pepper to the pan. Cook for 2 minutes to allow the flavors to meld. 3. Add the orange juice, orange zest, cooked black beans, and enough water to cover the beans by 3 inches. Bring the soup to a boil over high heat. 4. Reduce the heat to medium and simmer the soup, covered, for 25 minutes to allow the flavors to develop. Season with salt and freshly ground black pepper to taste. 5. Serve the Chipotle Black Bean Soup hot, optionally garnished with toppings such as chopped cilantro, diced avocado, or a dollop of sour cream.

Per Serving:

calories: 293 | fat: 1g | protein: 17g | carbs: 54g | fiber: 17g

Tofu Noodle Soup with Coconut Lemongrass Broth

Prep time: 15 minutes | Cook time: 10 minutes | Serves 6

4 cups vegetable stock
2 stalks fresh lemongrass, chopped
1 cup full-fat coconut milk
1 cup tightly packed fresh cilantro leaves
Salt and pepper, to taste
1 tablespoon virgin coconut oil (optional)
1 medium shallot, small diced
1 small green chili pepper, seeded and minced
1 (2-inch) piece fresh ginger, peeled and minced
1 cup snow peas
1½ cups small broccoli florets
1 block (14 ounces / 397 g) extra-firm tofu, drained and cut into ½-inch cubes
1 teaspoon gluten-free tamari soy sauce
2 tablespoons fresh lime juice
Serve:
Cooked rice or rice noodles
Lime wedges

1. In a large pot, bring the vegetable stock and chopped lemongrass to a boil. Remove from heat and allow the lemongrass to steep for 10 minutes. Strain the steeped broth, discarding the lemongrass. 2. Transfer the broth to a blender. Add the coconut milk, cilantro, salt, and pepper (if desired). Blend on high until completely smooth. Set aside. 3. In the same large pot, heat the coconut oil (if using) over medium heat. Add the shallots, chili pepper, and ginger. Stir and sauté until the shallots are translucent and slightly soft, about 2 minutes. 4. Add the snow peas and broccoli florets to the pot. Stir and season the vegetables with salt and pepper (if desired). Add the tofu cubes and stir. Pour in the coconut lemongrass broth and tamari soy sauce, and stir to combine. Taste the broth for seasoning and adjust if necessary. 5. Bring the soup to a boil, then reduce the heat to a simmer. Cook the soup, uncovered, until the broccoli is tender, about 4 minutes. Stir in the lime juice. 6. Serve the hot soup with cooked rice or rice noodles. Garnish with lime wedges on the side.

Per Serving:

calories: 204 | fat: 16g | protein: 10g | carbs: 9g | fiber: 2g

Cauliflower Soup

Prep time: 10 minutes | Cook time: 30 minutes | Makes 3 quarts

2 tablespoons extra-virgin coconut oil (optional)
1 medium yellow onion, diced
3 large garlic cloves, finely chopped
2 teaspoons fine sea salt, plus more to taste (optional)
2 small-medium cauliflower, cut into 1-inch florets
6 cups filtered water
Freshly ground black pepper
Tamari (optional)

1. In a large pot, warm the extra-virgin coconut oil (if using) over medium-high heat. Add the diced onion and cook for 6 to 8 minutes, until it begins to brown. Stir in the chopped garlic and salt (if using) and cook for an additional 3 to 4 minutes, until the garlic becomes golden and fragrant. 2. Add the cauliflower florets and water to the pot, increasing the heat to bring the mixture to a boil. Press down the cauliflower florets to submerge them as much as possible, although not all of them will be submerged. Cover the pot, reduce the heat to low, and simmer for 12 to 14 minutes, until the cauliflower becomes tender. Halfway through cooking, press the cauliflower down into the simmering liquid again. You can test the tenderness of the cauliflower by inserting a sharp knife into a floret; it should go in easily. 3. Remove the pot from the heat and scoop out 1 cup of the cooking liquid, setting it aside. Stir in freshly ground black pepper to taste and allow the soup to cool slightly. 4. Working in batches, transfer the soup to an upright blender, filling it no more than two-thirds full. Blend on high speed until the soup becomes smooth and velvety. If necessary, add some of the reserved cooking liquid to achieve the desired consistency. Pour the blended soup into a large bowl or another large pot. 5. Season the soup to taste with more salt, pepper, and tamari (if using). Serve the soup warm. 6. Store any leftover soup in jars in the refrigerator for up to 5 days, or freeze it for up to 3 months.

Per Serving: (1 quart)

calories: 141 | fat: 10g | protein: 4g | carbs: 13g | fiber: 4g

Curried Zucchini Soup

Prep time: 10 minutes | Cook time: 3 to 4 hours | Serves 4 to 6

1 medium onion, chopped
3 garlic cloves, minced
3 medium zucchini (about 1½ pounds / 680 g), chopped into 1-inch pieces
2 yellow potatoes (about ⅔ pound / 272 g), unpeeled and chopped
5 cups store-bought low-sodium vegetable broth
1 tablespoon curry powder
Ground black pepper
Salt (optional)

1. In a slow cooker, combine the chopped onion, minced garlic, chopped zucchini, chopped potatoes, vegetable broth, curry powder, a sprinkle of ground black pepper, and salt (if desired). 2. Cover the slow cooker and cook on High for 3 to 4 hours or on Low for 6 to 7 hours, until the vegetables are tender. 3. Before serving, blend the soup until smooth using an immersion blender directly in the slow cooker, or transfer the soup in batches to a blender and blend carefully, starting on low speed and gradually increasing speed to avoid hot soup splatters. 4. Taste and adjust the seasoning with salt and pepper, if needed. 5. Serve the curried zucchini soup hot.

Per Serving:
calories: 119 | fat: 1g | protein: 5g | carbs: 25g | fiber: 5g

Deep Immune Cup of Soup

Prep time: 15 minutes | Cook time: 15 minutes | Serves 4

1 teaspoon virgin olive oil (optional)
1 small yellow onion, diced
1 medium carrot, diced
1 stalk celery, diced
3 cloves garlic, minced
1 (2-inch) piece of fresh ginger, peeled and minced
2 teaspoons turmeric powder
½ teaspoon dried chili flakes, to taste
⅔ cup whole grain orzo pasta or other small, shaped pasta
4 cups vegetable stock
2 teaspoons mellow or light miso
1 teaspoon apple cider vinegar
⅓ cup chopped fresh flat-leaf parsley
Salt and pepper, to taste (optional)

1. Heat the olive oil in a large pot over medium heat. Add the onions, carrots, and celery. Sauté and stir vegetables until the onions are very soft and translucent, about 5 minutes. 2. Add the garlic, ginger, turmeric, and chili flakes, and stir until the spices are fragrant, about 30 seconds. Add the orzo and vegetable stock. Bring to a boil. Lower the heat to a simmer, and cook until pasta is just tender, about 7 minutes. 3. In a small bowl, stir together the miso and apple cider vinegar. Ladle 2 to 3 tablespoons of the warm broth into the small bowl to fully dissolve the miso. Add this mixture to the soup along with the chopped parsley. Season the soup with salt and pepper at this point if you like. Serve immediately.

Per Serving:
calories: 83 | fat: 2g | protein: 2g | carbs: 16g | fiber: 3g

Coconut Curry Soup

Prep time: 25 minutes | Cook time: 20 minutes | Serves 6

3 tablespoons water
¾ cup diced red, white, or yellow onion
1½ teaspoons minced garlic
1 cup diced green or red bell pepper
1 (14½ ounces / 411 g) can diced tomatoes with their juices
1 (15 ounces / 425 g) can chickpeas, drained and rinsed
4 cups vegetable broth
1½ teaspoons ground cumin
2½ teaspoons curry powder
1 (13½ ounces / 383 g) can full-fat coconut milk
½ cup cooked brown rice
Salt and pepper, to taste (optional)
Optional Toppings:
Red chili flakes
Minced cilantro

1. In a large pot, heat the water over medium heat. 2. Add the diced onion, minced garlic, and diced bell pepper. Cook, stirring occasionally, for about 5 minutes or until the vegetables are tender. 3. Add the diced tomatoes with their juices, drained and rinsed chickpeas, vegetable broth, ground cumin, and curry powder. Bring the mixture to a boil. 4. Reduce the heat to low and simmer gently, stirring occasionally, for 10 minutes. 5. Add the full-fat coconut milk and cooked brown rice to the pot. Continue cooking for an additional 5 minutes, stirring occasionally. 6. Taste the soup and season with salt and pepper if desired. 7. Serve the coconut curry soup hot, optionally garnished with red chili flakes and minced cilantro.

Per Serving:
calories: 126 | fat: 2g | protein: 5g | carbs: 24g | fiber: 6g

Golden Split Pea Soup

Prep time: 10 minutes | Cook time: 3 to 4 hours | Serves 5 to 7

1 medium onion, diced
3 carrots, diced
3 celery stalks, diced
3 garlic cloves, crushed
1 cup yellow split peas, rinsed and stones removed
1 yellow potato (about ⅓ pound / 136 g), unpeeled and cubed
4 cups low-sodium vegetable broth or water
1 bay leaf
¾ teaspoon ground cumin
¾ teaspoon ground turmeric
½ teaspoon dry mustard
Ground black pepper
Salt (optional)

1. Put the onion, carrots, celery, garlic, peas, potato, broth, bay leaf, cumin, turmeric, mustard, pepper, and salt (if using) in the slow cooker. Cover and cook on High for 3 to 4 hours or on Low for 7 to 8 hours. 2. Remove and discard the bay leaf. Using an immersion blender or a countertop blender, fully purée the soup before serving.

Per Serving:
calories: 207 | fat: 1g | protein: 11g | carbs: 40g | fiber: 13g

Indian Red Split Lentil Soup

Prep time: 5 minutes | Cook time: 50 minutes | Makes 4 bowls

- 1 cup red split lentils
- 2 cups water
- 1 teaspoon curry powder plus 1 tablespoon, divided, or 5 coriander seeds (optional)
- 1 teaspoon coconut oil, or 1 tablespoon water or vegetable broth
- 1 red onion, diced
- 1 tablespoon minced fresh ginger
- 2 cups peeled and cubed sweet potato
- 1 cup sliced zucchini
- Freshly ground black pepper, to taste
- Sea salt, to taste (optional)
- 3 to 4 cups vegetable stock or water
- 1 to 2 teaspoons toasted sesame oil (optional)
- 1 bunch spinach, chopped
- Toasted sesame seeds

1. In a large pot, combine the red split lentils, 2 cups of water, and 1 teaspoon of curry powder (or coriander seeds if using). Bring the mixture to a boil, then reduce the heat and simmer, covered, for about 10 minutes until the lentils are soft. 2. Meanwhile, heat a large pot over medium heat. Add coconut oil (or water or vegetable broth) and sauté the diced red onion and minced ginger until they become soft, for about 5 minutes. Add the cubed sweet potato and cook for about 10 minutes to soften it slightly. Then, add the sliced zucchini and cook until it starts to become shiny, for about 5 minutes. Add the remaining 1 tablespoon of curry powder, freshly ground black pepper, and sea salt (if using), and stir to coat the vegetables. 3. Pour in the vegetable stock or water and bring it to a boil. Reduce the heat to a simmer, cover the pot, and let the vegetables cook slowly for 20 to 30 minutes or until the sweet potato is tender. 4. Add the fully cooked lentils to the soup. Season with another pinch of salt (if needed), toasted sesame oil (if using), and chopped spinach. Stir the soup, allowing the spinach to wilt before removing the pot from the heat. 5. Serve the Indian Red Split Lentil Soup garnished with toasted sesame seeds.

Per Serving: (1 bowl)

calories: 238 | fat: 3g | protein: 15g | carbs: 38g | fiber: 9g

Minty Beet and Sweet Potato Soup

Prep time: 10 minutes | Cook time: 40 minutes | Makes 6 bowls

- 5 cups water, or salt-free vegetable broth (if salted, omit the sea salt below)
- 1 to 2 teaspoons olive oil or vegetable broth
- 1 cup chopped onion
- 3 garlic cloves, minced
- 1 tablespoon thyme, fresh or dried
- 1 to 2 teaspoons paprika
- 2 cups peeled and chopped beets
- 2 cups peeled and chopped sweet potato
- 2 cups peeled and chopped parsnips
- ½ teaspoon sea salt (optional)
- 1 cup fresh mint, chopped
- ½ avocado, or 2 tablespoons nut or seed butter (optional)
- 2 tablespoons balsamic vinegar (optional)
- 2 tablespoons pumpkin seeds

1. In a large pot, bring the water to a boil. 2. In another large pot, heat the olive oil (if using) or vegetable broth over medium heat. Sauté the chopped onion and minced garlic until softened, about 5 minutes. 3. Add the thyme, paprika, chopped beets, sweet potato, and parsnips to the pot. Pour in the boiling water (or salt-free vegetable broth) and add the sea salt if using. Cover the pot and let it gently boil for approximately 30 minutes, or until the vegetables are soft. 4. Set aside a little bit of chopped mint for garnishing and add the rest of the mint, along with the avocado (if using), to the pot. Stir until well combined. 5. Transfer the soup to a blender or use an immersion blender to purée the mixture until smooth. If desired, add the balsamic vinegar at this stage and blend again. 6. Serve the soup in bowls, topped with fresh mint leaves, pumpkin seeds, and optionally, chunks of the remaining half avocado.

Per Serving: (1 bowl)

calories: 157 | fat: 5g | protein: 3g | carbs: 26g | fiber: 6g

Minestrone

Prep time: 30 minutes | Cook time: 55 minutes | Serves 8 to 10

- 1 large onion, peeled and chopped
- 2 large carrots, peeled and chopped
- 2 celery stalks, chopped
- 4 cloves garlic, peeled and minced
- 8 cups vegetable stock, or low-sodium vegetable broth
- 2 tablespoons nutritional yeast (optional)
- 1 (28 ounces / 794 g) can diced tomatoes
- 2 teaspoons oregano
- 2 medium red-skin potatoes, scrubbed and cubed
- 4 cups packed chopped kale, ribs removed before chopping
- ½ cup uncooked brown basmati rice
- 6 cups cooked cannellini beans, or 3 (15 ounces / 425 g) cans, drained and rinsed
- Salt and freshly ground black pepper, to taste
- 1 cup finely chopped basil

1. Place the chopped onion, carrots, and celery in a large saucepan over medium heat. Sauté the vegetables for about 10 minutes, adding water 1 to 2 tablespoons at a time to prevent sticking. 2. Add the minced garlic and cook for another minute until fragrant. 3. Add the vegetable stock or low-sodium vegetable broth, nutritional yeast (if using), diced tomatoes, oregano, cubed potatoes, chopped kale, and brown basmati rice to the pot. Bring the mixture to a boil over high heat, then reduce the heat to medium-low and simmer for 30 minutes. 4. After 30 minutes, add the cooked cannellini beans (or drained and rinsed canned beans) to the pot and continue to simmer for an additional 15 minutes, or until the rice is tender. 5. Season the minestrone soup with salt and freshly ground black pepper according to your taste preferences. 6. Stir in the finely chopped basil just before serving. 7. Ladle the minestrone soup into bowls and enjoy.

Per Serving:

calories: 118 | fat: 2g | protein: 5g | carbs: 24g | fiber: 7g

Chapter 7 Snacks and Appetizers

Chocolate Cake Munch Cookies

Prep time: 10 minutes | Cook time: 10 minutes | Serves 12

½ cup dairy-free butter, softened
1 cup coconut sugar (optional)
1 tablespoon chia seeds or ground chia seeds
¾ cup soy milk
1 teaspoon vanilla
2 cups whole wheat flour
¼ cup protein powder
1 teaspoon baking powder
½ teaspoon baking soda
½ teaspoon salt (optional)
½ cup cocoa powder
1 cup chopped walnuts

1. In the bowl of a stand mixer, add the softened dairy-free butter and coconut sugar (if using). Mix on medium speed for about 5 minutes until creamy. 2. In a small bowl, mix the chia seeds with 3 tablespoons of water. Allow the mixture to thicken for a few minutes. 3. Add the chia seed mixture, soy milk, and vanilla extract to the bowl of the stand mixer with the butter and sugar. Mix well on medium speed. 4. In a separate medium-sized bowl, combine the whole wheat flour, protein powder, baking powder, baking soda, salt (if using), and cocoa powder. Mix well. 5. With the stand mixer on medium speed, gradually add the dry mixture to the wet mixture. Mix until well combined. Fold in the chopped walnuts. 6. Place the cookie dough in the refrigerator for at least one hour or overnight to firm up. 7. Preheat the oven to 400ºF (205ºC) and line a baking sheet with parchment paper. 8. Drop heaping tablespoons of the cookie dough onto the prepared baking sheet, spacing them about 2 inches apart. Roll the dough into balls and flatten each one by about half with the bottom of a measuring cup or a similar object. The cookies will bake up thick. 9. Bake the cookies for 8 minutes until they are set. Remove from the oven and let them cool on a wire rack.

Per Serving: (2 cookies)
calories: 239 | fat: 16g | protein: 7g | carbs: 21g | fiber: 4g

Gingerbread Protein Bars

Prep time: 20 minutes | Cook time: 15 minutes | Makes 8 bars

2 cups raw and unsalted almonds
10 pitted dates
4 tablespoons five-spice powder
2 scoops soy protein isolate, chocolate flavor
1 (4-inch) piece ginger, minced
Optional Toppings:
Cocoa powder
Shredded coconut

1. Preheat the oven to 257ºF (125ºC) and line a baking sheet with parchment paper. 2. Spread the almonds evenly on the lined baking sheet and roast them in the preheated oven for about 10 to 15 minutes, or until fragrant. Remove from the oven and let them cool. 3. In a small bowl, cover the dates with water and let them soak for about 10 minutes. Drain the dates thoroughly to remove any excess water. 4. In a food processor, add the roasted almonds, soaked dates, five-spice powder, soy protein isolate, and minced ginger. Blend the ingredients until a smooth mixture is formed. Alternatively, you can add all the ingredients to a medium bowl, cover it, and process using a handheld blender. 5. Line a loaf pan with parchment paper. Transfer the almond mixture to the loaf pan and spread it out evenly, pressing it down firmly until it is about 1 inch thick all over. 6. Place the loaf pan in the fridge and let it chill for about 45 minutes, or until it becomes firm. 7. Remove the chilled mixture from the loaf pan and cut it into 8 bars. 8. Serve the Gingerbread Protein Bars cold and, if desired, sprinkle them with cocoa powder or shredded coconut as optional toppings. 9. Store the bars in an airtight container in the refrigerator and consume them within 6 days. Alternatively, you can store them in the freezer for a maximum of 90 days. Thaw frozen bars at room temperature before enjoying.

Per Serving:
calories: 263 | fat: 18g | protein: 16g | carbs: 9g | fiber: 4g

Nori Snack Rolls

Prep time: 5 minutes | Cook time: 8 to 10 minutes | Makes 4 rolls

2 tablespoons almond, cashew, peanut, or other nut butter
2 tablespoons tamari or soy sauce
4 standard nori sheets
1 mushroom, sliced
1 tablespoon pickled ginger
½ cup grated carrots

1. Preheat the oven to 350ºF (180ºC). 2. In a small bowl, mix together the nut butter and tamari (or soy sauce) until smooth and very thick. 3. Lay out a nori sheet, rough side up, in front of you, positioned lengthwise. Spread a thin line of the nut butter and tamari mixture on the far end of the nori sheet, from side to side. 4. Place the mushroom slices, pickled ginger, and grated carrots in a line at the end of the nori sheet closest to you. 5. Fold the nori sheet over the vegetables, rolling toward the end with the nut butter and tamari mixture. The mixture will act as a seal for the roll. 6. Repeat the process to make a total of 4 rolls. 7. Place the rolls on a baking sheet and bake in the preheated oven for 8 to 10 minutes, or until the rolls are slightly browned and crispy at the ends. 8. Remove the rolls from the oven and let them cool for a few minutes. Then, slice each roll into 3 smaller pieces.

Per Serving:
(1 roll)
calories: 62 | fat: 4g | protein: 2g | carbs: 3g | fiber: 1g

Rich Chocolate Energy Cookies

Prep time: 15 minutes | Cook time: 15 minutes | Serves 12

½ cup softened dairy-free butter
1 cup coconut sugar (optional)
1 tablespoon chia seeds or ground chia seeds
2 cups (12 ounces) dairy-free chocolate chips, divided
1 tablespoon instant coffee
1¼ cups whole wheat flour
½ teaspoon baking soda
1 teaspoon baking powder
½ teaspoon salt (optional)
2 tablespoons raw shelled hempseed
1 cup chopped walnuts

1. Preheat the oven to 350ºF (180ºC). Cut a piece of parchment paper to fit on a baking sheet and set it aside. 2. In the bowl of a stand mixer, add the softened dairy-free butter and coconut sugar (if using). Cream the mixture on medium speed for about 5 minutes or until it becomes light and fluffy. 3. In a small bowl, mix the chia seeds with 3 tablespoons of water and set it aside to allow the mixture to thicken. 4. Melt ½ cup of the dairy-free chocolate chips either in the microwave or using a double boiler. Set the melted chocolate aside to cool slightly. 5. Boil 2 tablespoons of water and dissolve the instant coffee in it. Set it aside to cool. 6. In a separate bowl, combine the whole wheat flour, baking soda, baking powder, and salt (if using). Mix well by hand. 7. Add the prepared chia seed mixture and melted chocolate to the bowl of the stand mixer. Mix on medium speed until well combined. Add the flour mixture and continue mixing until just combined. Remove the mixing bowl from the stand mixer and fold in the remaining dairy-free chocolate chips, raw shelled hempseed, and chopped walnuts. Mix well. 8. Drop large, heaping tablespoons of the cookie dough onto the prepared baking sheet, spacing them about 2 inches apart. Flatten each cookie slightly. 9. Bake the cookies for approximately 12 minutes or until they are set. Remove them from the oven and let them cool on a wire rack.

Per Serving: (2 cookies)

calories: 222 | fat: 14g | protein: 7g | carbs: 21g | fiber: 2g

Skillet Spinach and Artichoke Dip

Prep time: 10 minutes | Cook time: 15 minutes | Serves 6

8 ounces (227 g) silken tofu
½ cup soy milk
2 tablespoons chickpea flour
¼ cup vegetable broth
10 ounces (283 g) frozen spinach
1 (12 ounces / 340 g) jar plain artichoke hearts, chopped
¼ cup nutritional yeast
2 teaspoons liquid aminos
1 teaspoon onion powder
1 teaspoon garlic powder

1. In a blender, combine the silken tofu, soy milk, and chickpea flour. Blend until the mixture is smooth and creamy. 2. In a sauté pan, heat the vegetable broth over medium heat. Add the frozen spinach to the pan and bring it to a simmer. Cover the pan and cook for 4 to 5 minutes, or until the spinach is heated through. 3. Add the tofu mixture, chopped artichoke hearts, nutritional yeast, liquid aminos, onion powder, and garlic powder to the pan. Stir well to combine all the ingredients. 4. Simmer the mixture, stirring occasionally, for 5 to 7 minutes, or until the dip has thickened. 5. Remove the skillet from the heat and transfer the spinach and artichoke dip to a serving dish. 6. Serve the dip warm with tortilla chips, crackers, or sliced vegetables for dipping.

Per Serving:

calories: 143 | fat: 2g | protein: 12g | carbs: 20g | fiber: 11g

Garlic Hummus

Prep time: 10 minutes | Cook time: 0 minutes | Makes 3 cups

3 garlic cloves
2 (15 ounces / 425 g) cans chickpeas, drained and rinsed
3 tablespoons extra-virgin olive oil, plus more as needed (optional)
Juice of 2 lemons
¼ cup tahini
½ teaspoon salt
½ teaspoon ground cumin
1 tablespoon sesame seeds, for garnish (optional)

1. In a blender or food processor, add the garlic cloves, drained and rinsed chickpeas, extra-virgin olive oil, lemon juice, tahini, salt, and ground cumin. 2. Blend the ingredients until smooth and creamy. If needed, add a bit more olive oil or water to achieve your desired consistency. You can adjust the flavors by adding more lemon juice, tahini, salt, or cumin according to your taste preference. 3. Once the hummus is smooth and creamy, transfer it to a serving bowl. 4. Drizzle a little extra olive oil on top for added flavor and presentation. You can also garnish with sesame seeds for a nice touch. 5. Serve the Garlic Hummus with your favorite vegetables, pita bread, or crackers. It makes a delicious dip or spread for snacks, appetizers, or sandwiches.

Per Serving:

calories: 58 | fat: 4g | protein: 2g | carbs: 5g | fiber: 2g

Endurance Snack Mix

Prep time: 5 minutes | Cook time: 0 minutes | Makes 3 cups

½ cup raw pistachios
1 cup raw pumpkin seeds
½ cup unsweetened large coconut flakes
¼ cup raisins
¼ cup goji berries
½ cup dried mulberries
Handful of dried dulse, or 1 sheet nori, cut into bite-sized pieces

1. In a medium-sized bowl, combine the raw pistachios, raw pumpkin seeds, unsweetened coconut flakes, raisins, goji berries, dried mulberries, and dried dulse (or cut nori sheet) pieces. 2. Toss all the ingredients together well, ensuring they are evenly distributed throughout the snack mix. 3. Portion the snack mix into several servings, using snack-sized paper bags, reusable bags, or small glass jars. This allows for convenient on-the-go snacking. 4. Store the snack mix in the refrigerator or freezer to keep it fresh. It can last for several weeks when stored properly.

Per Serving:

calories: 236 | fat: 17g | protein: 9g | carbs: 12g | fiber: 3g

Cacao Crush Smoothie

Prep time: 5 minutes | Cook time: 0 minutes | Serves 1

1½ cups unsweetened almond milk
½ cup frozen cauliflower
¼ avocado, peeled
1 tablespoon cacao powder
½ teaspoon ground cinnamon
½ teaspoon pure vanilla extract

1. In a high-powered blender, combine the unsweetened almond milk, frozen cauliflower, avocado, cacao powder, ground cinnamon, and pure vanilla extract. 2. Blend the ingredients until smooth and creamy. Make sure the cauliflower is completely blended to achieve a smooth consistency. 3. Once the smoothie is well blended, pour it into a glass over a handful of ice cubes to chill it and give it a refreshing texture. 4. Serve the Cacao Crush Smoothie immediately and enjoy!

Per Serving:

calories: 254 | fat: 7g | protein: 15g | carbs: 32g | fiber: 6g

Pressure Cooker Thai Nuggets

Prep time: 10 minutes | Cook time: 5 minutes | Serves 4

¾ cup plus 3 tablespoons vital wheat gluten
¼ cup chickpea flour
½ teaspoon ground ginger
½ teaspoon salt (optional)
¼ teaspoon garlic powder
¼ teaspoon paprika
¾ cup vegetable broth
2 teaspoons tamari, divided
4 teaspoons red curry paste, divided
1½ cups vegetable broth, divided

1. In a large bowl, combine the vital wheat gluten, chickpea flour, ground ginger, salt (if desired), garlic powder, and paprika. 2. In a separate small bowl, mix together ¾ cup vegetable broth, 1 teaspoon tamari, and 2 teaspoons red curry paste. Pour the wet mixture into the dry ingredients. 3. Mix and knead the ingredients for about 2 to 3 minutes until the dough becomes elastic. It will be a wet dough, but it should still be stretchy and pliable. Pinch off small pieces of the dough and roll them into small balls, approximately 1 to 1½ inches in diameter. They will expand slightly during cooking. 4. Place the seitan dough balls into an electric pressure cooker. 5. In another bowl, combine 1½ cups vegetable broth, 1½ cups water, and 2 teaspoons red curry paste. Stir well, and pour the mixture over the nuggets in the pressure cooker. 6. Close the lid of the pressure cooker and ensure the top knob is turned to the sealing position. Press the Manual button and set the cooking time to 4 minutes. The pressure cooker will take about 15 minutes to build pressure and cook. 7. After the cooking time is complete, let the pressure naturally release for about an hour. Do not vent the pressure manually during this time. 8. Once the pressure has released, vent the pressure manually and open the lid. 9. Remove the nuggets from the liquid and set them aside to cool. You can enjoy them immediately, use them in recipes, or refrigerate them overnight. They can also be frozen for later use.

Per Serving:

calories: 155 | fat: 2g | protein: 26g | carbs: 11g | fiber: 2g

Steamed Seitan Chipotle Links

Prep time: 15 minutes | Cook time: 40 minutes | Makes 4 links

⅓ cup plus 2 tablespoons vital wheat gluten
2 tablespoons chickpea flour
1 teaspoon garlic powder
1 teaspoon onion powder
1 teaspoon taco seasoning
2 tablespoons tomato sauce
1 teaspoon chipotle hot sauce

1. In a large bowl, combine the vital wheat gluten, chickpea flour, garlic powder, onion powder, and taco seasoning. 2. In a small bowl, mix together 1/4 cup water, tomato sauce, and chipotle hot sauce until well combined. 3. Pour the liquid mixture into the dry ingredients and mix well. Knead the dough for about 2 minutes until it becomes elastic and holds together. The dough should have a firm texture and not rise significantly during cooking. 4. Divide the dough into four equal pieces and shape each piece into a log shape, resembling links. 5. Fill a saucepan with 5 cups of water and bring it to a boil. Place a steamer basket inside the pan. 6. Reduce the heat to a simmer and carefully place the seitan links into the steamer basket. Cover the saucepan. 7. Steam the seitan links for 40 minutes. Make sure the water doesn't boil vigorously, as a gentle simmer is preferred for steaming. 8. Once the seitan links are cooked, remove them from the steamer and let them cool. 9. Store the steamed seitan links in the refrigerator for up to 5 days or in the freezer for up to 4 months.

Per Serving: (1 links)

calories: 120 | fat: 1g | protein: 30g | carbs: 8g | fiber: 1g

High-Protein Peanut Butter Cookie Dough

Prep time: 15 minutes | Cook time: 0 minutes | Makes 45 balls

1 cup crunchy peanut butter
1 cup maple syrup (optional)
½ teaspoon salt (optional)
1 cup chickpea flour
¾ cup almond meal flour
½ cup chopped peanuts
½ cup chopped cashews
½ cup old-fashioned oats
Finely ground peanuts, for coating (optional)

1. In a large bowl, mix together the peanut butter and maple syrup until well combined. If desired, add salt for additional flavor. 2. Add the chickpea flour, almond meal flour, chopped peanuts, chopped cashews, and old-fashioned oats to the bowl. Mix well until all the ingredients are evenly incorporated and a dough-like consistency is formed. 3. Shape the mixture into small balls using your hands. The size of the balls is up to your preference, but aim for bite-sized portions. 4. If desired, roll the balls in finely ground peanuts to give them a more refined appearance and added texture. This step is optional but can enhance the overall presentation. 5. Once shaped and coated (if desired), the high-protein peanut butter cookie dough balls are ready to be enjoyed. They can be eaten immediately or stored in the refrigerator for easier handling and to keep them firm.

Per Serving: (2 balls)

calories: 183 | fat: 7g | protein: 10g | carbs: 19g | fiber: 3g

Black Bean Tempeh Nachos with Cashew Cheese

Prep time: 20 minutes | Cook time: 10 minutes | Serves 4

Cashew Cheese:
- ¾ cup raw cashews, soaked from 1 hour to overnight and drained
- 1 tablespoon nutritional yeast
- 1 tablespoon tapioca starch or tapioca flour
- ½ teaspoon garlic powder
- ½ teaspoon onion powder
- 1 tablespoon lemon juice
- ½ cup water

Tempeh Nachos:
- 10 to 18 ounces (283 to 510 g) tortilla chips
- 1 (15 ounces / 425 g) can black beans, drained and rinsed
- ½ cup diced red onion
- 1 Roma tomato, diced small
- 8 ounces (227 g) tempeh, diced very small
- 1 hot chili pepper, sliced thin crosswise
- 2 tablespoons raw shelled hempseed
- 1 avocado
- Juice from one lime

1. Prepare the Cashew Cheese: In a blender, combine the soaked and drained cashews, nutritional yeast, tapioca starch, garlic powder, onion powder, lemon juice, and water. Blend until smooth and creamy. 2. Transfer the blended mixture into a small saucepan. Cook over medium heat, stirring continuously, until the sauce thickens slightly. This will take about 5 to 10 minutes. Remove from heat and let it cool slightly. 3. Assemble the Nachos: Arrange the tortilla chips on a platter. Sprinkle the drained and rinsed black beans evenly over the chips. Dot the cashew cheese on top of the beans. 4. Sprinkle the diced red onion, diced tomato, diced tempeh, sliced chili pepper, and hempseed over the nachos. 5. Dice the avocado and toss it in lime juice to prevent browning. Sprinkle the diced avocado over the nachos. 6. Serve the Black Bean Tempeh Nachos with Cashew Cheese immediately and enjoy!

Per Serving:
calories: 590 | fat: 26g | protein: 28g | carbs: 59g | fiber: 9g

Artichoke Quinoa Dip

Prep time: 20 minutes | Cook time: 25 minutes | Serves 4

- ½ cup quinoa
- 1 tablespoon extra virgin olive oil (optional)
- ½ cup diced onion
- 4 ounces (113 g) baby spinach, with stems chopped off
- ¼ cup raw shelled hempseed
- ½ teaspoon onion powder
- ½ teaspoon garlic powder
- 1 teaspoon salt (optional)
- ¼ teaspoon ground black pepper
- 8 ounces (227 g) artichoke hearts in water, drained
- 1 tablespoon lemon juice

1. Rinse the quinoa in a sieve under running water to remove any bitterness. In a small saucepan, combine the rinsed quinoa and 1 cup of water. Bring to a boil, then reduce the heat to low, cover, and simmer for 10 to 15 minutes, or until all the liquid is absorbed. Remove from heat and let it sit covered for 5 minutes. Fluff the quinoa with a fork. 2. In a large skillet, heat the olive oil (if using) over medium-high heat. Add the diced onion and sauté for about 10 minutes until the onion becomes translucent and slightly caramelized. Add the baby spinach to the skillet and cook for about a minute until it wilts. Stir in the hempseed, onion powder, garlic powder, salt (if using), and ground black pepper. Remove from heat. 3. Cut off the top of the artichoke hearts and discard the toughest outer leaves. Add the cooked quinoa, sautéed onion and spinach mixture, drained artichoke hearts, and lemon juice to a food processor. 4. Process the ingredients in the food processor until they are well combined and chopped into small pieces. You can adjust the texture to your preference—process it for a shorter time for a chunkier dip or longer for a smoother consistency. 5. Transfer the artichoke quinoa dip to a serving bowl. Serve it with homemade pita chips. To make pita chips, brush pita pockets or flatbread with oil, cut them into triangles, and bake at 400°F (205°C) for about 5 to 7 minutes, or until they are crispy and golden brown. Keep a close eye on them to avoid burning.

Per Serving:
calories: 155 | fat: 5g | protein: 10g | carbs: 23g | fiber: 6g

Calorie Bomb Cookies

Prep time: 15 minutes | Cook time: 30 minutes | Makes 24 cookies

- 4 cups old-fashioned rolled oats
- 1½ cups whole wheat flour
- 1 teaspoon baking powder
- ½ teaspoon salt (optional)
- 3 ripe bananas
- 1 cup coconut sugar (optional)
- ⅓ cup coconut oil (optional)
- ¼ cup plus 2 tablespoons water
- 2 tablespoons chia seeds or ground flaxseeds
- 2 teaspoons vanilla extract
- 1 cup dark chocolate chips
- 1 cup raw walnut pieces
- ½ cup raw sunflower seeds
- ½ cup unsweetened shredded coconut (optional)

1. Preheat the oven to 350°F (180°C) and line two baking sheets with parchment paper. 2. Place 2 cups of the oats in a food processor or blender and pulse until finely ground. Transfer the ground oats to a large bowl and add the whole wheat flour, baking powder, salt (if using), and the remaining rolled oats. 3. In the same food processor or blender, combine the ripe bananas, coconut sugar (if using), coconut oil (if using), water, chia seeds or ground flaxseeds, and vanilla extract. Blend until smooth. 4. Add the banana mixture to the oat mixture in the large bowl and stir with a sturdy wooden spoon until well combined. Fold in the dark chocolate chips, raw walnut pieces, sunflower seeds, and shredded coconut (if using). 5. With wet hands, form about ¼ cup of dough into a ball and flatten it to a thickness of ¾ to 1 inch. Place the flattened dough on the prepared baking sheets. Repeat with the remaining dough, leaving some space between each cookie. 6. Bake the cookies in the preheated oven for 30 minutes, or until they turn golden brown. 7. Remove the baking sheets from the oven and allow the cookies to cool completely before removing them from the parchment paper. 8. Store the cookies in an airtight container for up to 1 week, or freeze them for up to 3 months. For on-the-go eating, wrap them in parchment paper.

Per Serving: (2 cookies)
calories: 491 | fat: 24g | protein: 9g | carbs: 68g | fiber: 9g

Over-the-Top Bars to Go

Prep time: 20 minutes | Cook time: 15 minutes | Makes 16 squares

1½ cups old-fashioned oats
½ cup pecans
½ cup pistachios
½ cup cashews
½ cup dried cranberries
¼ cup dates, pitted and chopped
¼ cup sunflower seed kernels
¼ cup pepitas
2 tablespoons raw shelled hempseed
½ cup peanut butter
½ cup brown rice syrup
3 tablespoons maple syrup (optional)

1. Line an 8-inch square baking dish with parchment paper, leaving an overhang on opposite sides to act as handles for easy removal of the bars. 2. In a large bowl, combine the oats, pecans, pistachios, cashews, dried cranberries, dates, sunflower seed kernels, and pepitas. Mix well. 3. Add the peanut butter to the bowl and mix it in with a wooden spoon. Use your hands to thoroughly incorporate the peanut butter into the dry ingredients, making sure everything is well combined. 4. In a small saucepan, combine the brown rice syrup and maple syrup (if using). Bring the mixture to a boil and cook until it reaches the hard ball stage, which is 260°F (127°C) on a candy thermometer. 5. Pour the hot syrup mixture over the oat mixture and stir well to coat all the ingredients. 6. Transfer the mixture to the prepared baking dish and press it down firmly and evenly. You can use your fingertips or the bottom of a measuring cup to press it down. 7. Refrigerate the dish for at least 30 minutes to allow the bars to set. 8. Lift the bars out of the dish using the parchment paper handles. Place them on a cutting board and slice into sixteen squares.

Per Serving: (2 squares)
calories: 352 | fat: 22g | protein: 14g | carbs: 33g | fiber: 7g

Chocolate Sunflower Protein Cookies

Prep time: 15 minutes | Cook time: 10 minutes | Serves 12

1 cup dairy-free butter
¾ cup plus 2 tablespoons coconut sugar (optional)
2 tablespoons ground chia seeds
2¼ cups whole wheat pastry flour
¼ cup protein powder
1 teaspoon baking soda
½ teaspoon baking powder
¼ teaspoon salt (optional)
1 teaspoon vanilla extract
1 cup dairy-free chocolate chips
¼ cup sunflower seed kernels

1. Preheat the oven to 375°F (190°C) and line a baking sheet with parchment paper. Set it aside. 2. In the bowl of a stand mixer, add the dairy-free butter and coconut sugar (if using). Mix together on medium-low speed for about 5 minutes until creamy and well combined. 3. In a separate small bowl, mix the ground chia seeds with 6 tablespoons of water. Set aside and allow it to thicken for a few minutes. 4. In a medium bowl, whisk together the whole wheat pastry flour, protein powder, baking soda, baking powder, and salt (if using). 5. Add the vanilla extract and the chia mixture to the butter mixture in the stand mixer. Mix until well blended. 6. Gradually add the flour mixture to the wet ingredients, mixing on low speed until just combined. Stir in the dairy-free chocolate chips and sunflower seed kernels. 7. Form the cookie dough into round balls and place them about 2 inches apart on the prepared baking sheet. Flatten each cookie ball to about ½ inch thick. 8. Bake the cookies in the preheated oven for 8 to 9 minutes, or until they are lightly golden around the edges. 9. Remove the cookies from the oven and allow them to cool on a wire rack before serving.

Per Serving: (2 cookies)
calories: 281 | fat: g | protein: 7g | carbs: 16g | fiber: 3g

Skillet Cauliflower Bites

Prep time: 5 minutes | Cook time: 15 minutes | Serves 4 to 6

1 head cauliflower, cut into 1½- to 2-inch florets

1. Heat a nonstick skillet over medium heat. 2. Add the cauliflower florets to the skillet and spread them out in a single layer. You can add a small amount of oil or cooking spray to prevent sticking if desired, although it's not necessary with a nonstick skillet. 3. Cook the cauliflower for about 15 minutes, stirring every 3 to 5 minutes. The cauliflower should become browned and crisp-tender. 4. Once the cauliflower is browned and cooked to your desired tenderness, remove the skillet from the heat. 5. Serve the skillet cauliflower bites as a delicious and healthy side dish or snack.

Per Serving:
calories: 36 | fat: 0g | protein: 3g | carbs: 8g | fiber: 4g

Rainbow Veggie Protein Pinwheels

Prep time: 20 minutes | Cook time: 0 minutes | Serves 6

¼ cup hummus
¼ cup tempeh, crumbled in a food processor
2 large spinach tortillas
¼ cup thinly sliced red bell pepper
¼ cup thinly sliced yellow bell pepper
1 thinly sliced carrot
¼ cup thinly sliced purple cabbage

1. In a bowl, mix together the hummus and crumbled tempeh until well combined. 2. Lay out the spinach tortillas. Spread a thin layer of the hummus-tempeh mixture over the entire surface of each tortilla, leaving a 1-inch border around the edges. 3. Arrange a thin strip of each of the sliced red bell pepper, yellow bell pepper, carrot, and purple cabbage side by side over the hummus-tempeh mixture on each tortilla. 4. Roll each tortilla tightly, starting from one end, to form a log. If needed, you can use toothpicks to secure the pinwheels, but the hummus will help them stick together at the edges. 5. Using a sharp knife, cut each rolled tortilla crosswise into pinwheels. 6. Serve the rainbow veggie protein pinwheels as a nutritious and colorful appetizer, snack, or light meal.

Per Serving: (2 pinwheels)
calories: 66 | fat: 2g | protein: 9g | carbs: 8g | fiber: 4g

Spirulina Golden Berry Power Bars

Prep time: 2 minutes | Cook time: 0 minutes | Makes 8 bars

1 cup mixed raw seeds (pumpkin, sunflower, sesame, hemp)
1 tablespoon chia seeds
1 cup Medjool dates (about 10 large), pitted
2 tablespoons chopped fresh mint
2 teaspoons spirulina powder
1 tablespoon fresh lime juice
½ cup golden berries

1. In a food processor fitted with the S blade, combine all the ingredients, except the golden berries. 2. Process until a coarse dough has formed (this may take a couple of minutes). Stop the machine and check the consistency—pinch the dough between 2 fingers and make sure it sticks together easily so that your bars don't end up crumbly. If the dough is too dry, add a small amount of water—about ½ teaspoon at a time—and blend again until the desired stickiness is achieved. 3. Add the golden berries and pulse several times until they're just coarsely chopped, to give the bars a nice texture. 4. Place a large sheet of parchment paper on a flat surface and tip out the dough on top. Gather into a solid mass in the center, then fold the parchment paper over the top and, using a rolling pin, roll flat until about ¼ inch (6 mm) thick. 5. Place in the freezer for a few hours, then carefully use a knife or cookie cutter to cut the bars into your desired shapes. 6. Store in an airtight glass container for 2 to 3 weeks or in the freezer for up to 3 months.

Per Serving:
calories: 186 | fat: 8g | protein: 6g | carbs: 26g | fiber: 3g

Gluten-Free Energy Crackers

Prep time: 25 minutes | Cook time: 40 minutes | Serves 6

¼ cup flax seeds
¼ cup chia seeds
¾ cup water
1 tablespoon garlic, minced
½ tablespoon onion flakes
½ cup pumpkin seeds, chopped
¼ cup peanuts, crushed
¼ cup cashews, crushed
¼ cup sesame seeds
¼ teaspoon paprika powder
Salt and pepper to taste (optional)

1. Preheat the oven to 350°F (180°C). 2. Take a large bowl and combine the water, garlic, onion flakes, and paprika. Whisk until everything is combined thoroughly. Add the flax seeds, chia seeds, pumpkin seeds, peanuts, cashews, and sesame seeds to the bowl. Stir everything well, while adding pinches of salt (if desired) and pepper to taste, until it is thoroughly combined. 3. Line a baking sheet with parchment paper and spread out the mixture in a thin and even layer across the parchment paper. Bake for 20 to 25 minutes. Remove the pan from the oven and flip over the flat chunk so that the other side can crisp. Cut the chunk into squares or triangles, depending on preference and put the pan back into the oven and bake until the bars have turned golden brown, around 30 minutes. 4. Allow the crackers to cool before serving or storing.

Per Serving:
calories: 209 | fat: 16g | protein: 7g | carbs: 10g | fiber: 6g

Adventure Bars

Prep time: 5 minutes | Cook time: 0 minutes | Makes 8 bars

1 cup raw cashews
½ cup unsweetened shredded coconut
1 cup Medjool dates, pitted
½ cup dried apricots
½ cup dried tart cherries
4 tablespoons chia seeds
4 tablespoons hemp hearts
½ cup creamy almond butter

1. In a food processor fitted with the chopping blade, combine the cashews and coconut and pulse until finely chopped. Transfer to a bowl. 2. Place the dates in the food processor. Pulse a few times, then process the dates until they have turned into a paste. Add the apricots and cherries and pulse a few times. Return the cashew mixture to the fruit, along with the chia seeds, hemp hearts, and almond butter. Process until the ingredients are well combined—neither too dry nor too sticky—and hold together nicely when pressed. If the mixture is too crumbly, add a little more almond butter or a tiny bit of water and process again. 3. Lay a piece of parchment paper on a clean, flat surface and turn the mixture out onto it. Press the mixture together and form into an 8-inch square that is a little thicker than ¼ inch. Place in the fridge or freezer to firm up before cutting into 8 bars. 4. Wrap the bars individually in parchment paper. They will keep for several weeks in the fridge or several months in the freezer.

Per Serving:
calories: 322 | fat: 19g | protein: 8g | carbs: 34g | fiber: 6g

Amazing Lentil Energy Balls

Prep time: 15 minutes | Cook time: 25 minutes | Serves 9

½ cup lentils
½ cup dairy-free chocolate chips
2 cups quick-cooking oats
¼ cup sunflower seed kernels
¼ cup raw shelled hempseed
¼ cup unsweetened shredded coconut
½ cup almond butter
½ cup maple syrup (optional)

1. Rinse the lentils and drain them. Place 1 cup of water and the lentils in a medium-large saucepan. Bring to a boil over high heat. Once boiling, reduce the heat to medium-high and cook for 20 to 25 minutes, or until the lentils are tender and all the water is absorbed. Set aside to cool. 2. In a large bowl, combine the chocolate chips, oats, sunflower seed kernels, hempseed, and shredded coconut. 3. Once the lentils have cooled, add them to the bowl with the dry ingredients. Add almond butter and maple syrup, if using. Mix well until all the ingredients are evenly combined. 4. Form the mixture into thirty-six balls and place them in a glass container with a lid. 5. Refrigerate the energy balls for about 30 minutes to allow them to set. This will help them hold their shape. 6. After chilling, the energy balls are ready to enjoy. Store them in the refrigerator for up to 5 days or freeze them for up to 6 months.

Per Serving: (4 balls)
calories: 385 | fat: 18g | protein: 12g | carbs: 42g | fiber: 6g

Pepita and Almond Squares

Prep time: 20 minutes | Cook time: 15 minutes | Makes 16 squares

1 cup almonds, coarsely chopped
1 cup old-fashioned oats
⅔ cup pepitas
⅔ cup dried cranberries
½ cup unsweetened shredded coconut
¼ cup raw shelled hempseed
⅓ cup peanut butter
⅔ cup brown rice syrup
¼ cup maple syrup (optional)
2 teaspoons vanilla extract

1. Line an 8-inch square baking dish with parchment paper and come up about 3 inches on opposite sides. This will act as a handle to remove the squares from the dish. 2. In a large mixing bowl, add the almonds, oats, pepitas, cranberries, coconut, and hempseed. Mix well. Stir in the peanut butter and try to get it evenly combined. You can use your fingers when most of it is worked in. 3. Add the brown rice syrup, maple syrup (if desired), and vanilla to a small saucepan. Bring to a boil and continue boiling until it reaches the hard ball stage, 260°F (127°C), on a candy thermometer. When this temperature is reached, quickly pour over the almond mixture and stir well. It will start to harden up quickly. Pour into the prepared dish and press down firmly into the dish and as evenly as possible. Refrigerate for at least 30 minutes. 4. Grab the "handles" of the parchment paper and lift out of the dish. Place on a cutting sheet and slice into sixteen squares.

Per Serving: (2 squares)
calories: 198 | fat: 11g | protein: 12g | carbs: 22g | fiber: 4g

No-Bake Chocolate Peanut Butter Cookies

Prep time: 20 minutes | Cook time: 5 minutes | Makes 24 cookies

½ cup unsweetened dairy-free milk
3 tablespoons dairy-free butter
⅓ cup coconut sugar (optional)
1 tablespoon unsweetened cocoa powder
⅓ cup dairy-free semi-sweet chocolate chips
1 teaspoon vanilla extract
⅓ cup creamy peanut butter
Pinch of salt (optional)
2½ cups old-fashioned oats or quick-cooking oats
¼ cup raw shelled hempseed

1. Line a baking sheet with wax paper. 2. Place the milk, butter, sugar (if desired), cocoa powder, and chocolate chips in a large saucepan. Bring to a rolling boil and then look at the timer. Let boil for 2 minutes. Stir occasionally so that the chocolate chips don't stick to the bottom of the pan before they melt. Remove from the heat and add the vanilla, peanut butter, and salt (if desired) and mix until the peanut butter melts. Stir in the oats and hempseed. 3. With a spoon, drop dollops of the batter onto the prepared baking sheet. Within a minute or less you can handle them and shape into cookies. Let the cookies set for an hour or so. You can speed up the cooling and hardening process by placing them in the refrigerator.

Per Serving: (2 cookies)
calories: 220 | fat: 77g | protein: 7g | carbs: 29g | fiber: 5g

Basic Oil-Free Hummus

Prep time: 10 minutes | Cook time: 0 minutes | Makes 1½ cups

1 (15 ounces / 425 g) can chickpeas, drained and rinsed
1 tablespoon tahini
¼ teaspoon garlic powder
¼ teaspoon ground cumin
¼ cup lemon juice
1/16 teaspoon cayenne
¼ teaspoon za'atar

1. In a food processor, combine the chickpeas, tahini, garlic powder, cumin, lemon juice, cayenne, and za'atar. Process until smooth and creamy.

Per Serving:
calories: 136 | fat: 6g | protein: 3g | carbs: 21g | fiber: 3g

Vanilla Almond Date Balls

Prep time: 20 minutes | Cook time: 0 minutes | Makes 20 balls

1½ cups almond flour
16 pitted dates
4 tablespoons sunflower seed kernels
4 tablespoons vanilla protein powder
2 tablespoons flaxseed meal
1 teaspoon vanilla extract
Pinch of salt (optional)
2 tablespoons sunflower seed kernels, ground fine in a small food processor

1. Place all the ingredients except the ground sunflower seeds in a food processor. Process on high until all is combined well and forms a ball. Transfer into a large bowl and form twenty balls. This dough works well by squeezing each one a few times to form a ball. Roll in ground sunflower seeds.

Per Serving: (2 balls)
calories: 131 | fat: 4g | protein: 8g | carbs: 23g | fiber: 4g

Toast Points

Prep time: 5 minutes | Cook time: 20 minutes | Serves 2 to 4

8 whole grain bread slices (thawed if frozen)
Balsamic vinegar, for brushing (optional)
Garlic powder, for seasoning

1. Lay the bread flat on a parchment-lined baking sheet. 2. Brush the bread with a thin layer of vinegar (if using). 3. Sprinkle with garlic powder. 4. Transfer the baking sheet to a cold oven, and heat to 350°F (180°C). 5. When the oven reaches temperature, flip the bread over. Bake for another 5 to 15 minutes, or until crispy to your liking. Remove from the oven.

Per Serving:
calories: 165 | fat: 1g | protein: 8g | carbs: 31g | fiber: 6g

Strawberry Shortcake Rice Bites

Prep time: 20 minutes | Cook time: 25 minutes | Makes 8 balls

3 cups water
3 cups white sushi rice
½ cup coconut sugar (optional)
3 tablespoons fresh lemon juice
½ teaspoon vanilla extract
2 cups strawberries, hulled and quartered
3 tablespoons chia seeds
Salt (optional)

1. Bring the water to a boil in a large saucepan, then lower the heat to medium-low and stir in the rice. Cook, stirring often, until soft, about 15 to 20 minutes. You want it to be moist (but not soggy) and very sticky and tender. 2. Transfer the cooked rice to a large bowl. Working quickly, add the sugar, lemon juice, and vanilla. Stir thoroughly to combine and allow to cool slightly. 3. Spread out a sushi mat or silicone liner. Cover with plastic wrap and spread 1 cup rice on top of the plastic. With wet hands, press the rice into a uniform ½-inch thick layer. 4. Place a row of strawberries, end to end, about 1 inch from the bottom edge. Sprinkle with 1 teaspoon chia seeds. Starting with the edge closest to you, roll the rice tightly into a cylinder, using the plastic wrap and mat to assist. Be sure to pull the plastic and mat away from the rice as you roll. Repeat with the remaining ingredients. 5. Sprinkle the outside of the rolls with salt to taste, if desired. Let sit for 5 minutes, then slice each roll into 8 to 10 pieces using a very sharp knife. Wrap tightly in parchment paper and plastic wrap if eating on the go. Refrigerate for up to 2 days or freeze individual pieces for up to 3 months. (If frozen, allow to thaw overnight before eating.)

Per Serving:
calories: 385 | fat: 2g | protein: 9g | carbs: 87g | fiber: 5g

White Bean and Spinach Artichoke Dip

Prep time: 10 minutes | Cook time: 15 minutes | Serves 8

½ yellow onion, peeled and sliced
3 garlic cloves, coarsely chopped
1 tablespoon water
1 (15 ounces /425 g) can cannellini beans, drained and rinsed
½ cup nutritional yeast
2 tablespoons yellow (mellow) miso paste
1 tablespoon tapioca starch
1 cup unsweetened oat milk
1 (15 ounces /425 g) can pumpkin
1 (1-pound / 454 g) package chopped frozen spinach
1 (14 ounces / 397 g) can quartered artichoke hearts, drained

1. In a medium nonstick sauté pan or skillet, heat it over high heat. Add the sliced onion, chopped garlic, and water to the pan. Cook for about 3 minutes, stirring occasionally, until the onion becomes translucent and begins to brown slightly. Transfer the onion and garlic mixture to a blender. 2. To the blender, add the cannellini beans, nutritional yeast, yellow miso paste, tapioca starch, oat milk, and pumpkin. Purée the ingredients until smooth. Set aside. 3. Return the same pan to medium heat and add the frozen spinach. Cook for 4 to 7 minutes, stirring occasionally, until the spinach thaws. 4. Stir in the purée mixture from the blender. Cook for an additional 3 to 5 minutes, stirring occasionally, until the dip begins to bubble and thicken. 5. Add the drained artichoke hearts to the pan and stir to combine with the dip. 6. Serve the White Bean and Spinach Artichoke Dip warm. If desired, you can put the pan (if it's heat-safe) under the broiler for 1 to 2 minutes to give the top layer a little crust and char.

Per Serving:
calories: 147 | fat: 2g | protein: 12g | carbs: 23g | fiber: 9g

Crispy Chickpea Snackers

Prep time: 10 minutes | Cook time: 4 to 6 hours | Makes 7 to 8 cups

4 (14½ ounces / 411 g) cans chickpeas, drained and rinsed
Juice of 2 lemons
1 tablespoon garlic powder
1 tablespoon onion powder
2 teaspoons paprika
Salt (optional)

1. Put the chickpeas into the slow cooker. Add the lemon juice, garlic powder, onion powder, and paprika. Season with salt (if using). Toss gently to thoroughly coat every chickpea with the seasoning. 2. Cover the slow cooker and, using a wooden spoon or a chopstick, prop open the lid to allow the steam to escape. Cook on High for 4 to 6 hours or on Low for 8 to 10 hours, stirring every 30 to 45 minutes to keep the chickpeas from burning.

Per Serving:
calories: 56 | fat: 1g | protein: 3g | carbs: 9g | fiber: 3g

White Bean Tzatziki Dip

Prep time: 10 minutes | Cook time: 1 to 2 hours | Makes about 8 cups

4 (14½ ounces / 411 g) cans white beans, drained and rinsed
8 garlic cloves, minced
1 medium onion, coarsely chopped
¼ cup store-bought low-sodium vegetable broth, plus more as needed
Juice from one lemon, divided
2 teaspoons dried dill, divided
Salt (optional)
1 cucumber, peeled and finely diced

1. Place the beans, garlic, onion, broth, and half the lemon juice in a blender. Blend until creamy, about 1 minute, adding up to ¼ cup of additional broth as needed to make the mixture creamy. 2. Transfer the mixture to the slow cooker, stir in 1 teaspoon of dill, and season with salt (if using). Cover and cook on Low for 1 to 2 hours until heated through. 3. Meanwhile, in a medium bowl, mix the cucumber with the remaining 1 teaspoon of dill and the remaining half of the lemon juice. Toss to coat. Season with salt (if using). 4. Spoon the dip from the slow cooker into a serving bowl and top with the cucumber mixture before serving.

Per Serving:
calories: 59 | fat: 0g | protein: 3g | carbs: 11g | fiber: 4g

Slow Cooker Versatile Seitan Balls

Prep time: 15 minutes | Cook time: 6 hours | Makes 34 balls

1½ cups vital wheat gluten
½ cup chickpea flour
1 tablespoon mushroom powder
½ teaspoon dried oregano
½ teaspoon onion powder
¼ teaspoon garlic powder
¼ teaspoon nutmeg
¼ teaspoon ground ginger
¼ teaspoon ground cloves
¼ teaspoon ground sage
½ teaspoon salt (optional)
½ cup tomato sauce, divided
1 teaspoon liquid smoke
1½ cups vegetable broth, divided

1. Mix the gluten, flour, mushroom powder, oregano, onion and garlic powders, nutmeg, ginger, cloves, sage, and salt (if desired) in a large bowl. 2. In a small bowl, add ¼ cup tomato sauce, ¼ cup water, liquid smoke, and ½ cup vegetable broth. Mix well. 3. Make a well in the center of the dry ingredients and pour in the tomato sauce mixture. Mix well and start to knead. Knead for 1 minute or until the dough becomes mildly elastic. You will see the dough slightly pull back as you are kneading and it will be a bit sticky. Pour remaining ¼ cup tomato sauce, 1 cup vegetable broth, and 3 cups water into the slow cooker. Stir. 4. Tear off small chunks of the dough, squeeze into a round shape, and drop into the liquid in the slow cooker. There will be forty-four balls. You can also make seventeen larger balls and cut them after cooking and cooling. Or make two logs and cut into desired shapes. Cover and cook on low for 4 to 6 hours. They will grow in size as they cook. Check at 4 hours and see if you like the texture. They will become firmer as they sit in the refrigerator. 5. Remove from the pot and let cool. Store in the refrigerator for up to 5 days or freeze for up to 4 months.

Per Serving: (½ cup)
calories: 161 | fat: 1g | protein: 30g | carbs: 10g | fiber: 2g

Great Smoky Almonds

Prep time: 2 minutes | Cook time: 10 to 12 minutes | Serves 4

1 tablespoon avocado oil (optional)
2 teaspoons liquid smoke
1 teaspoon pure maple syrup (optional)
2 cups raw almonds
½ teaspoon sea salt (optional)
¼ teaspoon garlic powder

1. Preheat the oven to 350°F (180°C). Line a baking sheet with parchment paper. 2. In a medium mixing bowl, combine the oil (if using), liquid smoke, and maple syrup (if using). Add the almonds and stir until well coated. Sprinkle the salt (if using) and garlic powder over the almonds and stir again. 3. Spread the almonds on the prepared baking sheet. Bake for 10 to 12 minutes, or until the nuts are nicely toasted. Let cool completely before storing in an airtight container.

Per Serving:
calories: 450 | fat: 39g | protein: 15g | carbs: 16g | fiber: 9g

Crunchy Nuts and Seeds Protein Bars

Prep time: 15 minutes | Cook time: 0 minutes | Makes 16 bars

2 cups chickpea flour
1 cup plus 2 tablespoons almond flour
2 tablespoons flaxseed meal
1 cup dairy-free milk
1 cup cashew butter
½ cup maple syrup (optional)
½ cup slivered almonds
½ cup dried cranberries
¼ cup sunflower seed kernels
½ cup melted dairy-free chocolate chips

1. Line an 8-inch square baking dish with parchment paper and come up about 3 inches on opposite sides. This will act as a handle to remove the bars from the dish. 2. Combine the flours and flaxseed meal in a large bowl and mix well. With a heavy wooden spoon, mix in the milk, cashew butter, maple syrup (if desired), almonds, cranberries, and sunflower seeds. Lastly, mix in the melted chocolate. Add the batter to the prepared dish and press firmly into all corners and as evenly as possible. Refrigerate for at least 30 minutes. 3. Grab the "handles" of the parchment paper and lift out of the dish. Place on a cutting sheet and slice into sixteen bars.

Per Serving: (1 bar)
calories: 223 | fat: 9g | protein: 10g | carbs: 26g | fiber: 4g

Lemon-Oatmeal Cacao Cookies

Prep time: 30 minutes | Cook time: 35 minutes | Makes 14 cookies

12 pitted Medjool dates
Boiling water, for soaking the dates
1 cup unsweetened applesauce
1 tablespoon freshly squeezed lemon juice
1 teaspoon vanilla extract
1 tablespoon water, plus more as needed (optional)
1½ cups old-fashioned oats
1 cup oat flour
¾ cup coarsely chopped walnuts
2 tablespoons lemon zest
1 tablespoon cacao powder
½ teaspoon baking soda

1. In a small bowl, combine the dates with enough boiling water to cover. Let sit for 15 to 20 minutes to soften. 2. While the dates soak, preheat the oven to 300°F (150°C). Line 2 baking sheets with parchment paper or silicone mats. 3. Drain the excess liquid from the dates and put them in a blender, along with the applesauce, lemon juice, and vanilla. Purée until a thick paste forms. Add water, 1 tablespoon at a time, if the mixture isn't getting smooth. 4. In a large bowl, stir together the oats, oat flour, walnuts, lemon zest, cacao powder, and baking soda. Pour in the date mixture and stir to combine. One at a time, scoop ¼-cup portions of dough, gently roll into a ball, and press down lightly on the prepared baking sheets. The cookie should be about 1 inch thick and roughly 3 inches in diameter. 5. Bake for 30 to 35 minutes, or until the tops of the cookies look crispy and dry. Transfer to a wire rack to cool. 6. Store in an airtight container at room temperature for up to 1 week.

Per Serving: (1 cookie)
calories: 174 | fat: 6g | protein: 4g | carbs: 30g | fiber: 4g

Caribbean Chili

Prep time: 30 minutes | Cook time: 1 hour | Serves 4

2 tablespoons coconut oil (optional)
1 diced onion
1 diced green pepper
3 chopped Roma tomatoes
2 diced carrots
5 ounces (142 g) tomato paste
2 tablespoons chili powder
1 teaspoon salt (optional)
1 teaspoon ground cumin
½ teaspoon cinnamon
½ teaspoon allspice
½ teaspoon dried oregano
½ teaspoon cayenne pepper
¼ teaspoon garlic powder
¼ teaspoon garlic, minced
¼ teaspoon ground black pepper
1 (15 ounces / 425 g) can kidney beans, drained and rinsed
1 ear corn, kernels cut from the cob

1. Heat the oil (if desired) in a large skillet over medium-high heat and add the onion and bell pepper. Sauté until the onion is translucent, about 10 to 15 minutes. 2. Add the tomatoes, carrots, tomato paste, and ½ cup of water. Add the spices and herbs. Bring to a boil, cover, and turn down to simmer for 30 minutes. 3. Add the kidney beans and corn. Cook on a low simmer for another 15 minutes.

Per Serving:

calories: 259 | fat: 9g | protein: 13g | carbs: 36g | fiber: 10g

Mexikale Crisps

Prep time: 10 minutes | Cook time: 15 minutes | Serves 2

8 cups large kale leaves, chopped
2 tablespoons avocado oil (optional)
2 tablespoons nutritional yeast
1 teaspoon garlic powder
1 teaspoon ground cumin
½ teaspoon chili powder
1 teaspoon dried oregano
1 teaspoon dried cilantro
Salt and pepper to taste (optional)

1. Preheat the oven to 350°F (180°C) and line a baking tray with parchment paper. 2. Place the chopped kale leaves in a large bowl and use paper towels to absorb any remaining water. 3. Add the avocado oil (if using), nutritional yeast, garlic powder, ground cumin, chili powder, dried oregano, dried cilantro, salt (if desired), and pepper (if desired) to the bowl with the kale leaves. Mix and shake well to coat the kale leaves evenly with the seasonings. Feel free to adjust the amount of nutritional yeast and seasonings according to your taste preferences. 4. Spread out the seasoned kale leaves in a single layer on the prepared baking tray. 5. Bake the kale chips in the preheated oven for 10 to 15 minutes. Check the chips every minute after the 10-minute mark to prevent burning and remove them from the oven once they reach your preferred level of crispiness. 6. Take the baking tray out of the oven and set it aside to cool down. 7. Serve the Mexikale Crisps immediately or store them in a container for later. They can be enjoyed as a healthy snack or served as a side dish with your favorite Mexican-inspired meal.

Per Serving:

calories: 313 | fat: 14g | protein: 12g | carbs: 33g | fiber: 7g

Strawberry-Avocado Toast with Balsamic Glaze

Prep time: 5 minutes | Cook time: 0 minute | Serves 2

1 avocado, peeled, pitted, and quartered
4 whole-wheat bread slices, toasted
4 ripe strawberries, cut into ¼-inch slices
1 tablespoon balsamic glaze or reduction

1. Mash one-quarter of the avocado on a slice of toast. Layer one-quarter of the strawberry slices over the avocado, and finish with a drizzle of balsamic glaze. Repeat with the remaining ingredients, and serve.

Per Serving:

calories: 150 | fat: 8g | protein: 5g | carbs: 17g | fiber: 5g

Tropical Lemon Protein Bites

Prep time: 20 minutes | Cook time: 0 minutes | Makes 24 balls

1¾ cups cashews
¼ cup coconut flour
¼ cup unsweetened shredded coconut
3 tablespoons raw shelled hempseed
3 tablespoons maple syrup (optional)
3 tablespoons fresh lemon juice

1. Place the cashews in a food processor and process until very fine. Add the rest of the ingredients and process until well blended. Dump the mixture into a large bowl. 2. Take a clump of the dough and squeeze it into a ball. Keep squeezing and working it a few times until a ball is formed and solid.

Per Serving: (2 balls)

calories: 165 | fat: 9g | protein: 8g | carbs: 13g | fiber: 1g

Classic Italian Mushrooms

Prep time: 10 minutes | Cook time: 2 hours | Serves 4 to 6

2 pounds (907 g) white button mushrooms, stemmed
4 garlic cloves, minced
1 medium onion, sliced into half-moons
3 to 5 tablespoons store-bought low-sodium vegetable broth
3 teaspoons Italian seasoning
Ground black pepper
Salt (optional)

1. Cut any extra-large mushrooms in half. Place the mushrooms in the slow cooker. Add the garlic and onion. 2. Pour in the broth and sprinkle with the Italian seasoning. Season with black pepper and salt (if using). Stir to combine. Cover and cook on Low for 2 hours, or until the mushrooms are cooked through.

Per Serving:

calories: 68 | fat: 1g | protein: 8g | carbs: 12g | fiber: 3g

Kale Chips

Prep time: 5 minutes | Cook time: 20 minutes | Serves 4

¼ cup vegetable broth
1 tablespoon nutritional yeast
½ teaspoon garlic powder
½ teaspoon onion powder
6 ounces (170 g) kale, stemmed and cut into 2- to 3-inch pieces

1. Preheat the oven to 300°F (150°C). Line a baking sheet with parchment paper. 2. In a small bowl, mix together the broth, nutritional yeast, garlic powder, and onion powder. 3. Put the kale in a large bowl. Pour the broth and seasonings over the kale, and toss well to thoroughly coat. 4. Place the kale pieces on the baking sheet in an even layer. Bake for 20 minutes, or until crispy, turning the kale halfway through.

Per Serving:

calories: 41 | fat: 0g | protein: 4g | carbs: 7g | fiber: 2g

Legit Salsa

Prep time: 10 minutes | Cook time: 0 minutes | Makes 5 cups

2 jalapeño chile peppers, diced
1 yellow onion, quartered
1 small bunch fresh cilantro, leaves and tender stems
2 garlic cloves, halved
1 (28 ounces / 794 g) can diced tomatoes, undrained
¼ cup fresh lime juice
1 teaspoon sea salt (optional)

1. In a blender, combine all the ingredients and pulse until the desired texture is reached. Taste and add more salt (if using), if needed. Store in an airtight container in the refrigerator for up to 1 week.

Per Serving:

calories: 43 | fat: 0g | protein: 2g | carbs: 9g | fiber: 4g

Carrot Cake Balls

Prep time: 10 minutes | Cook time: 0 minutes | Makes 30 balls

2 cups unsweetened coconut flakes
1 carrot, coarsely chopped
2 cups old-fashioned oats
½ cup smooth natural peanut butter
½ cup pure maple syrup (optional)
¼ cup coarsely chopped pecans
1 teaspoon ground cinnamon
½ teaspoon vanilla extract
½ teaspoon ground ginger

1. In a sauté pan or skillet over medium-high heat, toast the coconut for 3 to 6 minutes, stirring or flipping occasionally, until lightly browned. Remove from the heat. 2. In a food processor, pulse the carrot until finely chopped but not puréed. Transfer the carrot to a bowl and set aside. 3. In the food processor (it is okay if there is a little carrot in the bowl from the previous step), combine the toasted coconut flakes and oats. Pulse until coarsely ground but not until the ingredients become a flour. 4. Return the carrots to the processor and add the peanut butter, maple syrup (if using), pecans, cinnamon, vanilla, and ginger. Pulse until the dough starts to form a ball. Divide the dough into 30 portions. Using your clean hands, press and form each portion into a ball. 5. Refrigerate in a sealable bag or airtight container for up to 2 weeks.

Per Serving: (2 balls)

calories: 203 | fat: 13g | protein: 4g | carbs: 19g | fiber: 4g

Oatmeal Granola Bar Bites

Prep time: 5 minutes | Cook time: 25 minutes | Serves 12

1½ cups rolled oats
⅓ cup unsweetened applesauce
¼ cup unsweetened natural peanut butter
2 tablespoons pure maple syrup
2 tablespoons ground flaxseed
1 tablespoon finely chopped pecans
1 tablespoon sliced almonds
1 tablespoon unsweetened raisins
1 tablespoon mini vegan chocolate chips

1. Preheat the oven to 350°F (180°C). Line an 8-by-8-inch baking dish and a baking sheet with parchment paper. 2. In a large bowl, using a wooden spoon or rubber spatula, mix together the oats, applesauce, peanut butter, maple syrup, flaxseed, pecans, almonds, raisins, and chocolate chips. 3. Using the back of a measuring cup, firmly press the mixture into the prepared baking dish. 4. Lift the pressed mixture out, and cut into 12 equal pieces. 5. Place the cut pieces in single layer on the prepared baking sheet. 6. Transfer the baking sheet to the oven, and bake for 20 to 25 minutes, flipping halfway through, or until the bars are golden brown. Remove from the oven.

Per Serving:

calories: 98 | fat: 5g | protein: 3g | carbs: 12g | fiber: 2g

Raw Date Chocolate Balls

Prep time: 20 minutes | Cook time: 0 minutes | Makes 24 balls

¾ cup sunflower seed kernels, ground
½ cup dates, pitted, chopped well
½ cup chopped walnuts
½ cup unsweetened cacao powder
½ cup maple syrup (optional)
½ cup creamy almond butter
½ cup old-fashioned oats (use gluten-free if desired)
¼ cup raw shelled hempseed
6 ounces (170 g) unsweetened coconut, for coating

1. Place the sunflower seeds, dates, walnuts, cacao powder, maple syrup (if desired), almond butter, oats, and hempseed in a large bowl. Mix well. 2. Pinch off pieces of dough and roll into twenty-four balls. Roll each ball in shredded coconut. Place in the refrigerator to harden for about 30 minutes.

Per Serving: (2 balls)

calories: 256 | fat: 16g | protein: 7g | carbs: 24g | fiber: 6g

Chapter 8 Desserts

Berry Chia Pudding

Prep time: 5 minutes | Cook time: 5 minutes | Makes 3 cups

4 cups fresh or frozen berries
1½ cups freshly squeezed orange juice
Pinch of fine sea salt (optional)
½ cup raw cashews or macadamia nuts
2 tablespoons coconut butter
2 teaspoons vanilla extract
6 tablespoons chia seeds

1. In a medium pot, combine the berries, orange juice, and salt (if using). Bring the mixture to a boil over high heat. 2. Reduce the heat to low, cover the pot, and simmer for 5 minutes, or until the berries have softened and released their juices. Remove from heat and allow to cool slightly. 3. Transfer the berry mixture to an upright blender. Add the cashews, coconut butter, and vanilla extract. Blend until completely smooth. 4. Pour the blended mixture into a wide-mouthed quart jar or a medium bowl. Add the chia seeds and whisk thoroughly, ensuring there are no clumps of seeds. 5. Allow the mixture to sit for a few minutes, then whisk again. Leave the whisk in place and refrigerate for at least 1 hour, or until completely chilled. Whisk the pudding every now and then to distribute the chia seeds evenly and help cool the pudding quickly. 6. The pudding will thicken further overnight. If it becomes too thick, you can stir in a splash of water or nut milk to adjust the consistency. 7. Store the berry chia pudding in an airtight glass jar or container in the refrigerator for up to 5 days.

Per Serving: (½ cup)
calories: 211 | fat: 14g | protein: 2g | carbs: 21g | fiber: 5g

Sweet Potato Spice Cake

Prep time: 5 minutes | Cook time: 45 minutes | Serves 6

1 sweet potato, cooked and peeled
½ cup unsweetened applesauce
½ cup plant-based milk
¼ cup maple syrup (optional)
1 teaspoon vanilla extract
2 cups whole-wheat flour
½ teaspoon baking soda
½ teaspoon ground cinnamon
¼ teaspoon ground ginger

1. Preheat the oven to 350°F (180°C). 2. In a large mixing bowl, use a fork or potato masher to mash the cooked and peeled sweet potato. 3. Mix in the unsweetened applesauce, plant-based milk, maple syrup (if desired), and vanilla extract. 4. Stir in the whole-wheat flour, baking soda, ground cinnamon, and ground ginger until the dry ingredients have been thoroughly combined with the wet ingredients. 5. Pour the batter into a nonstick baking dish or a baking dish lined with parchment paper. 6. Bake the cake for 45 minutes or until a knife inserted into the middle comes out clean. 7. Allow the cake to cool, then slice and serve.

Per Serving:
calories: 238 | fat: 1g | protein:5 g | carbs: 52g | fiber: 2g

Golden Banana Bread

Prep time: 5 minutes | Cook time: 50 minutes | Serves 10

Coconut oil, for pan (optional)
Dry Ingredients:
2 cups almond meal (ground almonds)
1 cup certified gluten-free rolled oats
¼ cup ground flaxseeds
2 tablespoons whole psyllium husk
2 teaspoons ground cinnamon
½ teaspoon ground turmeric
½ teaspoon Himalayan pink salt (optional)
Wet Ingredients:
4 very ripe bananas
¼ cup date syrup (optional)
3 tablespoons raw agave nectar (optional)
1 teaspoon vanilla bean powder
Suggested Add-Ins (optional):
½ cup raisins
½ cup chopped walnuts
1 cup diced banana
Garnish (optional):
1 very ripe banana, sliced
¼ cup chopped dark vegan chocolate

1. Preheat the oven to 375°F (190°C). If desired, coat the bottom and sides of an 8½ × 4½-inch loaf pan with coconut oil to prevent sticking. 2. In a high-speed blender or food processor, combine all the dry ingredients (almond meal, rolled oats, ground flaxseeds, psyllium husk, cinnamon, turmeric, and salt). Pulse together until well mixed, ensuring that some of the oats remain whole. Set aside. 3. In a large bowl, place the 4 ripe bananas and mash them using a fork until smooth. Add the date syrup, raw agave nectar (if using), and vanilla bean powder. Mix well to combine. 4. Add the dry mixture to the wet ingredients and mix until well combined. The mixture should form a dough-like texture due to the ground flaxseeds and psyllium husk. 5. Optionally, mix in your choice of add-ins such as raisins, chopped walnuts, or diced banana. 6. Scoop the dough mixture into the prepared loaf pan and press it firmly to remove any air pockets. For an optional garnish, slice a ripe banana lengthwise into 4 pieces and place them side by side on top of the loaf. 7. Bake the banana bread in the preheated oven for 50 minutes, or until a toothpick inserted into the center comes out clean. Ensure that the bread is thoroughly cooked. 8. Once baked, remove the loaf pan from the oven and allow the banana bread to cool in the pan. 9. If desired, garnish the cooled banana bread with additional banana slices or chopped dark vegan chocolate.

Per Serving:
calories: 284 | fat: 15g | protein: 8g | carbs: 39g | fiber: 7g

Chocolate Microwave Mug Cake

Prep time: 5 minutes | Cook time: 2 minutes | Serves 1

3 tablespoons whole-wheat flour
3 tablespoons unsweetened applesauce
1 tablespoon cocoa powder
1 tablespoon maple syrup (optional)
1 tablespoon plant-based milk
1 teaspoon vanilla extract
¼ teaspoon baking powder

1. In a microwave-safe coffee mug or bowl, combine the whole-wheat flour, unsweetened applesauce, cocoa powder, maple syrup (if desired), plant-based milk, vanilla extract, and baking powder. Stir the ingredients together until there are no clumps of dry flour left and the mixture is well combined. 2. Microwave the mug or bowl on high for 90 seconds, or until the cake has risen to the top of the mug and is cooked through. Cooking times may vary depending on the wattage of your microwave, so adjust accordingly. It's better to slightly undercook the cake than to overcook it, as it can become dry. 3. Once cooked, carefully remove the mug or bowl from the microwave and set it aside to cool for a minimum of 5 minutes. The cake will continue to cook slightly as it cools. 4. Serve the chocolate microwave mug cake as is or with your favorite toppings, such as a sprinkle of powdered sugar, a dollop of whipped cream or dairy-free alternative, or a drizzle of chocolate sauce.

Per Serving:
calories: 185 | fat: 1g | protein: 4g | carbs: 41g | fiber: 3g

Chocolate Tahini Muffins

Prep time: 10 minutes | Cook time: 20 minutes | Makes 12 muffins

½ teaspoon plus 2 tablespoons coconut oil, divided (optional)
2 tablespoons ground flaxseeds
6 tablespoons cold water
2 tablespoons tahini
2 tablespoons plain plant-based yogurt
1½ cups unsweetened plant-based milk
2 teaspoons baking powder
½ cup maple syrup (optional)
¼ cup unsweetened cocoa powder
½ teaspoon salt (optional)
2½ cups whole-wheat flour

1. Preheat the oven to 375°F (190°C). Lightly oil a 12-cup muffin tin with ½ tablespoon of coconut oil, or use muffin liners. 2. In a large bowl, mix together the ground flaxseeds and cold water to make 2 "flax eggs." Let the mixture sit for about 10 minutes to thicken. 3. In a microwave-safe bowl, microwave the remaining 2 tablespoons of coconut oil until melted, approximately 35 seconds. Be careful when handling the hot coconut oil. 4. Add the melted coconut oil, tahini, plant-based yogurt, plant-based milk, baking powder, and maple syrup (if using) to the bowl with the flax eggs. Mix well using a fork or whisk. 5. Add the cocoa powder, salt (if using), and whole-wheat flour to the bowl and mix until all the ingredients are well combined and there are no lumps. 6. Divide the batter evenly among the 12 muffin cups, filling each about three-fourths full. 7. Place the muffin tin in the preheated oven and immediately lower the heat to 350°F (180°C). Bake for approximately 20 minutes, or until a toothpick inserted into the center of a muffin comes out clean. 8. Remove the muffins from the oven and let them cool in the tin for a few minutes before transferring them to a wire rack to cool completely.

Per Serving:
calories: 187 | fat: 6g | protein: 5g | carbs: 31g | fiber: 4g

Almond-Date Energy Bites

Prep time: 5 minutes | Cook time: 0 minutes | Makes 24 bites

1 cup dates, pitted
1 cup unsweetened shredded coconut
¼ cup chia seeds
¾ cup ground almonds
¼ cup cocoa nibs or nondairy chocolate chips

1. In a food processor, combine the pitted dates, unsweetened shredded coconut, chia seeds, ground almonds, and cocoa nibs or nondairy chocolate chips. Process the mixture until it becomes crumbly and starts to stick together. If you don't have a food processor, you can mash soft Medjool dates by hand. If using harder baking dates, you may need to soak them and blend them in a blender. 2. Once the mixture is well combined and sticky, use your hands to form it into approximately 24 small balls. Place the energy bites on a baking sheet lined with parchment or waxed paper. 3. Put the baking sheet with the energy bites in the refrigerator for about 15 minutes to allow them to set.

Per Serving: (1 bite)
calories: 53 | fat: 3g | protein: 0g | carbs: 6g | fiber: 1g

Chocolate Dirt Yogurt Cup

Prep time: 15 minutes | Cook time: 0 minutes | Serves 2

¼ cup vegan chocolate chips
3 tablespoons sliced almonds
3 teaspoons cocoa powder, divided
2 teaspoons plus 2 tablespoons pure maple syrup, divided
1 cup nondairy vegan yogurt
2 tablespoons tahini
½ teaspoon vanilla extract
½ cup blueberries

1. In a food processor, combine the vegan chocolate chips, sliced almonds, 2 teaspoons of cocoa powder, and 2 teaspoons of pure maple syrup. Process the mixture until it becomes crumbly, resembling dirt. 2. In a medium bowl, mix together the nondairy vegan yogurt, remaining 2 tablespoons of pure maple syrup, tahini, vanilla extract, and the remaining 1 teaspoon of cocoa powder. Stir until well combined. 3. In small serving dishes or cups, start layering the dessert. Begin with 1 tablespoon of the chocolate "dirt" mixture as the base layer. Add ¼ cup of blueberries on top of the dirt layer, and then add a layer of the chocolate yogurt mixture. Repeat the layers for a second time, and finish with a sprinkling of the remaining chocolate "dirt" mixture on the top. 4. Refrigerate the yogurt cups until they are ready to be served.

Per Serving:
calories: 299 | fat: 17g | protein: 15g | carbs: 50g | fiber: 6g

Baked Apples

Prep time: 5 minutes | Cook time: 20 minutes | Serves 4

3 green apples, cored and evenly sliced
¼ cup apple juice
1½ teaspoons cinnamon
Optional Toppings:
1 tablespoon chopped pecans

1. Preheat the oven to 365ºF (185ºC). 2. In a 9 × 9-inch baking pan, spread the sliced apples in a single layer. 3. Pour the apple juice over the apples, ensuring they are evenly coated. 4. Sprinkle the cinnamon over the apples, distributing it evenly. 5. If desired, sprinkle the chopped pecans over the apples for added flavor and texture. 6. Cover the baking pan with aluminum foil to trap the moisture and flavors. 7. Place the pan in the preheated oven and bake for 15 to 18 minutes, or until the apples are a lighter color and have a soft texture. The baking time may vary depending on the thickness of the apple slices, so keep an eye on them to avoid overcooking. 8. Once baked, remove the pan from the oven and let the baked apples cool slightly before serving. 9. Serve the warm baked apples as is or with a scoop of vanilla ice cream, a dollop of whipped cream, or a sprinkle of powdered sugar, if desired.

Per Serving:
calories: 81 | fat: 0g | protein: 1g | carbs: 21g | fiber: 4g

Mango Sticky Rice

Prep time: 10 minutes | Cook time: 30 minutes | Serves 6

2½ cups water
1 cup short grain brown rice
½ cup light or full-fat coconut milk
2 tablespoons coconut sugar (optional)
1 to 2 tablespoons fresh lime juice, to taste
2 mangos, peeled and diced
Unsweetened shredded coconut (optional)

1. In a medium saucepan, bring the water to a boil over high heat. 2. Once the water is boiling, lower the heat to medium-low and stir in the brown rice. Cook the rice, stirring often, until the liquid is absorbed and the rice is tender, which usually takes about 30 minutes. 3. Remove the saucepan from the heat and stir in the coconut milk. If desired, add the coconut sugar for a touch of sweetness. Adjust the sweetness level according to your preference. 4. Add lime juice to taste, starting with 1 tablespoon and adding more if desired. Lime juice adds a refreshing tang to balance the sweetness of the dish. 5. Transfer the cooked rice mixture to a shallow glass dish, spreading it evenly. 6. Top the rice with the diced mangoes, arranging them in an attractive manner. 7. If desired, garnish the dish with a sprinkle of unsweetened shredded coconut to add a tropical flavor and texture. 8. Serve the mango sticky rice warm as a comforting dessert or allow it to cool and refrigerate it for a chilled treat. If refrigerating, wait to garnish with shredded coconut until just before serving.

Per Serving:
calories: 244 | fat: 5g | protein: 4g | carbs: 47g | fiber: 3g

Black Sesame–Ginger Quick Bread

Prep time: 20 minutes | Cook time: 50 minutes | Make 12 muffins

⅔ cup black sesame seeds
1 cup candied ginger
1½ cups plus 2 tablespoons whole wheat pastry flour
1 cup almond meal
2½ teaspoons baking powder
½ teaspoon salt (optional)
¾ cup almond milk, room temperature
¾ cup coconut sugar (optional)
½ cup melted coconut oil (optional)
2 tablespoons chia seeds
1 tablespoon fresh lemon juice
1 tablespoon ginger juice

1. Preheat the oven to 350ºF (180ºC). Line two muffin pans with liners. 2. In a food processor, pulse the black sesame seeds until ground. Transfer them to a large bowl and set aside. 3. Add the candied ginger and 2 tablespoons of the whole wheat pastry flour to the food processor. Pulse until the ginger is roughly chopped. The flour helps keep the ginger suspended in the batter as it bakes. 4. To the bowl with the ground sesame seeds, add the remaining whole wheat pastry flour, almond meal, baking powder, and salt (if using). Stir to combine, then stir in the ginger. Make a well in the center of the dry ingredients. 5. In the now-empty food processor, process the almond milk, coconut sugar (if using), melted coconut oil (if using), chia seeds, lemon juice, and ginger juice until completely combined. Transfer the mixture to the bowl with the dry ingredients and gently fold in the wet ingredients until just combined. The batter will be quite thick. 6. Scoop the batter into the prepared muffin pans, filling each liner about three-quarters full. Smooth the tops with a wet spatula. 7. Bake for approximately 30 minutes, or until a toothpick inserted into the center of a muffin comes out clean. 8. Allow the muffins to cool for 10 minutes in the pans, then transfer them to a wire rack to cool completely before slicing or peeling off the liners.

Per Serving: (2 muffins)
calories: 449 | fat: 30g | protein: 9g | carbs: 42g | fiber: 6g

Almond Truffles with Toasted Coconut

Prep time: 10 minutes | Cook time: 0 minutes | Makes 8

¼ cup almond meal
¼ cup toasted shredded coconut
2 tablespoons cacao powder
2 tablespoons maple syrup (optional)

1. In a medium bowl, combine the almond meal, toasted shredded coconut, cacao powder, and maple syrup (if using). Mix the ingredients together using a fork or by hand until you achieve a smooth consistency. 2. Scoop approximately 1 tablespoon of the dough and roll it between your hands to form a small ball. Repeat this process with the remaining dough to make a total of 8 truffles. 3. You can enjoy the almond truffles immediately, or if you prefer a firmer texture, refrigerate them for 10 to 20 minutes before serving.

Per Serving:
calories: 42 | fat: 3g | protein: 1g | carbs: 5g | fiber: 1g

Stone Fruit Compote

Prep time: 5 minutes | Cook time: 10 minutes | Makes 2½ cups

1½ pounds (680 g) ripe peaches, plums, apricots, or cherries
½ cup freshly squeezed orange juice or filtered water
Tiny pinch of fine sea salt (optional)
1 teaspoon arrowroot powder
2 teaspoons filtered water
½ teaspoon vanilla extract

1. If using peaches, plums, or apricots, halve and pit them. Cut each half into ½-inch wedges and slice the wedges in half crosswise. If using cherries, pit them. 2. Put the prepared fruit in a medium-sized pot and add the orange juice or filtered water. If desired, add a tiny pinch of fine sea salt. 3. Bring the mixture to a simmer over high heat. Once simmering, cover the pot, reduce the heat to low, and continue to simmer for 8 to 10 minutes, or until the fruit is soft and tender. 4. In a small cup, dissolve the arrowroot powder in the filtered water, creating a slurry. 5. Drizzle the arrowroot slurry into the pot, stirring constantly. Continue stirring until the compote returns to a simmer and thickens slightly. 6. Remove the pot from the heat and stir in the vanilla extract. 7. The stone fruit compote can be served warm or at room temperature. If not serving immediately, allow it to cool and then transfer to a sealed jar. Store the compote in the refrigerator for up to 5 days.

Per Serving: (½ cup)
calories: 77 | fat: 0g | protein: 1g | carbs: 19g | fiber: 2g

Coconut Crumble Bars

Prep time: 10 minutes | Cook time: 15 minutes | Makes 8 bars

2 cups raw and unsalted almonds
10 pitted dates
2 scoops soy protein isolate, chocolate flavor
½ cup cocoa powder
½ cup shredded coconut

1. Preheat the oven to 257°F (125°C) and line a baking sheet with parchment paper. 2. Put the almonds on the baking sheet and roast them for about 10 to 15 minutes or until they're fragrant. 3. Meanwhile, cover the dates with water in a small bowl and let them sit for about 10 minutes. Drain the dates after soaking and make sure no water is left. 4. Add the almonds, dates, chocolate protein and cocoa powder to a food processor and blend into a chunky mixture. 5. Alternatively, add all ingredients to a medium bowl, cover it, and process using a handheld blender. 6. Line a loaf pan with parchment paper. Add the almond mixture to the loaf pan, spread it out and press it down firmly until it's 1-inch-thick (2.5 cm) all over. 7. Add the shredded coconut in an even layer on top and press it down firmly to make it stick. 8. Divide into 8 bars, serve cold and enjoy! 9. Store the bars in an airtight container in the fridge, and consume within 6 days. Alternatively, store in the freezer for a maximum of 90 days.

Per Serving:
calories: 301 | fat: 21g | protein: 17g | carbs: 9g | fiber: 5g

Ginger Peach Muffins

Prep time: 10 minutes | Cook time: 27 minutes | Makes 12 muffins

1 cup unsweetened plant-based milk
1 tablespoon ground flaxseeds
1 teaspoon apple cider vinegar
2¼ cups spelt flour
¾ cup date sugar (optional)
1 tablespoon baking powder
½ teaspoon salt (optional)
2 teaspoons ground ginger
1 teaspoon ground cinnamon
¾ cup unsweetened applesauce
1 teaspoon pure vanilla extract
4 medium peaches, peeled, halved, pitted, and cut into ¼-inch slices (about 2 cups)

1. Preheat the oven to 350°F (180°C). Line a 12-cup muffin pan with silicone liners or have ready a nonstick or silicone muffin pan. 2. In a large measuring cup, use a fork to vigorously mix together the plant-based milk, flaxseeds, and vinegar. Mix for about a minute, or until it appears foamy. Set aside. 3. In a medium mixing bowl, sift together the flour, date sugar (if using), baking powder, salt (if using), ginger, and cinnamon. Make a well in the center of the mixture and pour in the milk mixture. Add the applesauce and vanilla and stir together with the milk mixture in the well. Incorporate the dry ingredients into the wet ingredients in the well just until the dry ingredients are moistened (do not overmix). Fold in the peaches. 4. Fill each muffin cup all the way to the top. Bake for 24 to 27 minutes, or until a knife inserted through the center comes out clean. 5. Remove the pan from the oven. Let the muffins cool completely, about 20 minutes, then carefully run a knife around the edges of each muffin to remove.

Per Serving:
calories: 146 | fat: 1g | protein: 4g | carbs: 25g | fiber: 3g

Apple-Oat Crisp

Prep time: 10 minutes | Cook time: 25 minutes | Serves 4 to 6

4 medium Granny Smith apples, cored and cut into ½-inch-thick slices
¾ cup pure maple syrup, divided
1 tablespoon lemon juice
½ teaspoon ground cinnamon
⅛ teaspoon ground nutmeg
¼ teaspoon tapioca starch
⅔ cup rolled oats
⅔ cup oat flour
⅓ cup unsweetened applesauce

1. Preheat the oven to 350°F (180°C). 2. In a medium bowl, mix together the apples, ½ cup of maple syrup, the lemon juice, cinnamon, nutmeg, and tapioca starch until the apples are well coated. 3. Spread the apples out in a single layer in an 8-by-8-inch glass baking dish or a 9-inch pie plate. 4. In a medium bowl, mix together the oats, oat flour, remaining ¼ cup of maple syrup, and the applesauce until well combined. Scoop the oat mixture in dollops onto the apples, and spread gently, trying to cover all the apples. 5. Transfer the baking dish to the oven, and bake for 20 to 25 minutes, or until the oat mixture is golden brown. Remove from the oven.

Per Serving:
calories: 344 | fat: 3g | protein: 5g | carbs: 80g | fiber: 9g

Two-Ingredient Peanut Butter Fudge

Prep time: 5 minutes | Cook time: 5 minutes | Serves 8

1 cup chocolate chips
½ cup natural peanut butter
Sea salt (optional)

1. In a small saucepan, combine the chocolate chips and peanut butter over medium-low heat. Stir often as you cook until the chocolate is melted and the mixture is well combined. This process usually takes about 5 minutes. 2. Once the mixture is smooth, use a spatula to transfer it into a pie plate or small glass container lined with parchment paper. Spread it evenly. If desired, sprinkle sea salt over the top for a touch of added flavor. 3. Place the pie plate or container in the refrigerator and let the fudge set for at least 1 hour, or ideally overnight. 4. Once the fudge has set, remove it from the refrigerator and slice it into squares. 5. Serve and enjoy! Alternatively, you can store the fudge in the refrigerator in an airtight container for up to 1 week.

Per Serving:
calories: 194 | fat: 12g | protein: 6g | carbs: 21g | fiber: 2g

Blueberry-Lime Sorbet

Prep time: 5 minutes | Cook time: 0 minutes | Serves 6

1 cup frozen blueberries
1 cup fresh blueberries
3 to 6 ice cubes
¼ cup unsweetened raisins
2 tablespoons lime juice

1. In a high-efficiency blender, combine the frozen blueberries, fresh blueberries, ice cubes, raisins, and lime juice. 2. Blend the ingredients for about 30 seconds or until smooth. You may need to use the tamping tool of the blender to move the frozen ingredients toward the blades. 3. Serve the blueberry-lime sorbet immediately.

Per Serving:
calories: 116 | fat: 1g | protein: 2g | carbs: 30g | fiber: 4g

Almond Anise Biscotti

Prep time: 5 minutes | Cook time: 40 minutes | Makes 18 slices

⅓ cup unsweetened plant-based milk
2 tablespoons ground flaxseeds
¾ cup date sugar (optional)
¼ cup unsweetened applesauce
¼ cup almond butter
½ teaspoon pure vanilla extract
½ teaspoon almond extract
1⅔ cups whole wheat pastry flour
2 tablespoons cornstarch
2 teaspoons baking powder
2 teaspoons anise seeds
½ teaspoon salt (optional)
1 cup slivered almonds

1. Preheat the oven to 350°F (180°C). Line a baking sheet with parchment paper or a Silpat baking mat. 2. In a large mixing bowl, use a fork to vigorously mix together the plant-based milk and ground flaxseeds until frothy. Mix in the date sugar (if using), unsweetened applesauce, almond butter, vanilla extract, and almond extract. 3. Sift in the whole wheat pastry flour, cornstarch, and baking powder. Add the anise seeds and salt (if using) to the bowl. Mix until all the ingredients are well combined. Knead in the slivered almonds using your hands, as the dough will be stiff. 4. On the prepared baking sheet, form the dough into a rectangle about 12 inches long by 3 to 4 inches wide. Bake for 26 to 28 minutes, or until lightly puffed and browned. Remove the baking sheet from the oven and let the dough cool for 30 minutes. 5. Increase the oven temperature to 375°F (190°C). Using a heavy, sharp knife, slice the biscotti loaf into ½-inch-thick slices. It is best to slice the loaf in one motion, pushing down, rather than sawing through the slices to prevent crumbling. Lay the slices flat on the baking sheet. 6. Bake the biscotti slices for 10 to 12 minutes, flipping them halfway through the baking time. They should become golden brown and crisp. Allow the biscotti to cool for a few minutes on the baking sheet before transferring them to cooling racks.

Per Serving:
calories: 127 | fat: 5g | protein: 3g | carbs: 16g | fiber: 2g

Apple Crisp

Prep time: 10 minutes | Cook time: 50 minutes | Serves 6 to 8

Filling:
3 pounds (1.4 kg) Granny Smith apples (about 8 apples), peeled, cored, and cut into ¼-inch slices
2 tablespoons cornstarch
1 teaspoon ground cinnamon
½ teaspoon ground ginger
⅛ teaspoon ground cloves
½ cup 100% pure maple syrup (optional)

Topping:
¼ cup 100% pure maple syrup (optional)
3 tablespoons cashew butter
2 tablespoons unsweetened applesauce
1 teaspoon pure vanilla extract
1½ cup rolled oats
½ teaspoon ground cinnamon
¼ teaspoon salt (optional)

1. Preheat the oven to 400°F (205°C). Line an 8 × 8-inch pan with parchment paper, making sure that the parchment goes all the way up the sides of the pan, or use an 8 × 8-inch nonstick or silicone baking pan. 2. In a large mixing bowl, combine the sliced apples, cornstarch, cinnamon, ginger, and cloves. Toss well to coat the apple slices evenly. If using maple syrup, pour it over the apple mixture and stir to combine. 3. Transfer the apple mixture to the prepared baking pan and spread it out evenly. 4. In a small bowl, stir together the maple syrup (if using), cashew butter, applesauce, and vanilla extract until relatively smooth. Add the rolled oats, ground cinnamon, and salt (if using), and toss to coat the oats evenly. 5. Spread the topping mixture over the apple mixture in the baking pan. 6. Place the pan in the preheated oven and bake for 20 minutes. Then, reduce the oven temperature to 350°F (180°C) and bake for an additional 30 minutes, or until the topping is golden and the apple filling is bubbly. 7. Remove the pan from the oven and place it on a cooling rack. Allow the crisp to cool slightly before serving.

Per Serving:
calories: 232 | fat: 4g | protein: 4g | carbs: 45g | fiber: 8g

Pumpkin Bread Pudding

Prep time: 10 minutes | Cook time: 25 minutes | Serves 8

1¼ cups pumpkin purée (a little over ½ of a 15 ounces / 425 g can)
1 cup unsweetened plant-based milk
½ cup 100% maple syrup (optional)
2 teaspoons pure vanilla extract
2 tablespoons cornstarch
½ teaspoon salt (optional)
½ teaspoon ground cinnamon
¾ teaspoon ground ginger
¼ teaspoon ground nutmeg
¼ teaspoon ground allspice
⅛ teaspoon ground cloves
8 slices stale whole wheat bread, cut into 1-inch cubes (about 6 cups)
½ cup golden raisins

1. Preheat the oven to 350°F (180°C). Grease or line an 8 × 8-inch nonstick or silicone baking pan. 2. In a large bowl, whisk together the pumpkin purée, plant-based milk, maple syrup (if using), and vanilla extract. 3. Add the cornstarch, salt (if using), cinnamon, ginger, nutmeg, allspice, and cloves to the bowl. Whisk well to combine all the ingredients. 4. Stir in the bread cubes and golden raisins. Toss the mixture gently to ensure that all the bread cubes are coated with the pumpkin mixture. 5. Transfer the mixture to the prepared baking pan, spreading it out evenly. 6. Bake in the preheated oven for 25 minutes, or until the top is golden brown and the pudding is firm to the touch. 7. Remove from the oven and let it cool slightly. Serve the pumpkin bread pudding warm.

Per Serving:
calories: 192 | fat: 1g | protein: 4g | carbs: 31g | fiber: 2g

Pumpkin Spice Bread

Prep time: 5 minutes | Cook time: 1 hour | Makes one 8 × 4-inch loaf

2 cups whole wheat pastry flour
2 teaspoons baking powder
1 teaspoon baking soda
2 teaspoons ground cinnamon
½ teaspoon ground ginger
¼ teaspoon ground allspice
⅛ teaspoon ground cloves
1 (15 ounces / 425 g) can pumpkin purée (about 2 cups)
½ cup 100% pure maple syrup (optional)
⅓ cup apple butter
1 teaspoon pure vanilla extract
½ cup golden raisins (optional)
½ cup chopped walnuts (optional)

1. Preheat the oven to 350°F (180°C). Grease an 8 × 4-inch nonstick or silicone baking pan and set it aside. 2. In a large mixing bowl, sift together the whole wheat pastry flour, baking powder, baking soda, cinnamon, ginger, allspice, and cloves. 3. In a separate mixing bowl, vigorously mix together the pumpkin puree, maple syrup (if using), apple butter, and vanilla extract. 4. Pour the wet mixture into the dry mixture and combine until everything is evenly moistened. The batter will be stiff. Fold in the golden raisins and chopped walnuts, if desired. 5. Spoon the batter into the prepared loaf pan, distributing it evenly along the length of the pan. Do not spread the batter to the edges, as it will spread as it bakes. 6. Bake for 50 to 60 minutes, or until a knife inserted through the center comes out clean. 7. Remove the pan from the oven and let the bread cool for at least 30 minutes. Run a knife around the edges and carefully invert the loaf onto a cooling rack. Make sure the bread is fully cooled before slicing.

Per Serving:
calories: 180 | fat: 3g | protein: 4g | carbs: 30g | fiber: 4g

Molasses ginger Oat Cookie Balls

Prep time: 10 minutes | Cook time: 15 minutes | Makes 1 dozen cookies

1 cup pitted dates
3 tablespoons unsalted, unsweetened almond butter
2 tablespoons blackstrap molasses
1 teaspoon vanilla extract
1 cup oat flour
¼ cup rolled oats
½ teaspoon baking powder
1 teaspoon ground ginger
½ teaspoon ground cinnamon
⅛ teaspoon ground nutmeg
⅛ teaspoon ground cardamom

1. Preheat the oven to 350°F (180°C). Line a baking sheet with parchment paper. 2. In a food processor, combine the pitted dates and almond butter. Blend until you achieve a creamy paste-like consistency. Transfer the mixture to a large bowl. 3. Stir in the blackstrap molasses and vanilla extract into the date and almond butter mixture. 4. In a medium bowl, thoroughly combine the oat flour, rolled oats, baking powder, ground ginger, ground cinnamon, ground nutmeg, and ground cardamom. 5. Fold the flour mixture into the molasses mixture, combining well to form a dough. 6. Take about 1 tablespoon of dough and roll it into a ball. Repeat this process to make 12 cookie balls. Place them on the prepared baking sheet about 1 inch apart. 7. Bake the cookie balls for 12 to 15 minutes, or until the edges are golden brown and the cookie balls are slightly firm to the touch. 8. Remove the cookie balls from the oven and let them cool on a wire rack before enjoying.

Per Serving:
calories: 275 | fat: 10g | protein: 6g | carbs: 44g | fiber: 6g

Vanilla Nice Cream

Prep time: 5 minutes | Cook time: 0 minutes | Serves 2

2 frozen sliced bananas
½ teaspoon vanilla extract
3 tablespoons unsweetened plant-based milk
1 teaspoon maple syrup (optional)

1. In a food processor or high-speed blender, combine the bananas, vanilla, plant-based milk, and maple syrup (if using) and blend until smooth and creamy. You will have to stop the machine to scrape down the sides two or three times before the desired consistency of soft-serve ice cream is achieved. 2. Serve immediately or store in an airtight container and freeze for later. Be sure to pull it out of the freezer 10 to 15 minutes before you want to serve it to let it soften. Otherwise, it will be hard to scoop.

Per Serving:
calories: 130 | fat: 1g | protein: 2g | carbs: 30g | fiber: 3g

Quinoa Banana Muffins

Prep time: 10 minutes | Cook time: 24 minutes | Makes 12 muffins

2 cups spelt flour
2 teaspoons baking powder
½ teaspoon baking soda
¾ teaspoon salt (optional)
½ teaspoon ground cinnamon
½ cup date sugar (optional)
1 cup mashed banana (from about 2 large bananas, peeled)
¼ cup plant-based milk
⅓ cup unsweetened applesauce
2 teaspoons pure vanilla extract
1 cup cooked quinoa, drained and rinsed until cool

1. Preheat the oven to 350°F (180°C). Line a 12-cup muffin pan with silicone liners or prepare a nonstick or silicone muffin pan. 2. In a medium mixing bowl, sift together the spelt flour, baking powder, baking soda, salt (if using), cinnamon, and date sugar (if using). Create a well in the center of the mixture. 3. Add the mashed banana, plant-based milk, applesauce, and vanilla to the well. Stir together the wet ingredients in the well. 4. Gradually incorporate the dry ingredients into the wet ingredients, mixing just until the dry ingredients are moistened. Be careful not to overmix. Fold in the cooked quinoa. 5. Fill each muffin cup all the way to the top with the batter. 6. Bake for 22 to 24 minutes, or until a knife inserted into the center of a muffin comes out clean. 7. Allow the muffins to cool completely for about 20 minutes. Then, carefully run a knife around the edges of each muffin to remove them from the pan.

Per Serving:

calories: 126 | fat: 0g | protein: 3g | carbs: 24g | fiber: 3g

Walnut Brownies

Prep time: 10 minutes | Cook time: 20 minutes | Makes 12 brownies

3 ounces (85 g) extra-firm silken tofu, drained
⅓ cup pitted prunes, rough stems removed
½ cup unsweetened plant-based milk, heated until very hot but not boiling
¾ cup 100% pure maple syrup (optional)
½ cup plus 2 tablespoons unsweetened cocoa powder
¾ cup water, heated until very hot but not boiling
2 teaspoons pure vanilla extract
1 cup whole wheat pastry flour
½ teaspoon baking soda
½ teaspoon salt (optional)
½ cup walnuts, roughly chopped

1. Preheat the oven to 325°F (165°C). Line an 8 × 8-inch pan with a 10-inch square of parchment paper or have an 8 × 8-inch nonstick or silicone baking pan ready. 2. In a blender, crumble the tofu and add the pitted prunes. Pour in the hot plant-based milk and blend for about 30 seconds until smooth. Add the maple syrup (if using) and continue blending until relatively smooth, without any tofu chunks. Scrape down the sides of the blender with a rubber spatula to ensure all ingredients are incorporated. 3. In a mixing bowl, sift the cocoa powder. Add the hot water and mix with a fork until well combined, creating a thick chocolate sauce. 4. Add the prune mixture from the blender to the chocolate sauce in the mixing bowl. Stir to combine and mix in the vanilla extract. 5. Sift in half of the whole wheat pastry flour and add the baking soda and salt (if using). Mix well. Add the remaining flour and fold in the chopped walnuts. 6. Spread the brownie batter evenly into the prepared baking pan. The batter will be thick, but it will spread as it bakes, so there's no need to push it into the corners. 7. Bake for 17 to 20 minutes. The top should be set and firm to the touch. 8. Remove the pan from the oven and let it cool for at least 20 minutes. Once cooled, slice the brownies into 12 squares and serve.

Per Serving:

calories: 148 | fat: 4g | protein: 3g | carbs: 26g | fiber: 2g

Graham Crackers

Prep time: 5 minutes | Cook time: 12 minutes | Makes 12 crackers

1½ cups spelt flour, plus additional for dusting
¼ cup plus 1 tablespoon date sugar (optional)
½ teaspoon baking soda
1 teaspoon ground cinnamon
½ teaspoon salt (optional)
¼ cup unsweetened applesauce
2 tablespoons molasses
1 teaspoon pure vanilla extract
¼ cup unsweetened plant-based milk
1 tablespoon ground flaxseeds

1. Preheat the oven to 350°F (180°C). 2. In a large bowl, mix together the flour, ¼ cup of date sugar (if using), the baking soda, ½ teaspoon of the cinnamon, and the salt (if using). Make a well in the middle of the bowl and add the applesauce, molasses, and vanilla. Mix the ingredients together with a fork until well combined and crumbly. 3. In a large measuring cup, whisk together the plant-based milk and ground flaxseeds. Pour the mixture into the dough and stir to combine. Use your hands to knead the dough a few times until it holds together; add an extra tablespoon of milk or water if needed. You should be able to form a pliable ball of dough. 4. Line a work surface with parchment paper or a Silpat baking mat. Place the dough on the parchment and flatten it into a rectangle. Sprinkle the dough lightly with spelt flour. Use a rolling pin to roll the dough into a roughly 10 × 14-inch rectangle. The dough should be about ⅛-inch thick. 5. Using a sharp knife, trim the edges so that you have a relatively even 8 × 12-inch rectangle. Cut the dough into eight crackers. Transfer the parchment onto a large baking sheet. Gather up the remaining scraps of dough and form them into a ball. On a separate sheet of parchment paper, roll out the scraps into a 4 × 8-inch rectangle, or whatever size you can manage to make. Trim the edges and cut into four crackers. Transfer the parchment to a baking sheet. 6. Mix together the remaining tablespoon of date sugar (if using) and ½ teaspoon of cinnamon and sprinkle evenly over the crackers. Score each cracker with a fork four times in two columns. You don't need to poke all the way through. Bake for 10 to 12 minutes. 7. Remove the crackers from the oven and let cool on the baking sheet for 5 minutes, and then transfer to a cooling rack to cool completely.

Per Serving:

calories: 78 | fat: 0g | protein: 2g | carbs: 16g | fiber: 2g

Salted Chocolate Truffles

Prep time: 5 minutes | Cook time: 5 minutes | Makes 18 truffles

12 ounces (340 g) vegan dark chocolate
⅔ cup full-fat coconut milk
1 teaspoon fine sea salt (optional)
½ cup unsweetened cocoa powder

1. Set up a double boiler with a medium saucepan and medium, nonreactive bowl. Break up the chocolate into pieces, and transfer them to the bowl along with the coconut milk and sea salt, if using. 2. Place the bowl over the simmering water. Let it sit for about a minute. Then, start stirring occasionally with a spatula. Once you have a melted, smooth mixture, remove the bowl from the heat. Let the truffle mixture cool to room temperature, and then place it in the refrigerator for at least 6 hours, preferably overnight. 3. Line a small baking sheet with parchment paper. 4. Once the truffle mixture is set and fully chilled, scoop out full tablespoons onto the parchment-lined sheet. Once you've scooped out all the truffles, transfer the baking sheet to the refrigerator for 30 minutes. 5. Place the cocoa powder in a shallow bowl. 6. Remove the scooped truffle mixture from the refrigerator. Working quickly, roll the portioned mixture into balls. Then, roll those balls in the cocoa powder. Try to gently shake off any excess cocoa powder, and then place the truffles back on the baking sheet. 7. The truffles will keep in a sealed container in the refrigerator for about 1 week.

Per Serving: (2 truffles)
calories: 278 | fat: 21g | protein: 4g | carbs: 21g | fiber: 6g

Pear Chia Pudding

Prep time: 10 minutes | Cook time: 10 minutes | Makes 3 cups

3 firm but ripe pears, peeled, cored, and cut into 1-inch dice
½ cup freshly squeezed orange juice or ¼ cup filtered water
Pinch of fine sea salt (optional)
½ cup raw cashews or macadamia nuts
2 tablespoons coconut butter
1 teaspoon vanilla extract
6 tablespoons chia seeds

1. Combine the pears, orange juice or water, and salt, if using, in a medium pot and bring to a boil over high heat. Cover, reduce the heat to low, and simmer for 8 to 10 minutes, until the pears have cooked through. Remove from the heat and allow to cool slightly. Transfer the mixture to an upright blender, add the cashews, coconut butter, and vanilla, and blend until completely smooth. Pour into a widemouthed quart jar or a medium bowl, add the chia seeds, and whisk thoroughly, making sure there are no clumps of seeds hiding anywhere. Allow to sit for a few minutes and then whisk again. Leave the whisk in place and refrigerate for at least 1 hour, or until completely chilled, whisking every now and then to distribute the chia seeds evenly and to help cool the pudding quickly. The pudding will thicken further overnight; if it gets too thick, stir in a splash of water or nut milk. Store the pudding in an airtight glass jar or other container in the fridge for up to 5 days.

Per Serving: (½ cup)
calories: 188 | fat: 13g | protein: 2g | carbs: 18g | fiber: 5g

Zesty Orange-Cranberry Energy Bites

Prep time: 10 minutes | Cook time: 0 minutes | Makes 12 bites

2 tablespoons almond butter, or cashew or sunflower seed butter
2 tablespoons maple syrup or brown rice syrup (optional)
¾ cup cooked quinoa
¼ cup sesame seeds, toasted
1 tablespoon chia seeds
½ teaspoon almond extract or vanilla extract
Zest of 1 orange
1 tablespoon dried cranberries
¼ cup ground almonds

1. In a medium bowl, mix together the nut or seed butter and syrup (if using) until smooth and creamy. 2. Stir in the rest of the ingredients, and mix to make sure the consistency is holding together in a ball. 3. Form the mix into 12 balls. Place them on a baking sheet lined with parchment or waxed paper and put in the fridge to set for about 15 minutes.

Per Serving: (1 bite)
calories: 71 | fat: 4g | protein: 2g | carbs: 6g | fiber: 1g

Peach Cobbler

Prep time: 15 minutes | Cook time: 1 to 2 hours | Serves 6 to 8

Filling:
2 (15 ounces / 425 g) cans peaches in juice
½ teaspoon ground cinnamon
½ teaspoon ground ginger
3 tablespoons maple syrup or date syrup (optional)
2 tablespoons cornstarch

Topping:
1 cup rolled oats
¼ teaspoon ground cinnamon
2 tablespoons coconut cream
1 tablespoon liquid from the canned peaches
4 tablespoons date syrup (optional)

1. Make the filling: Remove the peaches from the cans, reserving the juice. Slice the peaches into bite-size chunks and put them in the slow cooker. Stir in the cinnamon, ginger, syrup (if using), and cornstarch. 2. Make the topping and cook: In a medium bowl, combine the oats, cinnamon, coconut cream, canned peach liquid, and date syrup (if using). Stir together until the oats are wet and crumbly. Sprinkle over the peaches in the slow cooker. 3. To keep the condensation that forms on the inside of the lid away from the topping, stretch a clean dish towel or several layers of paper towels over the top of the slow cooker, but not touching the food, and place the lid on top of the towel(s). If you skip this step, you will have a soggy result. Cook on High for 1 to 2 hours or on Low for 2 to 3 hours.

Per Serving:
calories: 196 | fat: 2g | protein: 3g | carbs: 44g | fiber: 4g

Chapter 9 Salads

Summer Quinoa Salad

Prep time: 15 minutes | Cook time: 25 minutes | Serves 4

1 cup dry quinoa
2 cups vegetable stock
2 tablespoons balsamic vinegar
1 tablespoon extra-virgin olive oil (optional)
1 tablespoon fresh lemon juice
Sea salt and ground black pepper, to taste
¼ cup raisins, soaked in water for 10 minutes and drained
1 carrot, finely grated
1 cup kale, stems removed and thinly sliced
2 scallions, thickly sliced
2 tablespoons sunflower seeds
2 tablespoons pepitas

1. If the quinoa is not prerinsed, place it in a fine-mesh sieve and rinse thoroughly with cool water to remove any bitter saponins. Drain well. 2. In a medium pot, combine the rinsed quinoa and stock. Bring to a boil, then reduce the heat to low and cover the pot. Cook for about 20 minutes, or until the quinoa is cooked through and the liquid is absorbed. Let it stand for 10 minutes, then transfer the cooked quinoa to a shallow freezer container and place it in the freezer for 20 minutes to quickly cool it down. 3. In a small bowl, whisk together the vinegar, oil (if using), and lemon juice to make the dressing. Season with salt and pepper to taste. 4. Once the quinoa is chilled, transfer it to a medium bowl. Add the raisins, carrot, kale, scallions, sunflower seeds, and pepitas. Drizzle the dressing over the salad and toss well to combine all the ingredients.

Per Serving:
calories: 283 | fat: 10g | protein: 8g | carbs: 40g | fiber: 4g

Bulgur Lettuce Cups

Prep time: 10 minutes | Cook time: 20 minutes | Serves 2 to 4

Sauce:
½ cup unsweetened natural peanut butter
¼ cup soy sauce
3 tablespoons seasoned rice vinegar
2 tablespoons lime juice
1 teaspoon liquid aminos
1 teaspoon sriracha
Cups:
1 cup bulgur
½ cup soy sauce
¼ cup seasoned rice vinegar
½ teaspoon garlic powder
½ teaspoon ground ginger
¼ teaspoon red pepper flakes
1 cup shredded carrots
1 cup shredded cabbage
½ cup sliced scallions, green and white parts
1 head red leaf lettuce or Bibb lettuce

Make the Sauce: In a small bowl, whisk together the peanut butter, soy sauce, vinegar, lime juice, liquid aminos, and sriracha until well combined. Set the sauce aside. Make the Bulgur: In a medium saucepan, cook the bulgur according to the package instructions, typically for about 12 minutes. Once cooked, remove the saucepan from the heat and drain any excess water from the bulgur. Make the Flavorful Mixture: In a small bowl, combine the soy sauce, vinegar, garlic powder, ginger, and red pepper flakes. Mix well to create a flavorful mixture. 1. Combine the Ingredients: In a large bowl, add the cooked bulgur and the prepared soy sauce mixture. 2. Then, add the carrots, cabbage, and scallions to the bowl. 3. Mix everything thoroughly to ensure the flavors are well distributed. 4. Assemble the Lettuce Cups: Scoop the bulgur mixture into individual lettuce leaves, creating lettuce cups. Drizzle each lettuce cup with the prepared peanut sauce for added flavor.

Per Serving:
calories: 532 | fat: 17g | protein: 25g | carbs: 79g | fiber: 18g

Garden Salad with Sumac Vinaigrette

Prep time: 15 minutes | Cook time: 0 minutes | Serves 2

Dressing:
Juice of 1 lemon
1 tablespoon cider vinegar
2 tablespoons extra-virgin olive oil (optional)
1 tablespoon agave nectar (optional)
1 tablespoon minced or grated fresh ginger
½ teaspoon sumac powder
½ teaspoon ground cumin
Salt and freshly ground black pepper, to taste (optional)
Salad:
½ medium cucumber, chopped
1 small zucchini, chopped
1 bell pepper, seeded and chopped
2 small carrots, chopped
1 cup cherry tomatoes, halved
½ cup fresh parsley, finely chopped
2 tablespoons finely chopped fresh mint

1. Start by preparing the dressing. In a large bowl, combine all the dressing ingredients, including the optional salt and black pepper to taste. Mix well to ensure the ingredients are thoroughly combined. 2. Next, prepare the salad. Add the cucumber, zucchini, bell pepper, carrots, tomatoes, and herbs to the bowl with the dressing. Mix everything together thoroughly, ensuring that the vinaigrette coats all the vegetables evenly. 3. Serve the Garden Salad with Sumac Vinaigrette and enjoy!

Per Serving:
calories: 189 | fat: 14g | protein: 3g | carbs: 15g | fiber: 4g

Blueprint: Lifesaving Bowl

Prep time: 20 minutes | Cook time: 0 minutes | Makes 1 bowl

1 cup cooked quinoa
1 cup shredded or chopped raw vegetables
½ avocado, sliced
¼ cup prepared kimchi
2 tablespoons nutritional yeast
1 tablespoon lime juice or vinegar
Sesame or hemp seeds

1. Start by selecting a base for your bowl. This can be a grain such as quinoa, brown rice, or couscous, or you can opt for a bed of leafy greens like spinach or kale. 2. Add a variety of colorful vegetables to your bowl. This can include sliced bell peppers, cherry tomatoes, shredded carrots, cucumber, radishes, or any other vegetables of your choice. This adds freshness, crunch, and a range of nutrients. 3. Incorporate a source of protein. This can be grilled chicken, tofu, tempeh, chickpeas, lentils, or any other protein-rich ingredient. If you prefer seafood, you can add grilled shrimp or flaked salmon. 4. Include a healthy fat component. This can be sliced avocado, toasted nuts or seeds, or a drizzle of olive oil. Healthy fats provide satiety and contribute to the overall flavor and texture of the bowl. 5. For added flavor and complexity, consider including herbs, spices, or dressings. Fresh herbs like cilantro, basil, or mint can add a burst of freshness. Sprinkle some spices like cumin, paprika, or turmeric for extra flavor. You can also drizzle a dressing of your choice, such as a tangy vinaigrette or a creamy tahini sauce. 6. Finish off with a garnish. This can be a sprinkle of sesame seeds, chopped scallions, or a squeeze of lemon or lime juice. 7. Layer all the ingredients in a bowl in the order of your preference, considering both aesthetics and taste. 8. Once all the ingredients are assembled, it's time to dig in and enjoy your lifesaving bowl! Mix the ingredients together to combine flavors, and savor each bite.

Per Serving: (¼ bowl)
calories: 149 | fat: 5g | protein: 6g | carbs: 20g | fiber: 6g

Zingy Melon and Mango Salad

Prep time: 5 minutes | Cook time: 0 minutes | Serves 2

1 large mango, peeled, pitted, and cut into 1-inch pieces (about 1 cup)
½ small cantaloupe or watermelon, peeled and cut into 1-inch pieces (about 2 cups)
Juice of 1 lime
¼ cup chopped fresh cilantro
1 teaspoon chili powder

1. In a large bowl, combine the mango and cantaloupe cubes. 2. Add the freshly squeezed lime juice and finely chopped cilantro to the bowl. 3. Gently toss the ingredients together until the fruits are coated with the lime juice and cilantro. 4. Spoon the salad into individual serving bowls or plates. 5. Sprinkle a pinch of chili powder over the top of each serving for an extra zingy kick. 6. Serve and enjoy the refreshing and flavorful melon and mango salad.

Per Serving:
calories: 171 | fat: 1g | protein: 3g | carbs: 42g | fiber: 5g

Lemon Garlic Chickpeas Salad

Prep time: 10 minutes | Cook time: 0 minutes | Serves 2

1 cup cooked or canned chickpeas
½ cup fresh spinach
¼ cup lemon juice
¼ cup tahini
1 clove garlic minced
¼ cup water
Optional Toppings:
Fresh cilantro
Raisins

1. If using dry chickpeas, soak and cook ⅓ cup of dry chickpeas according to the package instructions until tender. Drain and set aside. Alternatively, you can use canned chickpeas for convenience. 2. In a small airtight container or bowl, combine tahini, minced garlic, lemon juice, and water. 3. Whisk the tahini, lemon juice, garlic, and water together until the dressing becomes thinner and smooth. Add more water if you prefer a thinner consistency. Alternatively, you can shake the container with the ingredients to thoroughly mix them. 4. Rinse the spinach thoroughly under running water in a strainer to clean it. Drain well. 5. In a large bowl, combine the spinach and cooked chickpeas. 6. Mix the spinach and chickpeas together, ensuring they are well coated with the dressing. 7. Divide the salad between two bowls. Garnish with tangerines and any optional toppings you prefer. 8. Serve and enjoy! You can store any leftovers in an airtight container in the refrigerator for up to 2 days. If desired, you can also freeze the salad for a maximum of 30 days and thaw it at room temperature before serving. The salad can be enjoyed cold.

Per Serving:
calories: 406 | fat: 22g | protein: 19g | carbs: 33g | fiber: 11g

Larb Salad

Prep time: 15 minutes | Cook time: 5 minutes | Serves 4

1 teaspoon canola oil (optional)
1 (14 ounces / 397 g) block extra-firm tofu, pressed and crumbled
3 tablespoons lime juice, divided
2½ tablespoons minced cilantro
2 tablespoons soy sauce
1 green onion, sliced
½ tablespoon minced jalapeño
¼ cup thinly sliced red, white, or yellow onion
2 tablespoons minced mint
8 iceberg or romaine lettuce leaves

1. Heat oil (if desired) in a saucepan over medium heat. Add the tofu and 1 tablespoon of lime juice. Sauté for 4 to 5 minutes, or until the tofu is lightly browned. 2. Transfer the cooked tofu to a medium bowl. Add the remaining 2 tablespoons of lime juice, cilantro, soy sauce, green onion, jalapeño, onion, and mint. Mix well to combine all the ingredients. 3. To serve, place the larb mixture inside lettuce leaves, using them as cups or wraps for the salad. You can also garnish with additional cilantro or mint if desired.

Per Serving:
calories: 245 | fat: 10g | protein: 18g | carbs: 26g | fiber: 9g

Tomato, Corn and Bean Salad

Prep time: 20 minutes | Cook time: 10 minutes | Serves 4

6 ears corn
3 large tomatoes, diced
2 cups cooked navy beans, or 1 (15 ounces / 425 g) can, drained and rinsed
1 medium red onion, peeled and diced small
1 cup finely chopped basil
2 tablespoons balsamic vinegar
Salt and freshly ground black pepper, to taste

1. Start by bringing a large pot of water to a boil. Once boiling, add the corn and cook for 7 to 10 minutes, until tender. Drain the water from the pot, and then rinse the corn under cold water to cool it down. Once cooled, cut the kernels from the cob. 2. In a large bowl, combine the cooked corn kernels, tomatoes, beans, onion, basil, balsamic vinegar, and season with salt and pepper to taste. Toss everything together until well mixed. 3. Chill the Tomato, Corn, and Bean Salad in the refrigerator for at least 1 hour before serving. This will allow the flavors to meld together and enhance the taste of the salad.

Per Serving:
calories: 351 | fat: 2g | protein: 15g | carbs: 66g | fiber: 17g

Purple Potato and Kale Salad

Prep time: 10 minutes | Cook time: 15 minutes | Serves 4

5 to 6 small purple potatoes
2 cups chopped kale
½ cup chopped tomatoes
1¾ teaspoons fresh lime juice
1 cup chopped cilantro, plus more for garnish
1 clove garlic, peeled and chopped
¼ cup plus 2 tablespoons tahini
½ teaspoon salt, or to taste (optional)
1 teaspoon cayenne pepper

1. In a medium saucepan, place the purple potatoes and add enough water to cover them. Bring the water to a boil, then reduce the heat to medium and cook the potatoes for about 10 minutes or until they are tender when pierced with a fork. Drain the potatoes and allow them to cool. Once cooled, you may choose to peel them or leave the skin on, then cut them into ½-inch cubes. 2. In a skillet or saucepan, add the kale and tomatoes. Sauté them over medium heat for 2 to 3 minutes, until the kale has slightly softened. To prevent sticking, add 1 to 2 tablespoons of water at a time. Add ¼ teaspoon of lime juice to the skillet and let the mixture cool. 3. In a blender, combine the cilantro, garlic, tahini, salt (if desired), cayenne pepper, remaining 1½ teaspoons of lime juice, and 2 tablespoons of water. Blend the ingredients until you have a smooth dressing. 4. To serve, create a bed of the cooked kale and tomatoes in a large salad bowl. Top the kale and tomatoes with the boiled purple potato cubes. Spoon the dressing over the salad, coating the ingredients. If desired, garnish with chopped cilantro.

Per Serving:
calories: 261 | fat: 7g | protein: 7g | carbs: 43g | fiber: 7g

Mock Tuna Salad

Prep time: 10 minutes | Cook time: 0 minutes | Serves 4

Salad:
2 cups raw sunflower seeds, soaked in water for 2 hours
3 to 4 ribs celery, diced
2 scallions, diced
2 tablespoons dulse flakes
¼ cup fresh dill
Dressing:
⅔ cup hemp hearts
¼ cup coconut water or purified water
3 cloves garlic, peeled
½ cup fresh lemon juice
1 teaspoon sea salt (optional)
2 tablespoons stone ground mustard

1. Start by preparing the salad. In a food processor, pulse the sunflower seeds until they reach a slightly chunky pâté consistency. Transfer the pulsed seeds to a bowl. 2. Add the celery, scallions, dulse flakes, and dill to the bowl with the sunflower seed pâté. Stir the ingredients well to combine. Set the salad aside. 3. Next, prepare the dressing. In a blender, combine all the dressing ingredients. Blend the mixture until it becomes smooth and well combined. 4. Pour the dressing over the salad in the bowl. Toss the salad gently to ensure the dressing is evenly distributed and coats all the ingredients. Serve the Mock Tuna Salad and enjoy!

Per Serving:
calories: 403 | fat: 30g | protein: 13g | carbs: 19g | fiber: 9g

Fava Bean Salad

Prep time: 25 minutes | Cook time: 0 minutes | Serves 4

4 cups cooked fava beans, or 2 (15 ounces / 425 g) cans, drained and rinsed
2 large tomatoes, chopped
4 green onions (white and green parts), sliced
1 large cucumber, peeled, halved, seeded, and diced
½ cup finely chopped cilantro
1 jalapeño pepper, minced (for less heat, remove the seeds)
Zest of 1 lemon and juice of 2 lemons
2 cloves garlic, peeled and minced
1 teaspoon cumin seeds, toasted and ground
Salt and freshly ground black pepper, to taste

1. In a large bowl, combine the cooked fava beans, chopped tomatoes, sliced green onions, diced cucumber, finely chopped cilantro, minced jalapeño pepper, lemon zest, lemon juice, minced garlic, toasted and ground cumin seeds, salt, and black pepper. 2. Mix all the ingredients well to ensure they are evenly distributed. Adjust the seasoning according to your taste preferences. 3. Chill the fava bean salad in the refrigerator for at least 1 hour before serving. This will allow the flavors to meld together and enhance the taste. 4. Serve the chilled fava bean salad as a refreshing and nutritious side dish or as a light and satisfying main course. It can be enjoyed on its own or paired with grilled meats, roasted vegetables, or a side of crusty bread.

Per Serving:
calories: 152 | fat: 1g | protein: 11g | carbs: 31g | fiber: 12g

Strawberry-Pistachio Salad

Prep time: 10 minutes | **Cook time:** 0 minutes | **Serves 6**

- ¼ cup orange juice
- 2 tablespoons fresh lime juice
- ¼ teaspoon salt, plus more to taste (optional)
- ⅛ teaspoon black pepper, plus more to taste
- ½ small red onion, chopped or sliced
- 2 cups cooked grains, cooled
- 2 cups strawberries, hulled and chopped
- 1½ cups cooked cannellini beans, drained and rinsed
- 1 (5 to 6 ounces / 142 to 170 g) container mixed baby greens
- ½ cup chopped cilantro
- ½ cup roasted, shelled pistachios, chopped
- ½ avocado, diced
- High-quality balsamic vinegar

1. Combine the orange juice, lime juice, ¼ teaspoon salt (if desired), and ⅛ teaspoon pepper in a large bowl. Toss the onions in the dressing; add the grains, strawberries, and beans and toss to combine. 2. Season with salt and pepper to taste. (At this point, the salad can be refrigerated until ready to serve, up to 1 day.) 3. Add the greens and cilantro and toss to combine. Sprinkle with the pistachios, top with the avocado, and drizzle with the vinegar. Serve.

Per Serving:

calories: 393 | fat: 10g | protein: 11g | carbs: 67g | fiber: 8g

Curried Kale Slaw

Prep time: 20 minutes | **Cook time:** 0 minutes | **Serves 4**

- Dressing:
- ⅔ cup water
- 2 tablespoons apple cider vinegar
- 2 tablespoons pure maple syrup (optional)
- 1 garlic clove, minced
- 1 teaspoon grated peeled fresh ginger
- 1 teaspoon Dijon mustard
- ½ teaspoon curry powder
- Freshly ground black pepper, to taste
- Slaw:
- 1 apple, shredded
- 1 tablespoon freshly squeezed lemon juice
- 3 cups thinly sliced kale
- 1 carrot, shredded
- 1 cup shredded fennel
- ¼ cup golden raisins
- ¼ cup sliced almonds, plus more for garnish

Make the Dressing: 1. In a blender, combine the water, vinegar, maple syrup (if using), garlic, ginger, mustard, and curry powder. Season with pepper. Purée until smooth. Set aside. Make the Slaw: 2. In a large bowl, toss together the apple and lemon juice. 3. Add the kale, carrot, fennel, raisins, and almonds and toss to combine the slaw ingredients. 4. Add about three-quarters of the dressing and toss to coat. Taste and add more dressing as needed. Let sit for 10 minutes to allow the kale leaves to soften. Toss again and top with additional sliced almonds to serve.

Per Serving:

calories: 147 | fat: 4g | protein: 3g | carbs: 26g | fiber: 4g

Fiery Couscous Salad

Prep time: 5 minutes | **Cook time:** 5 minutes | **Serves 3**

- 1 cup cooked or canned chickpea
- ½ cup dry couscous
- 3 tangerines
- 1 (2-inch) piece ginger, minced
- ¼ cup tahini
- ½ cup water
- Optional Toppings:
- Cinnamon
- Fresh mint
- Raisins

1. If using dry chickpeas, soak and cook ⅓ cup of dry chickpeas if necessary. Cook the couscous for about 5 minutes. 2. Meanwhile, add the tahini, minced ginger and water to a small airtight container or bowl. Whisk the tahini and ginger in the bowl into a smooth dressing, adding more water if necessary. Alternatively, shake the container with tahini, ginger and water until everything is thoroughly mixed, adding more water if you want a thinner and less creamy dressing. 3. Add the couscous, dressing, and chickpeas to a large bowl and mix thoroughly. 4. Peel and section the tangerines and set them aside to garnish the salad. 5. Divide the salad between two bowls, garnish with the tangerines and optional toppings, serve and enjoy! 6. Store the salad in an airtight container in the fridge and consume within 2 days. Alternatively, store in the freezer for a maximum of 30 days and thaw at room temperature. The salad can be served cold.

Per Serving:

calories: 349 | fat: 14g | protein: 14g | carbs: 41g | fiber: 8g

Ancient Grains Salad

Prep time: 20 minutes | **Cook time:** 55 minutes | **Serves 6**

- ¼ cup farro
- ¼ cup raw rye berries
- 2 ripe pears, cored and coarsely chopped
- 2 celery stalks, coarsely chopped
- 1 green apple, cored and coarsely chopped
- ½ cup chopped fresh parsley
- ¼ cup golden raisins
- 3 tablespoons freshly squeezed lemon juice
- ¼ teaspoon ground cumin
- Pinch cayenne pepper

1. Cook the Grains: In an 8-quart pot, combine the farro, rye berries, and enough water to cover them by 3 inches. Bring the pot to a boil over high heat. Once boiling, reduce the heat to medium-low, cover the pot, and simmer for 45 to 50 minutes, or until the grains are firm and chewy but not hard. Drain the cooked grains and set them aside to cool. 2. Prepare the Salad: In a large bowl, gently stir together the cooled grains, diced pears, celery, apple, parsley, raisins, lemon juice, cumin, and cayenne pepper. Make sure all the ingredients are well combined. 3. Serve or Store: You can serve the Ancient Grains Salad immediately, or if you prefer, you can refrigerate it in an airtight container for up to 1 week. This salad can be enjoyed as a side dish or a light meal on its own.

Per Serving:

calories: 127 | fat: 1g | protein: 3g | carbs: 31g | fiber: 5g

Creamy Fruit Salad

Prep time: 15 minutes | Cook time: 0 minutes | Serves 4

4 red apples, cored and diced
1 (15 ounces / 425 g) can pineapple chunks, drained, or 2 cups fresh pineapple chunks
¼ cup raisins
¼ cup chopped pecans or walnuts
1 cup plain plant-based yogurt
2 teaspoons maple syrup (optional)

1. In a large bowl, combine the apples and pineapples and toss well to make sure the apples are covered in pineapple juice to prevent browning. Add the raisins, nuts, yogurt, and maple syrup (if using) and mix well. Cover and refrigerate for at least 2 hours to develop the flavors.

Per Serving:
calories: 267 | fat: 5g | protein: 6g | carbs: 54g | fiber: 6g

Creamy Chickpea and Avocado Salad

Prep time: 20 minutes | Cook time: 0 minutes | Serves 2

1 (15 ounces / 425 g) can chickpeas, drained and rinsed
1 avocado, peeled and pitted
2 tablespoons slivered almonds
1 celery stalk, minced
1 large carrot, peeled and grated or minced
3 cherry tomatoes, diced small
6 Kalamata olives, pitted and chopped
Juice of 1 lemon
2 tablespoons chopped fresh parsley
½ teaspoon salt (optional)

1. In a medium bowl, combine the chickpeas and avocados and mash with a fork, until the avocado is smooth and the chickpeas are mostly broken but still chunky. 2. Add the almonds, celery, carrot, tomatoes, olives, lemon juice, parsley, and salt and mix until well combined. Serve immediately.

Per Serving:
calories: 396 | fat: 22g | protein: 12g | carbs: 43g | fiber: 17g

Raw Carrot and Date Walnut Salad

Prep time: 15 minutes | Cook time: 0 minutes | Serves 4 to 6

2 tablespoons apple cider vinegar
¼ cup water
1 teaspoon Dijon mustard
1 tablespoon lemon zest
1 tablespoon pure maple syrup (optional)
¼ teaspoon freshly ground black pepper
½ teaspoon cayenne pepper
10 carrots
1 small red onion
4 dates, finely chopped
¼ cup golden raisins
½ cup walnuts, chopped

1. In a small bowl, whisk together the vinegar, water, mustard, lemon zest, maple syrup (if using), black pepper, and cayenne pepper to combine. Set aside. 2. Using a mandoline, cut the carrots and red onion with the julienne blade. Transfer to a large bowl and add the dates, raisins, and walnuts. Toss to combine. 3. Pour in the dressing and toss until fully incorporated. Serve immediately or refrigerate in an airtight container overnight.

Per Serving:
calories: 229 | fat: 10g | protein: 4g | carbs: 34g | fiber: 6g

Orange, Fennel and White Bean Salad

Prep time: 15 minutes | Cook time: 0 minutes | Serves 4

6 large oranges, peeled and segmented
2 tablespoons fresh lemon juice
2 tablespoons balsamic vinegar
1 medium fennel bulb, trimmed and thinly sliced
2 tablespoons minced fresh fennel fronds
2 cups cooked navy beans, or 1 (15 ounces / 425 g) can, drained and rinsed
Salt, to taste (optional)
Cayenne pepper, to taste
4 cups arugula

1. In a large bowl, combine the orange sections, lemon juice, balsamic vinegar, fennel bulb and fronds, white beans, salt (if using), and a pinch of cayenne pepper. Mix well to combine all the ingredients. Allow the salad to sit for 1 hour to let the flavors meld together. 2. To serve, divide the arugula among 4 individual plates, creating a bed of greens on each plate. 3. Spoon the prepared orange, fennel, and white bean salad on top of the arugula, distributing it evenly among the plates. 4. Serve the salad immediately as a refreshing and flavorful appetizer or light lunch option.

Per Serving:
calories: 267 | fat: 1g | protein: 10g | carbs: 56g | fiber: 18g

Winter Sunshine Salad

Prep time: 15 minutes | Cook time: 0 minutes | Serves 6

2 small fennel bulbs, cored and thinly sliced
2 ruby red grapefruits with juice reserved
2 cups shredded red cabbage
1 red or orange bell pepper, thinly sliced
1 tablespoon fresh lime juice
Salt and black pepper (optional)
½ cup chopped cilantro
1 avocado, diced or sliced
¼ cup walnut pieces

1. Combine the fennel, grapefruit segments and juice, cabbage, bell pepper, and lime juice in a large bowl. Season with salt (if desired) and pepper to taste, then toss to combine. 2. When ready to serve, add the cilantro and toss to combine. Divide into bowls, then divide avocado and walnuts evenly between salads.

Per Serving:
calories: 157 | fat: 8g | protein: 4g | carbs: 21g | fiber: 7g

Greek Salad in a Jar

Prep time: 10 minutes | Cook time: 10 minutes | Serves 4

Salad:
1 cup uncooked quinoa
1 cucumber, diced
2 cups cherry tomatoes, halved
2 bell peppers, seeded and chopped
½ cup walnuts, chopped
¼ cup sun-dried black olives, sliced
4 cups chopped mixed greens (romaine is great, too)
Dressing:
¼ cup extra-virgin olive oil
(optional)
½ cup fresh lemon juice
1 tablespoon Dijon mustard
3 cloves garlic, minced, or 2 teaspoons garlic powder
¼ cup basil, finely chopped, or 1 tablespoon dried
1 tablespoon chopped fresh oregano, or 1 teaspoon dried
Himalayan pink salt and freshly ground black pepper (about ¼ teaspoon each)

1. Begin the salad: Cook the quinoa according to the package directions. Set aside to cool. 2. Meanwhile, prepare the dressing: In a small jar or other container with a lid, combine all the dressing ingredients. Screw the lid on the jar and shake to combine. 3. Assemble the salad: Add 1 to 4 tablespoons of dressing to the bottom of each jar, depending on personal preference. 4. Add the cucumber, cooked quinoa, tomatoes, bell peppers, walnuts and olives. Finish by adding the chopped mixed greens to fill the jar. 5. Screw the lid on the jar and store the salad in the refrigerator for up to 4 days. 6. When you're ready to eat, unscrew the lid and pour the salad into a bowl. As you do so, the dressing will coat the ingredients. If not, use your fork to gently toss the salad.

Per Serving:
calories: 399 | fat: 24g | protein: 10g | carbs: 39g | fiber: 6g

Pinto Salsa Bowl

Prep time: 10 minutes | Cook time: 0 minutes | Serves 2

2 cups cooked or canned pinto beans
1 small Hass avocado, peeled, stoned, and cubed
10 halved cherry tomatoes
¼ cup lime juice
¼ cup chopped fresh cilantro
Optional Toppings:
Red onion
Jalapeño slices
Sweet corn

1. When using dry pinto beans, soak and cook ⅔ cup of dry pinto beans if necessary. 2. Transfer the pinto beans to a large bowl, and add the halved cherry tomatoes, avocado cubes, and chopped cilantro. 3. Add the lime juice, stir thoroughly using a spatula and make sure everything is mixed evenly. 4. Divide the pinto salsa between two bowls, garnish with the optional toppings, serve and enjoy! 5. Store the salad in an airtight container in the fridge, and consume within 2 days. Alternatively, store in the freezer for a maximum of 30 days and thaw at room temperature. The salad can be served cold.

Per Serving:
calories: 399 | fat: 10g | protein: 20g | carbs: 57g | fiber: 22g

Classic French Vinaigrette

Prep time: 5 minutes | Cook time: 0 minutes | Serves 4

3 tablespoons apple cider vinegar
2 tablespoons minced shallot
1 tablespoon balsamic vinegar
1 teaspoon gluten-free Dijon mustard
½ teaspoon dried thyme
2 teaspoons olive oil (optional)
Salt and black pepper (optional)

1. In a medium jar with a tight-fitting lid, combine the apple cider vinegar, shallot, and balsamic vinegar. Let it sit for 5 minutes to allow the flavors to meld. 2. Stir in the mustard and thyme to the vinegar mixture. 3. Gradually whisk in the oil in a slow and steady stream until the vinaigrette emulsifies and thickens slightly. 4. Season with salt and pepper to taste, if desired. 5. Transfer the vinaigrette to the refrigerator and store it for up to 5 days.

Per Serving:
calories: 24 | fat: 2g | protein: 0g | carbs: 2g | fiber: 0g

Quinoa Tabbouleh

Prep time: 25 minutes | Cook time: 0 minutes | Serves 4

2½ cups quinoa, cooked and cooled to room temperature
Zest of 1 lemon and juice of 2 lemons, or to taste
3 Roma tomatoes, diced
1 cucumber, peeled, halved, seeded, and diced
2 cups cooked chickpeas, or 1 (15 ounces / 425 g) can chickpeas, drained and rinsed
8 green onions (white and green parts), thinly sliced
1 cup chopped parsley
3 tablespoons chopped mint
Salt and freshly ground black pepper, to taste

1. Combine all ingredients in a large bowl. Chill for 1 hour before serving.

Per Serving:
calories: 319 | fat: 4g | protein: 14g | carbs: 57g | fiber: 12g

Green Mix Salad

Prep time: 10 minutes | Cook time: 0 minutes | Serves 2

1 head romaine lettuce, chopped
2 cups baby arugula
1 cup baby spinach
1 cup fresh cilantro, chopped
1 cup fresh parsley, chopped

1. In a big salad bowl, combine all the greens. Eat fresh or store in a closed container in the fridge for 2 to 3 days.

Per Serving:
calories: 74 | fat: 1g | protein: 5g | carbs: 13g | fiber: 8g

Creamy Potato Salad

Prep time: 10 minutes | Cook time: 20 minutes | Serves 4

5 large red or golden potatoes, cut into 1-inch cubes
1 cup silken tofu or 1 large avocado
¼ cup chopped fresh chives
2 tablespoons Dijon mustard
½ tablespoon freshly squeezed lemon juice
½ teaspoon garlic powder
½ teaspoon onion powder
½ teaspoon dried dill
¼ teaspoon freshly ground black pepper

1. Bring a large pot of water to a boil over high heat. Immerse the potatoes in the hot water gently and carefully. Boil for 10 minutes, or until the potatoes can be easily pierced with a fork. Then drain. 2. Put the potatoes in a large bowl, and refrigerate for a minimum of 20 minutes. 3. Meanwhile, put the tofu in a separate large bowl. Using a fork or mixing spoon, smash the tofu until creamy. Whisk in the chives, mustard, lemon juice, garlic powder, onion powder, dill, and pepper until well combined. 4. Stir the cooled potatoes into the creamy dressing. Mix gently until the potatoes are well coated. Refrigerate the dish for at least 30 minutes or until ready to serve.

Per Serving:
calories: 341 | fat: 1g | protein: 10g | carbs: 74g | fiber: 12g

Lentil, Lemon and Mushroom Salad

Prep time: 10 minutes | Cook time: 25 minutes | Serves 2

½ cup dry lentils of choice
2 cups vegetable broth
3 cups mushrooms, thickly sliced
1 cup sweet or purple onion, chopped
4 teaspoons extra virgin olive oil (optional)
2 tablespoons garlic powder or 3 garlic cloves, minced
¼ teaspoon chili flakes
1 tablespoon lemon juice
2 tablespoons cilantro, chopped
½ cup arugula
Salt and pepper to taste (optional)

1. Sprout the lentils for 2 to 3 days. 2. Place the vegetable stock in a deep saucepan and bring it to a boil. Add the lentils to the boiling broth, cover the pan, and cook for about 5 minutes over low heat until the lentils are slightly tender. Remove the pan from heat and drain the excess water. 3. Heat a frying pan over high heat and add 2 tablespoons of olive oil. Add the onions, garlic, and chili flakes, and cook while stirring until the onions are almost translucent, about 5 to 10 minutes. Add the mushrooms to the pan and mix well. Continue cooking until the onions are completely translucent and the mushrooms have softened. Remove the pan from heat. 4. In a large bowl, combine the cooked lentils, onions, mushrooms, and garlic. Add the lemon juice and the remaining olive oil. Toss or stir to thoroughly combine everything. 5. Serve the mushroom and onion mixture over a bed of arugula in a bowl. Season with salt and pepper to taste, if desired. Alternatively, you can store the salad for later enjoyment.

Per Serving:
calories: 262 | fat: 10g | protein: 16g | carbs: 28g | fiber: 15g

Dill Potato Salad

Prep time: 15 minutes | Cook time: 20 minutes | Serves 4

6 medium potatoes, scrubbed and chopped into bite-size pieces
1 zucchini, chopped (same size pieces as the potatoes)
¼ cup chopped fresh dill, or about 2 tablespoons dried
1 to 2 teaspoons Dijon mustard
⅛ teaspoon sea salt (optional)
Freshly ground black pepper, to taste
1 tablespoon nutritional yeast (optional)
Nondairy milk or water (optional)
3 celery stalks, chopped
1 green or red bell pepper, seeded and chopped
1 tablespoon chopped chives or scallions

1. Fill a large pot about a quarter of the way with water and bring to a boil. Add the potatoes and boil 10 minutes. Add the zucchini to the pot after 10 minutes, and boil an additional 10 minutes. Remove the pot from the heat and drain the water, reserving about 1 cup liquid. Set the cooked vegetables aside in a large bowl to cool. 2. Take about ½ cup potatoes and transfer them to a blender or food processor, along with the reserved cooking liquid and the dill, mustard, salt (if using), pepper, and nutritional yeast (if using). Purée until smooth. If you need to, add a little nondairy milk or water for the consistency you want. 3. Toss the celery, bell pepper, and chives in with the cooked potatoes and zucchini. Pour the dressing over them and toss to coat.

Per Serving:
calories: 264 | fat: 0g | protein: 8g | carbs: 58g | fiber: 8g

Lentil Salad with Lemon and Fresh Herbs

Prep time: 10 minutes | Cook time: 45 minutes | Serves 4

1½ cups green lentils, rinsed
3 cups vegetable stock, or low-sodium vegetable broth
Zest of 1 lemon and juice of 2 lemons
2 cloves garlic, peeled and minced
½ cup finely chopped cilantro
2 tablespoons finely chopped mint
4 green onions (white and green parts), finely chopped, plus more for garnish
Salt and freshly ground black pepper, to taste
4 cups arugula

1. Place the lentils in a medium saucepan with the vegetable stock and bring to a boil over high heat. Reduce the heat to medium, cover, and cook for 35 to 45 minutes, or until the lentils are tender but not mushy. 2. Drain the lentils and place them in a large bowl. Add the lemon zest and juice, garlic, cilantro, mint, green onions, and salt and pepper and mix well. 3. To serve, divide the arugula among 4 individual plates. Spoon the lentil salad on top of the greens and garnish with freshly chopped green onions.

Per Serving:
calories: 277 | fat: 0g | protein: 18g | carbs: 51g | fiber: 8g

Blueprint: Classic Kale Salad

Prep time: 20 minutes | Cook time: 0 minutes | Serves 6

2 bunches kale, stemmed and chopped into bite-size pieces
2 tablespoons gluten-free vinegar or citrus juice, plus more to taste
½ teaspoon salt, plus more to taste (optional)
¼ teaspoon dried herbs or spices (optional)
2 cups shredded or chopped mixed crunchy vegetables
¼ cup finely chopped red onion, or 2 scallions, sliced
Black pepper
½ cup seeds or chopped nuts
¼ cup dried fruit

1. Place the kale in a large bowl and drizzle with the vinegar, then add ½ teaspoon salt (if desired) and the herbs, if desired. Use your hands to massage the kale thoroughly, until it starts to darken in color and look slick. 2. Add the mixed vegetables and onion and toss to combine. Refrigerate for 8 hours or overnight, until ready to serve. 3. Just before serving, season with salt, pepper, and vinegar to taste and sprinkle with the nuts and dried fruit. Serve immediately or refrigerate for up to 3 days.

Per Serving:
calories: 125 | fat: 5g | protein: 6g | carbs: 17g | fiber: 5g

Chapter 10 Staples, Sauces, Dips, and Dressings

Spanish Red Pepper Spread (Romesco)

Prep time: 5 minutes | Cook time: 10 minutes | Serves 12

½ cup raw almonds or walnuts
1 slice whole wheat bread, chopped
2 garlic cloves
1 (15 ounces / 425 g) jar roasted red peppers, drained with liquid reserved, and rinsed
3 tablespoons chopped flat-leaf parsley
¼ cup olive oil (optional)

1. In a small skillet over medium heat, toast the almonds for about 3 minutes, shaking occasionally, until they turn golden brown and become fragrant. Remove from heat and transfer to a food processor. 2. In the same skillet, add the torn bread and minced garlic. Cook for about 3 minutes until the bread is toasted and the garlic is softened. 3. Transfer the toasted bread and garlic to the food processor with the almonds. Pulse a few times to break them down. 4. Add the roasted red peppers and parsley to the food processor. Pulse until the mixture is well blended. 5. Drizzle in the olive oil and a small amount of the reserved liquid from the red pepper jar while pulsing, until the dip reaches a uniform texture. Add salt and pepper to taste. 6. Serve the Romesco spread as a dip or sauce. 7. Store any leftovers in an airtight container in the refrigerator for up to 5 days.

Per Serving:
calories: 81 | fat: 7g | protein: 1g | carbs: 4g | fiber: 1g

Cheesy Vegetable Sauce

Prep time: 10 minutes | Cook time: 25 minutes | Makes 4 cups

1 cup raw cashews
1 russet potato, peeled and cubed
2 carrots, cubed
½ cup nutritional yeast
2 tablespoons yellow (mellow) miso paste
1 teaspoon ground mustard
2 cups unsweetened oat milk (or almond or cashew if gluten-free)
1 tablespoon arrowroot powder, cornstarch, or tapioca starch
1 onion, chopped
3 garlic cloves, minced
1 tablespoon water, plus more as needed

1. In a large pot, combine the cashews, potato, and carrots. Add enough water to cover them by 2 inches. Bring the pot to a boil over high heat, then reduce the heat to simmer. Cook for 15 minutes, or until the vegetables are tender. 2. In a blender, add the nutritional yeast, miso paste, ground mustard, milk, and arrowroot powder. 3. Drain the cooked cashews, potato, and carrots, and transfer them to the blender. Do not blend yet. 4. Rinse the pot and place it over high heat. Add the onion and garlic, cooking for 3 to 4 minutes. Add water 1 tablespoon at a time if needed to prevent burning. 5. Transfer the cooked onion and garlic to the blender with the other ingredients. Blend everything until smooth, scraping the sides as needed. 6. Pour the blended cheese sauce back into the pot and place it over medium heat. Cook, stirring, until the sauce comes to a simmer. 7. Your cheesy vegetable sauce is now ready to be used. You can use it immediately or refrigerate it in a sealable container for up to 1 week.

Per Serving: (½ cup)
calories: 191 | fat: 10g | protein: 9g | carbs: 20g | fiber: 4g

Cashew Cheese Spread

Prep time: 5 minutes | Cook time: 0 minutes | Serves 5

1 cup water
1 cup raw cashews
1 teaspoon nutritional yeast
½ teaspoon salt (optional)
1 teaspoon garlic powder (optional)

1. Soak the cashews in water for 6 hours or overnight. Drain the cashews and rinse them well. 2. In a food processor or high-speed blender, combine the soaked cashews, 1 cup of water, nutritional yeast, lemon juice, garlic powder, onion powder, and salt. Blend until smooth and creamy. If needed, add a little more water to achieve the desired consistency. 3. Taste the cashew cheese spread and adjust the seasonings to your preference. You can add more lemon juice, garlic powder, or salt if desired. 4. Transfer the cashew cheese spread to an airtight container or jar. 5. Refrigerate the cashew cheese spread for at least 1 hour before serving to allow the flavors to develop and the spread to thicken. 6. Serve the cashew cheese spread chilled and use it as a delicious dip, spread, or topping for sandwiches, crackers, or vegetables. 7. Store the cashew cheese spread in the refrigerator for up to 5 days.

Per Serving:
calories: 151 | fat: 11g | protein: 5g | carbs: 9g | fiber: 1g

Creamy Mushroom Gravy

Prep time: 10 minutes | Cook time: 15 minutes | Makes 3 cups

8 ounces (227 g) baby portabella mushrooms, diced
4 ounces (113 g) shiitake mushrooms, stemmed and diced
1 small yellow onion, diced
1 garlic clove, minced
1 tablespoon water, plus more as needed
3 tablespoons whole wheat flour
2 tablespoons tamari or coconut aminos
½ teaspoon freshly ground black pepper
¼ teaspoon ground white pepper
2 cups oat milk

1. In a large sauté pan or skillet over medium-high heat, cook the portabella and shiitake mushrooms for 3 to 5 minutes, or until all their moisture evaporates and the edges of the mushrooms begin to blacken. Add the diced onion and minced garlic. Cook for 5 minutes more, adding water, 1 tablespoon at a time, to prevent burning. The onion should be browned. 2. Stir in the all-purpose flour, tamari (or soy sauce), black pepper, and white pepper, stirring to coat and combine the cooked vegetables. 3. Pour in the plant-based milk and whisk the mixture. Cook, whisking, until the gravy bubbles. Turn the heat to low and cook for 5 minutes, whisking occasionally, until the gravy thickens to your desired consistency. 4. Serve the creamy mushroom gravy fresh or reheat as needed. You can refrigerate any leftovers in a sealable glass container for up to 1 week, or freeze for up to 4 months.

Per Serving: (½ cup)
calories: 81 | fat: 1g | protein: 4g | carbs: 15g | fiber: 3g

Lentil Tacos

Prep time: 15 minutes | Cook time: 30 minutes | Serves 6

3 tablespoons water
½ cup diced red, white, or yellow onion
1 teaspoon minced garlic
1 cup uncooked lentils, rinsed
1½ tablespoons store-bought taco seasoning
1 cup vegetable broth
6 corn tortillas
Optional Toppings:
Dollop of vegan sour cream
Sliced avocado
Diced tomatoes
Shredded lettuce
½ cup salsa
Squeeze of lime juice

1. In a medium pan or pot with a lid, heat the water over medium-high heat. 2. Add the onion and garlic to the pan and sauté for about 3 minutes, or until the onion is tender and translucent. 3. Add the lentils and taco seasoning to the pan, followed by the vegetable broth. Stir well to combine. 4. Bring the mixture to a boil, then reduce the heat to low and cover the pan with the lid. Allow the lentils to simmer for 25 to 30 minutes, or until they are tender and have absorbed most of the liquid. Stir occasionally to prevent sticking. 5. Once the lentils are cooked, remove the pan from the heat and let them cool slightly. 6. Warm the tortillas in a dry skillet or microwave. 7. Spoon a portion of the lentil mixture onto each tortilla, spreading it out evenly. 8. Serve the lentil tacos immediately with your favorite toppings, such as shredded lettuce, diced tomatoes, salsa, guacamole, or vegan sour cream. 9. Enjoy your delicious lentil tacos!

Per Serving:
calories: 79 | fat: 1g | protein: 3g | carbs: 17g | fiber: 2g

Coconut Whipped Cream

Prep time: 5 minutes | Cook time: 0 minutes | Serves 5

1 cup coconut cream
1 teaspoon vanilla extract
2 tablespoons cocoa powder (optional)

1. Chill a can of full-fat coconut milk in the refrigerator overnight. This will help separate the cream from the liquid. 2. Open the can of chilled coconut milk and scoop out the solid coconut cream that has risen to the top, leaving behind the liquid. 3. Place the coconut cream in a large bowl or the bowl of a stand mixer. 4. Add any desired sweetener, such as powdered sugar or maple syrup, and vanilla extract to the bowl. 5. Using an electric mixer with beaters or a whisk, whip the coconut cream on medium-high speed for about 5 minutes, or until it becomes light and fluffy, resembling the texture of whipped cream. 6. Stop occasionally to scrape down the sides of the bowl and continue whipping until well combined. 7. Taste the whipped cream and adjust the sweetness if desired. 8. Serve the coconut whipped cream chilled as a topping for desserts, fruit, or beverages. 9. Store any leftover whipped cream in an airtight container in the refrigerator for up to 2 days. 10. Alternatively, you can freeze the whipped cream in a freezer-safe container for up to 60 days. Thaw it at room temperature before using.

Per Serving:
calories: 40 | fat: 1g | protein: 0g | carbs: 7g | fiber: 0g

Oat Milk

Prep time: 5 minutes | Cook time: 0 minutes | Makes 4 cups

1 cup rolled oats
3 dates, pitted (optional)
4 cups water

1. In a blender, add the oats, dates (if using), and water. 2. Blend on high speed for about 45 seconds, or until the mixture is creamy and the oats are well blended. Avoid overblending to prevent a slimy texture. 3. Place a nut milk bag, cheesecloth, or fine-mesh sieve over a large bowl or pitcher. Pour the blended mixture into the bag or sieve. 4. Gently squeeze or press the bag or sieve to strain out the liquid while separating it from the oat pulp. Continue until you've extracted as much milk as possible. 5. Transfer the strained oat milk into an airtight storage container. 6. Refrigerate the oat milk for up to 4 days to keep it fresh and chilled. 7. Before using the oat milk, give it a quick shake or stir as separation may occur.

Per Serving:
calories: 90 | fat: 3g | protein: 1g | carbs: 13g | fiber: 0g

Kalamata Olives and White Bean Dip

Prep time: 5 minutes | Cook time: 0 minutes | Makes 1 cup

5 jumbo Kalamata olives, pitted
1 cup cooked cannellini beans (no added salt)
1 tablespoon tahini (no added sugar or salt)
1 garlic clove
1 tablespoon freshly squeezed lemon juice
1 tablespoon water

1. In a food processor, combine the kalamata olives, white beans, tahini, garlic, lemon juice, and water. 2. Blend the mixture in the food processor until it reaches your desired consistency. You can blend it for a shorter time for a chunkier dip or longer for a smoother dip. 3. Once blended to your liking, taste the dip and adjust the flavors by adding more lemon juice, garlic, or salt if needed. 4. Transfer the dip to a serving bowl and garnish with a drizzle of olive oil, chopped fresh herbs, or additional kalamata olives if desired. 5. Serve the Kalamata Olives and White Bean Dip with sliced vegetables, pita bread, crackers, or your preferred dippers. 6. Store any leftover dip in an airtight container in the refrigerator for up to 5 days. 7. Enjoy the delicious and savory Kalamata Olives and White Bean Dip as a flavorful appetizer or snack.

Per Serving:
calories: 95 | fat: 3g | protein: 5g | carbs: 13g | fiber: 4g

Fall and Winter All-Purpose Seasoning

Prep time: 5 minutes | Cook time: 0 minutes | Makes ½ cup

3 tablespoons dried rosemary
2 tablespoons plus 2 teaspoons dried sage
2 tablespoons plus 2 teaspoons dried thyme
1 teaspoon black pepper
¼ teaspoon ground ginger (optional)

1. Using a mortar and pestle or a coffee grinder, grind the rosemary and sage until they are roughly crushed. You want to break them down to release their flavors but not create a fine powder. 2. Transfer the crushed rosemary and sage to a jar with a tight-fitting lid. 3. Add the thyme, pepper, and ginger (if desired) to the jar. 4. Close the lid tightly and shake the jar vigorously to thoroughly mix the ingredients together. 5. Store the seasoning in a cool, dry place for up to 6 months. Make sure the jar is properly sealed to maintain the freshness and potency of the flavors. 6. When using the fall and winter all-purpose seasoning, sprinkle it on roasted vegetables, soups, stews, or any other dish that could benefit from the warm and aromatic flavors of rosemary, sage, thyme, pepper, and ginger. 7. Feel free to adjust the quantities of the ingredients to suit your taste preferences. 8. Enjoy the rich and flavorful seasoning throughout the fall and winter seasons!

Per Serving: (½ cup)
calories: 26 | fat: 1g | protein: 1g | carbs: 5g | fiber: 3g

Green Goddess Dressing

Prep time: 10 minutes | Cook time: 0 minutes | Makes 1 cup

½ cup tahini
2 tablespoons apple cider vinegar
Juice of 1 lemon
¼ cup tamari or soy sauce
2 garlic cloves, minced or pressed
½ cup water
½ cup fresh basil, minced
½ cup fresh parsley, minced
½ cup scallions or chives, minced
¼ teaspoon sea salt (optional)
Pinch freshly ground black pepper (optional)
1 tablespoon maple syrup (optional)

1. Place all the ingredients for the Green Goddess Dressing in a blender or food processor. 2. Blend the ingredients on high speed until smooth and creamy, usually for about 30 to 45 seconds. 3. If the dressing appears too thick, you can add a little water, a tablespoon at a time, to achieve the desired consistency. 4. Once the dressing is smooth and creamy, taste it and adjust the seasoning as needed by adding more salt, pepper, or lemon juice. 5. Transfer the Green Goddess Dressing to a container or jar with a tight-fitting lid for storage. 6. Use the dressing immediately or refrigerate it for later use. It should keep well in the refrigerator for about 5 to 7 days. 7. Enjoy the vibrant and flavorful Green Goddess Dressing on salads, sandwiches, or as a dip for vegetables.

Per Serving: (1 tablespoon)
calories: 211 | fat: 16g | protein: 7g | carbs: 12g | fiber: 1g

Maple Caramel

Prep time: 5 minutes | Cook time: 15 minutes | Makes 1¼ cups

1 cup full-fat coconut milk
¾ cup pure maple syrup (optional)
1 teaspoon pure vanilla extract
1 teaspoon fresh lemon juice
¾ teaspoon fine sea salt (optional)

1. In a medium saucepan, combine the coconut milk and maple syrup (if using) over medium-high heat. 2. Bring the mixture to a boil, then reduce the heat to a strong simmer. 3. The caramel will continue to bubble, so whisk it every couple of minutes to prevent burning. 4. Keep simmering and whisking the caramel for about 15 minutes, or until the liquid has reduced by 1/3 and thickened slightly. 5. Remove the saucepan from heat and stir in the vanilla, lemon juice, and sea salt (if using) while the caramel is still warm. 6. Transfer the caramel to a bowl or glass jar and let it come to room temperature. 7. Once cooled, cover the caramel and store it in the refrigerator. 8. For the best texture, refrigerate the caramel overnight before using. 9. The caramel will keep for up to 1 week when stored properly in the refrigerator.

Per Serving: (¼ cup)
calories: 256 | fat: 11g | protein: 1g | carbs: 35g | fiber: 1g

Spicy Tomato and Pepper Sauce

Prep time: 10 minutes | **Cook time:** 10 minutes | **Makes 1 cup**

2 medium ripe tomatoes, halved and seeded
½ cup chopped red bell pepper
¼ cup chopped walnuts
4 medium garlic cloves
1 tablespoon ground coriander
1 teaspoon red pepper flakes
1 teaspoon ground fenugreek
½ teaspoon freshly ground black pepper

1. Place the tomatoes, red bell peppers, walnuts, garlic, coriander, red pepper flakes, fenugreek, and black pepper in a food processor. Blend the ingredients until you achieve a thick salsa-like consistency. 2. Transfer the mixture from the food processor to a small saucepan. Bring it to a boil, then reduce the heat and let it simmer for 3 minutes. 3. Allow the spicy tomato and pepper sauce to cool down. Store it in an airtight container in the refrigerator for up to 5 days.

Per Serving:
calories: 35 | fat: 2g | protein: 1g | carbs: 2g | fiber: 1g

Vegan Basil Pesto

Prep time: 5 minutes | **Cook time:** 0 minutes | **Serves 6**

2 bunches basil, leaves only
1 cup spinach
¼ cup roasted almonds
¼ cup toasted pine nuts
4 raw Brazil nuts, chopped
2 garlic cloves
¼ cup water
¼ to ½ teaspoon salt (optional)

1. In a food processor, combine the basil, spinach, almonds, pine nuts, Brazil nuts, and garlic. Pulse the ingredients until they are well combined and finely chopped. 2. With the food processor running, slowly stream in the water until the pesto reaches the desired consistency. Add ¼ teaspoon of salt and taste. Adjust the salt to your preference. 3. Transfer the vegan basil pesto to an airtight container and refrigerate for up to 5 days. Alternatively, you can freeze the pesto in single portions by scooping it into ice cube trays, freezing it, and then transferring the frozen pesto cubes to an airtight container. The frozen pesto can be stored for up to 6 months.

Per Serving:
calories: 81 | fat: 8g | protein: 2g | carbs: 2g | fiber: 1g

Tofu Veggie Gravy Bowl

Prep time: 15 minutes | **Cook time:** 10 minutes | **Serves 4**

Gravy:
6 tablespoons water
¼ cup diced red, white, or yellow onion
2 tablespoons whole wheat or all-purpose flour
1 cup vegetable broth
Veggie Base:
1 cup evenly sliced broccoli, steamed
1 cup evenly chopped zucchini, steamed
1 cup chopped carrots, steamed
½ (14 ounces / 397 g) block extra-firm tofu, pressed and cut into ½-inch cubes

1. Heat water and onion in a medium pan over medium heat. Cook for about 3 minutes until the onion becomes tender and translucent. 2. Reduce the heat to low and add the flour to the pan. Stir well until the mixture forms a smooth roux with a paste-like consistency, about 2 to 3 minutes. 3. Pour in the broth and continue stirring over low heat. Cook for 3 to 4 minutes until the gravy thickens. 4. Arrange the broccoli, zucchini, carrots, and tofu on a plate. Pour the gravy over the vegetables and tofu. Serve the tofu veggie gravy bowl immediately.

Per Serving:
calories: 86 | fat: 4g | protein: 7g | carbs: 9g | fiber: 2g

Pomegranate Ginger Sauce

Prep time: 5 minutes | **Cook time:** 0 minutes | **Serves 8**

2 cups fresh or frozen pomegranate seeds
10 dried pitted plums
1 (2-inch) piece ginger
1 tablespoon black pepper

1. Place all the ingredients in a blender or food processor. Blend until the mixture becomes smooth and well combined, forming a pomegranate ginger sauce. 2. Transfer the sauce to an airtight container and store it in the refrigerator. Consume the sauce within 3 days for optimal freshness. Alternatively, you can freeze the sauce by placing it in a freezer-safe container. Ensure the container is tightly sealed. The sauce can be stored in the freezer for up to 60 days. When ready to use, thaw the sauce at room temperature before serving.

Per Serving:
calories: 65 | fat: 0g | protein: 1g | carbs: 15g | fiber: 3g

Spicy Tahini Dressing

Prep time: 10 minutes | **Cook time:** 0 minutes | **Serves 8**

½ cup tahini
2 tablespoons lemon juice
1 clove garlic, minced
1 tablespoon paprika powder
½ cup water

1. In a small bowl or jar, combine the tahini, lemon juice, water, soy sauce or tamari, maple syrup or honey, sriracha or hot sauce, minced garlic, salt, and pepper. 2. Whisk the ingredients together vigorously or shake the jar until the dressing is smooth and well combined. 3. Serve the tahini dressing chilled as a topping or a side. 4. Store the tahini dressing in the refrigerator in an airtight container for up to 4 days or in the freezer for up to 60 days. Thaw frozen dressing at room temperature before using.

Per Serving:
calories: 102 | fat: 8g | protein: 4g | carbs: 2g | fiber: 1g

Curry Powder

Prep time: 10 minutes | Cook time: 5 minutes | Makes ½ cup

¼ cup coriander seeds
2 tablespoons cumin seeds
1 (3-inch) stick cinnamon, broken into pieces
1 teaspoon whole cardamom pods
1 teaspoon black peppercorns
8 whole cloves
2 tablespoons ground turmeric
2 tablespoons ground ginger
¼ teaspoon cayenne pepper

1. Heat a skillet over medium heat and add the coriander, cumin, cinnamon, cardamom, peppercorns, and cloves. Toast the spices for 2 to 3 minutes, or until they become fragrant. 2. Remove the skillet from the heat and transfer the toasted spices to an electric spice grinder. Grind the spices until they become a fine powder. 3. Transfer the ground spices to a bowl and add the turmeric, ginger, and cayenne. Stir the ingredients well to combine. 4. Store the curry powder in a tightly sealed jar for up to 3 months, ensuring it is kept in a cool, dry place.

Per Serving: (½ cup)
calories: 238 | fat: 8g | protein: 8g | carbs: 48g | fiber: 22g

Raw Date Paste

Prep time: 10 minutes | Cook time: 0 minutes | Makes 2½ cups

1 cup Medjool dates, pitted and chopped
1½ cups water

1. Place the dates and water in a blender and blend until you achieve a smooth consistency. 2. Transfer the raw date paste to an airtight container and store it in the refrigerator for up to 7 days.

Per Serving:
calories: 21 | fat: 0g | protein: 0g | carbs: 5g | fiber: 1g

Perfect Marinara Sauce

Prep time: 10 minutes | Cook time: 20 minutes | Makes 7 cups

2 (28 ounces / 794 g) cans crushed tomatoes in purée
4 garlic cloves, minced
2 tablespoons Italian seasoning
2 teaspoons pure maple syrup
2 teaspoons onion powder
2 teaspoons paprika
¼ teaspoon freshly ground black pepper

1. In a medium saucepan, combine the tomatoes, garlic, Italian seasoning, maple syrup, onion powder, paprika, and pepper. 2. Stir the ingredients together and bring the mixture to a simmer over medium heat. 3. Once simmering, reduce the heat to low and cover the saucepan. Allow the sauce to simmer for 15 to 20 minutes, or until it becomes fragrant and the flavors have melded together. 4. Remove the saucepan from the heat and your Italian tomato sauce is ready to use in your favorite recipes.

Per Serving:
calories: 39 | fat: 0g | protein: 2g | carbs: 8g | fiber: 2g

Jerk Spices

Prep time: 5 minutes | Cook time: 0 minutes | Makes ⅓ cup

1 tablespoon garlic powder
2 teaspoons dried thyme
2 teaspoons onion powder
1 teaspoon black pepper
1 teaspoon dried parsley
1 teaspoon sweet paprika
1 teaspoon whole allspice
½ teaspoon cayenne pepper
½ teaspoon crushed red pepper
¼ teaspoon cumin seeds
¼ teaspoon freshly grated nutmeg
¼ teaspoon ground cinnamon

1. Gather all the ingredients for the jerk spices. 2. Place the ingredients in a clean coffee grinder or spice grinder. 3. Pulse the grinder until the ingredients are thoroughly combined and have a uniform texture. 4. Transfer the jerk spices to an airtight container with a tight-fitting lid. 5. Label the container with the name and date for easy reference. 6. Store the jerk spices in a cool, dry place away from direct sunlight. 7. The spices will retain their flavor for up to 6 months if stored properly. 8. Use the jerk spices to season meats, vegetables, or other dishes for a delicious Caribbean-inspired flavor.

Per Serving: (⅓ cup)
calories: 83 | fat: 1g | protein: 3g | carbs: 18g | fiber: 5g

Strawberry-Peach Vinaigrette

Prep time: 5 minutes | Cook time: 0 minutes | Makes 1¼ cups

1 peach, pitted
4 strawberries
¼ cup water
2 tablespoons balsamic vinegar

1. Wash and remove the pits from the peach. Wash the strawberries as well. 2. In a blender, add the peach, strawberries, water, and vinegar. 3. Blend on high speed for 1 to 2 minutes, or until the ingredients are thoroughly blended and the dressing has a smooth consistency. 4. Taste the vinaigrette and adjust the sweetness or tartness by adding a little more vinegar or a sweetener if desired. 5. Transfer the vinaigrette to a refrigerator-safe container with a tight lid. 6. Store the vinaigrette in the refrigerator for up to 3 days to allow the flavors to meld together. 7. Shake well before using to ensure the ingredients are evenly distributed. 8. Drizzle the Strawberry-Peach Vinaigrette over your favorite salads or use it as a flavorful dressing for other dishes.

Per Serving: (2 tablespoons)
calories: 10 | fat: 0g | protein: 0g | carbs: 2g | fiber: 0g

Italian Seasoning

Prep time: 5 minutes | Cook time: 0 minutes | Makes 9 tablespoons

8 teaspoons dried marjoram
8 teaspoons dried basil
4 teaspoons dried thyme
2 teaspoons dried rosemary
2 teaspoons dried sage
2 teaspoons dried oregano
1 teaspoon garlic powder

1. Get an airtight container with a lid, or repurpose a spice jar for this purpose. 2. Combine the marjoram, basil, thyme, rosemary, sage, oregano, and garlic powder in the container. 3. Close the lid tightly and shake the container or mix the ingredients well until they are thoroughly combined. 4. Your homemade Italian seasoning is now ready to use! 5. Store the seasoning in a cool, dry place with the lid tightly closed to maintain its freshness and flavor. 6. Use the Italian seasoning in your favorite Italian dishes, such as pasta sauces, soups, stews, marinades, or as a seasoning for roasted vegetables or grilled meats.

Per Serving:
calories: 7 | fat: 0g | protein: 0g | carbs: 2g | fiber: 1g

Everyday Pesto

Prep time: 5 minutes | Cook time: 5 minutes | Makes 1 cup

4 cups packed fresh basil leaves
¼ cup raw cashews
2 tablespoons nutritional yeast
1 garlic clove
¼ teaspoon freshly ground black pepper
3 tablespoons boiling water, plus more as needed

1. Place the basil, cashews, nutritional yeast, garlic, pepper, and boiling water in a food processor. 2. Blend the ingredients until smooth, scraping down the sides of the processor as needed. 3. If needed, add more water to achieve the desired consistency. The pesto should be smooth and slightly thick. 4. Transfer the pesto to a sealed jar or container. 5. Refrigerate the pesto for up to 1 month to allow the flavors to develop. 6. Use the everyday pesto as a versatile and flavorful sauce for pasta, sandwiches, pizzas, or as a dip.

Per Serving: (2 tablespoons)
calories: 35 | fat: 2g | protein: 3g | carbs: 2g | fiber: 1g

Simple Berry-Chia Jam

Prep time: 2 minutes | Cook time: 0 minutes | Makes 1½ cups

2 cups frozen organic berries, any variety or a mixture
1 teaspoon fresh lemon juice
2 tablespoons chia seeds
1 to 2 tablespoons date syrup or agave nectar (optional)

1. Place the berries in a food processor and pulse until they are well chopped but not completely pureed. You want to have some texture remaining. 2. Add the lemon juice, chia seeds, and syrup (if using) to the food processor. Pulse a few more times to combine the ingredients evenly. 3. Transfer the mixture into an airtight jar or container, ensuring it is tightly sealed. 4. Refrigerate the jam overnight to allow the chia seeds to absorb the liquid and thicken the mixture. 5. The next day, your homemade berry chia jam will be ready to enjoy! It can be stored in the refrigerator for 5 to 7 days. 6. Use this delicious jam on toast, pancakes, oatmeal, or as a topping for yogurt or desserts. 7. Feel free to experiment with different types of berries or add spices like cinnamon or vanilla extract for extra flavor.

Per Serving:
calories: 53 | fat: 1g | protein: 1g | carbs: 10g | fiber: 2g

Balsamic Vinaigrette

Prep time: 2 minutes | Cook time: 0 minutes | Makes 1 cup

½ cup flax oil, hemp oil or extra-virgin olive oil (optional)
½ cup high-quality balsamic vinegar
2 tablespoons agave nectar (optional)
1½ teaspoons stone ground mustard
Pinch of sea salt (optional)

1. In a lidded glass jar, combine the balsamic vinegar, olive oil, Dijon mustard, honey (or maple syrup), garlic, salt, and black pepper in the order listed. 2. Secure the lid tightly on the jar and shake it vigorously until all the ingredients are well mixed and emulsified. 3. Taste the vinaigrette and adjust the flavors by adding more salt, pepper, or sweetener if desired. 4. Serve the Balsamic Vinaigrette immediately on your favorite salad, or refrigerate it for later use. Before using, give the jar a good shake to recombine any separated ingredients. 5. The vinaigrette can be stored in the refrigerator for about 2 weeks. 6. Enjoy the tangy and flavorful Balsamic Vinaigrette to enhance the taste of your salads.

Per Serving:
calories: 270 | fat: 27g | protein: 0g | carbs: 6g | fiber: 0g

Harissa

Prep time: 5 minutes | Cook time: 0 minutes | Makes ½ cup

2 tablespoons caraway seeds
2 tablespoons coriander seeds
2 tablespoons cumin seeds
2 teaspoons dried mint
2 teaspoons garlic powder
1 teaspoon sweet paprika
1 teaspoon crushed red pepper (optional)

1. Grind the caraway, coriander, and cumin in a clean coffee grinder. Transfer to a jar with a tight-fitting lid; add the mint, garlic powder, paprika, and crushed red pepper, if desired; and shake until combined. Store for up to 6 months.

Per Serving: (⅓ cup)
calories: 150 | fat: 7g | protein: 8g | carbs: 24g | fiber: 12g

Strawberry Chia Jam

Prep time: 2 minutes | Cook time: 10 minutes | Makes 1½ cups

3 cups frozen strawberries
4 dates, pitted and chopped small
¼ cup water
3 tablespoons chia seeds

1. In a medium saucepan, combine the strawberries, dates, and water. Place the saucepan over medium-high heat and bring the mixture to a boil. 2. Reduce the heat to medium-low and let the mixture simmer for about 10 minutes, stirring occasionally. 3. Remove the saucepan from the heat and use a potato masher to gently mash the mixture until you achieve a smooth consistency with some small chunks of strawberries. 4. Add the chia seeds to the mixture and stir well to combine. Let the jam cool. 5. Transfer the strawberry chia jam to a small jar and cover it. Allow it to cool completely, and as it cools, it will thicken to a jam-like consistency. 6. Store the jam in the refrigerator in an airtight container for up to 5 days. 7. Enjoy the delicious and nutritious Strawberry Chia Jam on toast, pancakes, oatmeal, or as a filling for pastries.

Per Serving:

calories: 43 | fat: 1g | protein: 1g | carbs: 8g | fiber: 3g

Homemade Beans

Prep time: 5 minutes | Cook time: 2 hours | Makes 3 cups

8 ounces (227 g) dried black beans, picked over and rinsed
3½ cups water
Pinch kelp granules

1. In a Dutch oven or saucepan, combine the beans, water, and kelp. Bring to a boil over high heat. 2. Reduce the heat to low. Cover, and simmer for about 1½ hours. Remove from the heat.

Per Serving:

calories: 110 | fat: 1g | protein: 11g | carbs: 29g | fiber: 16g

Corn Bread Muffins

Prep time: 10 minutes | Cook time: 20 minutes | Makes 12 muffins

Oil, for preparing the muffin pan (optional)
½ cup canned corn
1½ cups unsweetened oat milk or other nondairy milk
¼ cup agave syrup or pure maple syrup (optional)
¼ cup unsweetened applesauce
1¼ cups whole wheat flour
1 cup cornmeal
4 teaspoons baking powder
½ teaspoon salt (optional)

1. Preheat the oven to 400°F (205°C). Lightly coat a muffin pan with oil (if using), or line it with parchment paper. 2. In a large bowl, mash the corn slightly with a potato masher or heavy spoon. Stir in the oat milk, agave syrup (if using), and applesauce. 3. In a medium bowl, whisk together the flour, cornmeal, baking powder, and salt (if using) to combine. Using a spatula, fold the dry ingredients into the wet ingredients until combined. Evenly divided the batter among the prepared muffin cups. 4. Bake for 16 to 20 minutes. The tops of the muffins should be lightly browned, and a toothpick inserted into the middle of a muffin should come out clean. Let cool for 5 minutes before transferring the muffins to a wire rack to cool completely. 5. Store in a resealable bag or airtight container at room temperature for up to 1 week or freeze for 1 to 2 months.

Per Serving: (1 muffin)

calories: 121 | fat: 2g | protein: 3g | carbs: 25g | fiber: 2g

Sweet Peanut Butter Dipping Sauce

Prep time: 10 minutes | Cook time: 0 minutes | Makes 1 cup

½ cup creamy peanut butter (no added sugar or salt)
2 tablespoons rice vinegar
¼ cup unsweetened coconut milk
1 tablespoon maple syrup (optional)
2 garlic cloves
½-inch piece fresh ginger, peeled and grated
¼ teaspoon red pepper flakes

1. In a food processor, add the peanut butter, rice vinegar, coconut milk, maple syrup (if using), garlic, ginger, and red pepper flakes. Blend the ingredients until you achieve a smooth and creamy consistency. 2. Transfer the peanut butter dipping sauce to an airtight container and store it in the refrigerator. 3. The sauce can be refrigerated for up to 5 days, allowing the flavors to meld together and intensify. 4. When ready to serve, remove the sauce from the refrigerator and give it a good stir before using as a delicious dip or sauce.

Per Serving:

calories: 107 | fat: 8g | protein: 4g | carbs: 6g | fiber: 1g

Barbecue Sauce

Prep time: 10 minutes | Cook time: 0 minutes | Makes 2 cups

1 (8 ounces / 227 g) can tomato sauce
3 pitted dates
¼ cup apple cider vinegar
3 tablespoons blackstrap molasses
2 tablespoons whole grain mustard
1½ teaspoons onion powder
1½ teaspoons smoked paprika
½ teaspoon garlic powder
⅛ teaspoon cayenne

1. In a high-efficiency blender or food processor, combine the tomato sauce, dates, vinegar, molasses, mustard, onion powder, paprika, garlic powder, and cayenne. Process until smooth. Store leftovers in an airtight container in the refrigerator for up to 1 week.

Per Serving:

calories: 45 | fat: 0g | protein: 1g | carbs: 11g | fiber: 1g

Coconut Butter

Prep time: 5 minutes | Cook time: 0 minutes | Makes 1 cup

4 cups unsweetened shredded dried coconut or 7 cups unsweetened flaked dried coconut

1. Put the coconut in a food processor and process for 10 to 15 minutes, scraping down the sides every couple of minutes, until the butter is completely smooth and quite liquid. Store in a tightly sealed glass jar at room temperature for up to 1 month.

Per Serving: (½ cup)
calories: 280 | fat: 28g | protein: 3g | carbs: 10g | fiber: 7g

Quick Tahini Sauce

Prep time: 10 minutes | Cook time: 0 minutes | Makes 1¼ cups

- ½ cup tahini
- ½ cup filtered water
- 2 tablespoons extra-virgin olive oil (optional)
- 2 tablespoons freshly squeezed lemon juice
- 1 small garlic clove, finely grated or pressed
- ½ teaspoon fine sea salt, plus more to taste (optional)

1. Combine the tahini, water, olive oil, lemon juice, garlic, and salt, if using, in a food processor and blend until smooth. Season to taste. Serve immediately, or store the sauce in a glass jar in the fridge for up to 5 days. Bring to room temperature before using and add water to thin if needed.

Per Serving: (¼ cup)
calories: 193 | fat: 18g | protein: 4g | carbs: 6g | fiber: 2g

Zucchini Dressing

Prep time: 10 minutes | Cook time: 0 minutes | Makes 1 cup

- 1 medium zucchini, cut into 1-inch chunks
- 1 (3-inch) piece scallion, white and light green parts only, coarsely chopped
- 3 tablespoons freshly squeezed lime juice
- 3 tablespoons extra-virgin olive oil (optional)
- ½ teaspoon fine sea salt, plus more to taste (optional)

1. Combine the zucchini, scallion, lime juice, oil, and salt, if using, in an upright blender and blend until smooth, starting on a lower speed and gradually increasing it as the dressing comes together. Use a rubber spatula (with the blender off) to help move the ingredients around as necessary, or use the tamper stick if using a high-powered blender. Adjust the seasoning to taste. Scrape down the sides and blend again. 2. Serve immediately, or store in a glass jar in the fridge for up to 3 days. Shake well before using. The dressing will thicken once chilled; thin it out with a little water if needed.

Per Serving: (¼ cup)
calories: 98 | fat: 10g | protein: 0g | carbs: 2g | fiber: 0g

Easy One-Pot Vegan Marinara

Prep time: 10 minutes | Cook time: 15 minutes | Makes 2¼ cups

- 1 cup water
- 1 cup tomato paste
- 2 tablespoons maple syrup (optional)
- 1 teaspoon dried oregano
- 1 teaspoon dried thyme
- 1 teaspoon garlic powder
- 1 teaspoon onion powder
- ½ teaspoon dried basil
- ¼ teaspoon red pepper flakes

1. In a medium saucepan, bring the water to a rolling boil over high heat. Reduce the heat to low, and whisk in the tomato paste, maple syrup (if desired), oregano, thyme, garlic powder, onion powder, basil, and red pepper flakes. 2. Cover and simmer for 10 minutes, stirring occasionally. Serve warm.

Per Serving: (½ cup)
calories: 87 | fat: 0g | protein: 3g | carbs: 21g | fiber: 3g

Sour Cream

Prep time: 5 minutes | Cook time: 0 minutes | Serves 10

- 1 cup coconut cream
- 2 tablespoons lemon juice
- ½ teaspoon apple cider vinegar
- ½ teaspoon salt (optional)

1. Add all of the ingredients to a food processor or blender and blend until smooth. Alternatively, put all ingredients into a medium bowl and whisk using hand mixers until smooth. 2. Serve the sour cream chilled and enjoy as a topping or a side! 3. Store the sour cream in the fridge, using an airtight container, and consume within 4 days. Alternatively, store the sour cream in the freezer for a maximum of 60 days and thaw at room temperature.

Per Serving:
calories: 20 | fat: 1g | protein: 0g | carbs: 3g | fiber: 0g

Minimalist Guacamole

Prep time: 5 minutes | Cook time: 0 minutes | Serves 2

- 1 avocado, mashed
- 2 tablespoons fresh lime juice
- 1 scallion, sliced thin
- Crushed red pepper
- Salt (optional)

1. Combine the avocado, lime juice, and scallion in a small bowl. Season with crushed red pepper and salt (if desired) and serve.

Per Serving:
calories: 170 | fat: 15g | protein: 2g | carbs: 10g | fiber: 7g

Nut Milk

Prep time: 5 minutes | Cook time: 0 minutes | Makes 5 cups

1 cup raw cashews or almonds, soaked overnight and drained
3 dates, pitted (optional)
1 teaspoon vanilla extract (optional)
4 cups water

1. In a blender combine the soaked nuts, dates (if using), vanilla (if using), and water and blend on high for 3 to 4 minutes, until the nuts are all pulverized and the liquid looks creamy. 2. Pour the blended mix through a nut milk bag, cheesecloth, or a fine-mesh sieve and pour it into an airtight storage container. Chill and use within 4 days.

Per Serving:
calories: 25 | fat: 2g | protein: 0g | carbs: 1g | fiber: 0g

Garam Masala

Prep time: 5 minutes | Cook time: 0 minutes | Makes ½ cup

2 tablespoons black peppercorns
2 tablespoons coriander seeds
2 tablespoons cumin seeds
1 teaspoon freshly grated nutmeg or 1¼ teaspoons ground nutmeg
1 teaspoon ground cinnamon
1 teaspoon whole cloves
¼ teaspoon cardamom seeds

1. Pulse all the ingredients in a clean coffee grinder until thoroughly combined. Store in an airtight container for up to 6 months.

Per Serving: (½ cup)
calories: 132 | fat: 6g | protein: 5g | carbs: 23g | fiber: 11g

Smoky Mushrooms

Prep time: 10 minutes | Cook time: 10 minutes | Makes 2 cups

2 tablespoons soy sauce
2 tablespoons pure maple syrup
1 tablespoon liquid smoke
1 tablespoon liquid aminos
¼ teaspoon freshly ground black pepper
1 pound (454 g) cremini mushrooms, cut into ½-inch-thick slices

1. In a sauté pan or skillet, whisk together the soy sauce, maple syrup, liquid smoke, liquid aminos, and pepper. 2. Add the mushrooms, and cook over medium-high heat, stirring frequently, for about 10 minutes, or until the liquid evaporates but the mushrooms are still tender and glistening. Remove from the heat. Store in an airtight container in the refrigerator until ready to use.

Per Serving:
calories: 45 | fat: 0g | protein: 3g | carbs: 8g | fiber: 1g

Spicy Satay Sauce

Prep time: 5 minutes | Cook time: 10 minutes | Serves 8

1 cup peanut butter
2 tablespoons lime juice
¼ cup sweet soy sauce
2 small onions, minced
2 cloves garlic, minced
2 cups water
Optional Toppings:
Red chili flakes
Minced ginger
Fresh cilantro

1. Put all ingredients in a food processor and blend until smooth, add more water if the sauce is too thick. Alternatively, mix everything in a medium bowl, using a handheld mixer. 2. Heat up the sauce in a saucepan over a medium heat. Let it cook for about 10 minutes while stirring continuously as the sauce thickens. 3. Turn off the heat and let the sauce cool down for a minute while stirring. 4. Serve warm with the optional toppings and enjoy! 5. Store the satay sauce in an airtight container in the fridge and consume within 4 days. The satay sauce can also be stored in the freezer for a maximum of 90 days. Thaw at room temperature before serving.

Per Serving:
calories: 217 | fat: 15g | protein: 8g | carbs: 10g | fiber: 2g

Whipped Lentil Chipotle Dip

Prep time: 10 minutes | Cook time: 10 minutes | Makes 2 cups

1 cup split red lentils, rinsed
3 cloves garlic, peeled
2 chipotle peppers in adobo
1 tablespoon adobo sauce from the can (optional)
3 tablespoons raw cashew butter
1 tablespoon fresh lemon juice
1 teaspoon tomato paste
1½ teaspoons ground cumin
Salt and pepper, to taste (optional)
Garnishes (optional):
Virgin olive oil (optional)
Ground cumin
Sweet paprika

1. Place the lentils in a medium saucepan and cover them with 3 cups of filtered water. Bring to a boil over medium-high heat. Lower to a simmer and cook until the lentils are mushy and falling apart, about 8 minutes. 2. While the lentils are cooking, combine the garlic, chipotles, adobo, if using, cashew butter, lemon juice, tomato paste, and cumin in a blender. 3. Drain the cooked lentils, and scrape them into the blender with the garlic and chipotle mixture. Season with salt and pepper, if using. Whiz everything on high until the dip is completely smooth. You may have to stop the blender and scrape down the sides a couple of times. 4. The dip will be quite warm. For optimal serving, scrape the dip into a container and cover it with plastic wrap, pressing it onto the surface of the dip. Refrigerate the dip for at least 1 hour before serving. 5. You can garnish the top with a drizzle of olive oil, some extra ground cumin, and a sprinkle of paprika if you like.

Per Serving: (½ cup)
calories: 261 | fat: 7g | protein: 14g | carbs: 38g | fiber: 6g

Beer "Cheese" Dip

Prep time: 10 minutes | Cook time: 10 minutes | Serves 12

¾ cup brown ale
¾ cup water
½ cup raw cashews, soaked in hot water for at least 15 minutes, then drained
½ cup raw walnuts, soaked in hot water for at least 15 minutes, then drained
2 tablespoons fresh lemon juice
2 tablespoons tomato paste or 1 roasted red pepper
1 tablespoon apple cider vinegar
½ cup nutritional yeast
1 tablespoon arrowroot powder
½ teaspoon sweet or smoked paprika
1 tablespoon red miso

1. Purée the beer, water, cashews, walnuts, lemon juice, tomato paste, and vinegar in a high-speed blender until completely smooth. 2. Transfer to a medium saucepan set over medium heat. Whisk in the nutritional yeast, arrowroot powder, and paprika. Cook, whisking often, until the mixture thickens, about 7 minutes. Remove from the heat, whisk in the miso paste, and serve immediately. 3. Store in an airtight container in the refrigerator for up to 5 days.

Per Serving:
calories: 85 | fat: 5g | protein: 5g | carbs: 7g | fiber: 1g

Potato Wedges

Prep time: 10 minutes | Cook time: 40 minutes | Serves 2 to 4

3 or 4 medium red potatoes, cut into ½-inch wedges (about 1 pound / 454 g)

1. Preheat the oven to 450°F (235°C). Line a baking sheet with parchment paper. 2. Spread the potatoes out in a single layer on the prepared baking sheet. 3. Bake for 15 to 20 minutes, or until the potatoes are browned and crispy. 4. Flip the potatoes over, and bake for 15 to 20 minutes, or until crispy. Remove from the oven. Serve immediately.

Per Serving:
calories: 149 | fat: 0g | protein: 4g | carbs: 34g | fiber: 4g

Cilantro and Lime Chutney

Prep time: 10 minutes | Cook time: 0 minutes | Makes 1 cup

2 green chiles, stemmed
1 tablespoon grated peeled fresh ginger
1 teaspoon lime zest
Juice of 1 large lime
2 tablespoons water, plus more as needed
2 cups fresh cilantro, washed and shaken dry
1 tablespoon agave syrup, or pure maple syrup (optional)
½ teaspoon ground cumin
¼ teaspoon ground coriander

1. In a blender, combine the green chiles, ginger, lime zest and juice, and 2 tablespoons of water. Purée until smooth. 2. Add the cilantro, agave syrup (if using), cumin, and coriander. Purée again until smooth. Scrape down the sides, as needed, and add up to 2 tablespoons more water to reach your desired consistency. 3. Refrigerate in an airtight container for up to 2 weeks or freeze for up to 6 months.

Per Serving: (1 tablespoon)
calories: 8 | fat: 0g | protein: 0g | carbs: 2g | fiber: 0g

Appendix 1: Measurement Conversion Chart

MEASUREMENT CONVERSION CHART

VOLUME EQUIVALENTS (DRY)

US STANDARD	METRIC (APPROXIMATE)
1/8 teaspoon	0.5 mL
1/4 teaspoon	1 mL
1/2 teaspoon	2 mL
3/4 teaspoon	4 mL
1 teaspoon	5 mL
1 tablespoon	15 mL
1/4 cup	59 mL
1/2 cup	118 mL
3/4 cup	177 mL
1 cup	235 mL
2 cups	475 mL
3 cups	700 mL
4 cups	1 L

VOLUME EQUIVALENTS (LIQUID)

US STANDARD	US STANDARD (OUNCES)	METRIC (APPROXIMATE)
2 tablespoons	1 fl.oz.	30 mL
1/4 cup	2 fl.oz.	60 mL
1/2 cup	4 fl.oz.	120 mL
1 cup	8 fl.oz.	240 mL
1 1/2 cup	12 fl.oz.	355 mL
2 cups or 1 pint	16 fl.oz.	475 mL
4 cups or 1 quart	32 fl.oz.	1 L
1 gallon	128 fl.oz.	4 L

TEMPERATURES EQUIVALENTS

FAHRENHEIT (F)	CELSIUS (C) (APPROXIMATE)
225 °F	107 °C
250 °F	120 °C
275 °F	135 °C
300 °F	150 °C
325 °F	160 °C
350 °F	180 °C
375 °F	190 °C
400 °F	205 °C
425 °F	220 °C
450 °F	235 °C
475 °F	245 °C
500 °F	260 °C

WEIGHT EQUIVALENTS

US STANDARD	METRIC (APPROXIMATE)
1 ounce	28 g
2 ounces	57 g
5 ounces	142 g
10 ounces	284 g
15 ounces	425 g
16 ounces (1 pound)	455 g
1.5 pounds	680 g
2 pounds	907 g

Appendix 2: The Dirty Dozen and Clean Fifteen

The Dirty Dozen and Clean Fifteen

The Environmental Working Group (EWG) is a nonprofit, nonpartisan organization dedicated to protecting human health and the environment Its mission is to empower people to live healthier lives in a healthier environment. This organization publishes an annual list of the twelve kinds of produce, in sequence, that have the highest amount of pesticide residue-the Dirty Dozen-as well as a list of the fifteen kinds of produce that have the least amount of pesticide residue-the Clean Fifteen.

THE DIRTY DOZEN

- The 2016 Dirty Dozen includes the following produce. These are considered among the year's most important produce to buy organic:

Strawberries	Spinach
Apples	Tomatoes
Nectarines	Bell peppers
Peaches	Cherry tomatoes
Celery	Cucumbers
Grapes	Kale/collard greens
Cherries	Hot peppers

- The Dirty Dozen list contains two additional items kale/collard greens and hot peppers-because they tend to contain trace levels of highly hazardous pesticides.

THE CLEAN FIFTEEN

- The least critical to buy organically are the Clean Fifteen list. The following are on the 2016 list:

Avocados	Papayas
Corn	Kiw
Pineapples	Eggplant
Cabbage	Honeydew
Sweet peas	Grapefruit
Onions	Cantaloupe
Asparagus	Cauliflower
Mangos	

- Some of the sweet corn sold in the United States are made from genetically engineered (GE) seedstock. Buy organic varieties of these crops to avoid GE produce.

Appendix 3 Recipes Index

A

Adventure Bars	65
Almond Anise Biscotti	75
Almond Truffles with Toasted Coconut	73
Almond-Date Energy Bites	72
Amazing Lentil Energy Balls	65
Ancient Grains Salad	82
Anti-Inflammatory Miso Soup	51
Apple Crisp	75
Apple-Oat Crisp	74
Applesauce Crumble Muffins	30
Artichoke Quinoa Dip	63
Avocado Tartare	48
Avocado Toast	31
Avocado Toast with Tomato and Hemp Hearts	28

B

Baby Potatoes with Dill, Chives, and Garlic	46
Baked Apples	73
Baked Spaghetti Squash with Spicy Lentil Sauce	48
Balsamic Vinaigrette	92
Banana Zucchini Pancakes	24
Barbecue Sauce	93
Basic Baked Granola	30
Basic Oil-Free Hummus	66
Beer "Cheese" Dip	96
Beet Sushi and Avocado Poke Bowls	42
Berbere-Spiced Red Lentils	38
Berry Chia Pudding	71
Black and White Bean Chili	33
Black Bean Tempeh Nachos with Cashew Cheese	63
Black Beans and Rice	38
Black Sesame–Ginger Quick Bread	73
Blackened Sprouts	43
Black-Eyed Pea and Collard Stew with Spicy Tahini	49
BLAT (Bacon, Lettuce, Avocado and Tomato) Pitas	39
Bloody Caesar Gazpacho	53
Blueberry Scones	24
Blueberry-Lime Sorbet	75
Blueprint: Classic Kale Salad	86
Blueprint: Lifesaving Bowl	80
Breakfast Scramble	28
Broccoli and "Cheddar" Soup	55
Brown Lentil Stew with Avocado Salsa	54
Buckwheat Sesame Milk	23
Bulgur Chickpea Pilaf	37
Bulgur Lettuce Cups	79
Butter Bean Pâté	34

C

Cabbage and Millet Pilaf	36
Cacao Crush Smoothie	62
Calorie Bomb Cookies	63
Caribbean Chili	69
Carrot Cake Balls	70
Carrot Cake Oatmeal	27
Carrot Ginger Soup	51
Cashew Cheese Spread	87
Cauliflower Soup	57
Chana Masala	36
Cheesy Vegetable Sauce	87
Chickpea Caponata	33
Chickpea Country Gravy	26
Chickpea Masala	39
Chickpea of the Sea Salad	43
Chickpea Pâté	34
Chickpea Quiche	27
Chickpea Tortilla Fajita Stack	36
Chickpea Vegetable Soup	55
Chilean Bean Stew	49
Chili Powder	22
Chipotle Black Bean Soup	57
Chocolate Banana Hemp Smoothie Bowl	31
Chocolate Cake Munch Cookies	60
Chocolate Cherry Oats Bowl	32
Chocolate Dirt Yogurt Cup	72
Chocolate Microwave Mug Cake	72
Chocolate Sunflower Protein Cookies	64
Chocolate Tahini Muffins	72
Cilantro and Lime Chutney	96
Classic French Vinaigrette	84
Classic Italian Mushrooms	69
Cleansing Morning Lemonade	28
Coconut Butter	94
Coconut Crumble Bars	74
Coconut Curry Soup	58
Coconut Whipped Cream	88
Congee with Dates and Spices	27
Corn Bread Muffins	93
Corn Chowder	56
Cozy Lentil Soup	54

Crazy Quinoa Protein Muffins	25
Creamy Chickpea and Avocado Salad	83
Creamy Curried Potatoes and Peas	41
Creamy Fruit Salad	83
Creamy Herbed Hemp Dressing	20
Creamy Mushroom Gravy	88
Creamy Potato Salad	85
Crispy Chickpea Snackers	67
Crispy Maple Mustard Cabbage	45
Croutons	19
Crunchy Nuts and Seeds Protein Bars	68
Cumin-Citrus Roasted Carrots	46
Curried Kale Slaw	82
Curried Zucchini Soup	58
Curry Powder	91

D

Daikon Beet Pickle with Lime	48
Date Syrup	22
Deep Immune Cup of Soup	58
Dill Potato Salad	85

E

Easy DIY Pizza Crust	22
Easy One-Pot Vegan Marinara	94
Easy-Peasy Almond Milk	18
Endurance Snack Mix	61
Everyday Pesto	92

F

Fall and Winter All-Purpose Seasoning	89
Fall Harvest Vegetable Chowder	50
Farro Tabbouleh	40
Fava Bean Salad	81
Fennel and Ginger Butternut Squash Soup	50
Fiery Couscous Salad	82
Fried Rice with Tofu Scramble	40
Fruited Barley	32

G

Garam Masala	95
Garden Salad with Sumac Vinaigrette	79
Garlic Hummus	61
Ginger Peach Muffins	74
Ginger, Shiitake, Pecan, and Apricot Pilaf	44
Gingerbread Protein Bars	60
Gluten-Free Blueberry Blender Pancakes	30
Gluten-Free Energy Crackers	65

Golden Banana Bread	71
Golden Split Pea Soup	58
Graham Crackers	77
Great Smoky Almonds	68
Greek Salad in a Jar	84
Green Banana Smoothie	27
Green Chile Rice with Black Beans	39
Green Goddess Dressing	89
Green Mix Salad	84
Green Split Peas	21
Greener Guacamole	22
Gut-Healing Sauerkraut	21

H

Harissa	92
Hemp and Vanilla Bircher Breakfast	29
Herbed Millet Pizza Crust	19
High-Protein Peanut Butter Cookie Dough	62
Homemade Beans	93
Hot and Sour Soup	54

I

Indian Red Split Lentil Soup	59
Italian Lentil Soup	54
Italian Seasoning	92

J

Jerk Spices	91

K

Kalamata Olives and White Bean Dip	89
Kale and White Bean Soup	52
Kale Chips	70
Kasha Varnishkes (Buckwheat Groats with Bow-Tie Pasta)	37

L

Larb Salad	80
Legit Salsa	70
Lemon Garlic Chickpeas Salad	80
Lemon-Oatmeal Cacao Cookies	68
Lemon-Tahini Dressing	23
Lemon-Thyme Dressing	19
Lemony Herbed Lentil Soup	56
Lentil Salad with Lemon and Fresh Herbs	85
Lentil Tacos	88
Lentil, Lemon and Mushroom Salad	85
Lime-Mint Soup	56

Loaded Breakfast Burrito	28
Loaded Frijoles	45
Lucky Black-Eyed Pea Stew	35

M

Mama Mia Marinara Sauce	23
Mango Satay Tempeh Bowl	38
Mango Sticky Rice	73
Mango-Orange Dressing	21
Maple Caramel	89
Maple glazed Butternut Squash and Brussels Sprouts	45
Maple-Dijon Dressing	21
Mayonnaise	23
Mexikale Crisps	69
Millet Stew	53
Minestrone	59
Minimalist Guacamole	94
Minty Beet and Sweet Potato Soup	59
Miso Noodle Soup with Shiitake Mushrooms	51
Mock Tuna Salad	81
Molasses ginger Oat Cookie Balls	76
Mushroom Barley Risotto	39
Mushroom Risotto	40
Mustard-Roasted Broccoli Pâté	42

N

No-Bake Chocolate Peanut Butter Cookies	66
Nori Snack Rolls	60
Not-So-Fat Guacamole	19
Nut Butter and Jelly Breakfast Cookies	25
Nut Milk	95
Nut-Crusted Tofu	35

O

Oat Milk	88
Oatmeal Granola Bar Bites	70
Orange, Fennel and White Bean Salad	83
Orzo "Risotto"	34
Overnight Chocolate Chia Pudding	31
Overnight Pumpkin Spice Chia Pudding	31
Over-the-Top Bars to Go	64

P

Pan con Tomate	26
Peach Cobbler	78
Peanut Milk	23
Pear Chia Pudding	78
Pepita and Almond Squares	66
Perfect Marinara Sauce	91
Pineapple Chutney	22
Pinto Salsa Bowl	84
Plantains with Black Beans and Avocado	28
Plant-Based Parmesan	20
Plant-Powered Pancakes	31
Pomegranate Ginger Sauce	90
Portabella Mushroom Gyro	47
Potato Wedges	96
Potatoes	19
Powerhouse Green Juice	26
Pressure Cooker Thai Nuggets	62
Pumpkin and Anasazi Bean Stew	55
Pumpkin Bread Pudding	76
Pumpkin Spice Bread	76
Pure Nut Mylk	20
Purple Potato and Kale Salad	81

Q

Quick Marinated Arame	46
Quick Panfried Tempeh	37
Quick Tahini Sauce	94
Quinoa Banana Muffins	77
Quinoa Mylk	21
Quinoa Tabbouleh	84

R

Rainbow Veggie Protein Pinwheels	64
Raw Carrot and Date Walnut Salad	83
Raw Date Chocolate Balls	70
Raw Date Paste	91
Red Lentil Dal	40
Red Lentil Pâté	35
Rich Chocolate Energy Cookies	61
Roasted Balsamic Beets	41
Roasted Carrots with Ginger Maple Cream	47
Roasted Cauliflower with Green Tahini	47
Roasted Red Pepper Spread	23
Roasted Veggies with Tofu	46
Salted Chocolate Truffles	78
Sautéed Root Vegetables with Parsley, Poppy Seeds, and Lemon	46

S

Savory Oatmeal	25
Savory Rosemary–Black Pepper Scones	24
Savory Squash Soup	49
Shiitake Bakin'	29
Simple Berry-Chia Jam	92
Skillet Cauliflower Bites	64
Skillet Spinach and Artichoke Dip	61

Slow Cooker Apples and Oats	26
Slow Cooker Versatile Seitan Balls	68
Slow-Cooked Steel-Cut Oats	27
Smoky Cajun Bowl	33
Smoky Mushrooms	95
Sour Cream	94
Spanish Chickpea Stew	52
Spanish Red Pepper Spread (Romesco)	87
Spicy Carrots with Coriander	44
Spicy Cilantro Pesto	18
Spicy Satay Sauce	95
Spicy Tahini Dressing	90
Spicy Tomato and Pepper Sauce	90
Spirulina golden Berry Power Bars	65
Spring Steamed Vegetables with Savory Goji Berry Cream	42
Steamed Kabocha Squash with Nori and Scallions	48
Steamed Seitan Chipotle Links	62
Steel-Cut Oats with Cranberries and Nuts	32
Stir-Fried Vegetables with Miso and Sake	45
Stone Fruit Compote	74
Stovetop Blueberry Oatmeal	29
Strawberries and Cream Overnight Oatmeal	30
Strawberry Chia Jam	93
Strawberry Shortcake Rice Bites	67
Strawberry, Banana, and Granola Yogurt Bowls	25
Strawberry-Avocado Toast with Balsamic Glaze	69
Strawberry-Peach Vinaigrette	91
Strawberry-Pistachio Salad	82
Summer Quinoa Salad	79
Superfood Salad Topper	18
Sweet and Savory Root Veggies and Butternut Squash	43
Sweet Peanut Butter Dipping Sauce	93
Sweet Potato and Black Bean Hash	32
Sweet Potato and Cauliflower Rice Pilaf	37
Sweet Potato Spice Cake	71
Sweet Potato Tacos	34
Sweet Potato Toasts with Avocado Mash and Tahini	29

T

Tahini Dressing	20
Tangy Cabbage, Apples, and Potatoes	44
Tempeh Bacon	18
Toast Points	66
Tofu Noodle Soup with Coconut Lemongrass Broth	57
Tofu Veggie Gravy Bowl	90
Tom Yum Goong (Thai Hot-and-Sour Soup)	56
Tomato and Red Pepper Soup	55
Tomato Sauce	20
Tomato, Corn and Bean Salad	81
Tropical Lemon Protein Bites	69
Tuscan Bean Stew	52
Two-Ingredient Peanut Butter Fudge	75

U

Ultimate Veggie Wrap with Kale Pesto	44

V

Vanilla Almond Date Balls	66
Vanilla Nice Cream	76
Vegan Basil Pesto	90
Vegetable Goulash	50
Vegetable Spring Rolls with Spicy Peanut Dipping Sauce	41

W

Walnut Brownies	77
Weeknight Chickpea Tomato Soup	52
Weeknight Root Vegetable Dhal	53
Whipped Lentil Chipotle Dip	95
White Bean and Spinach Artichoke Dip	67
White Bean Tzatziki Dip	67
Whole grain Corn Muffins	35
Whole-Wheat Blueberry Muffins	32
Wild Rice, Cabbage and Chickpea Pilaf	38
Winter Squash Soup	50
Winter Sunshine Salad	83

Z

Zesty Orange-Cranberry Energy Bites	78
Zingy Melon and Mango Salad	80
Zucchini "Parmesan"	43
Zucchini Bisque	51
Zucchini Bread Oatmeal	26
Zucchini Dressing	94

Made in the USA
Monee, IL
01 September 2023